THE HISTORY OF NATIONS

Spain

Other books in the History of Nations series:

THE HISTORY OF NATIONS

Spain

Laurie Stoff, *Book Editor*

Daniel Leone, *President*
Bonnie Szumski, *Publisher*
Scott Barbour, *Managing Editor*

**GREENHAVEN
PRESS ®**

THOMSON
GALE

San Diego • Detroit • New York • San Francisco • Cleveland
New Haven, Conn. • Waterville, Maine • London • Munich

For more information, contact
Greenhaven Press
27500 Drake Rd.
Farmington Hills, MI 48331-3535
Or you can visit our Internet site at http://www.gale.com

LIBRARY OF CONGRESS CATALOGING-IN-PUBLICATION DATA
Spain / Laurie Stoff, book editor.
p. cm. — (History of nations)
Includes bibliographical references and index.
ISBN 0-7377-1851-X (pbk. : alk. paper) — ISBN 0-7377-1850-1 (lib. : alk. paper)
1. Spain—History. I. Stoff, Laurie. II. History of nations (Greenhaven Press)
DP66.S62 2004
946—dc21   2003048329

Contents

vate army, he seized the territory of Valencia, ruling it
until his death in 1099.

Chapter 3: The Golden Age of Spain and Its Decline

Spanish Catholic Church. He used the Spanish Inquisition to eradicate heresy and promoted the interests of Catholicism beyond Spain's borders.

Chapter 4: The Eighteenth and Nineteenth Centuries

Chapter 5: Twentieth-Century Spain

Chapter 6: Contemporary Spain

FOREWORD

In 1841, the journalist Charles MacKay remarked, "In reading the history of nations, we find that, like individuals, they have their whims and peculiarities, their seasons of excitement and recklessness." At the time of MacKay's observation, many of the nations explored in the Greenhaven Press History of Nations series did not yet exist in their current form. Nonetheless, whether it is old or young, every nation is similar to an individual, with its own distinct characteristics and unique story.

The History of Nations series is dedicated to exploring these stories. Each anthology traces the development of one of the world's nations from its earliest days, when it was perhaps no more than a promise on a piece of paper or an idea in the mind of some revolutionary, through to its status in the world today. Topics discussed include the pivotal political events and power struggles that shaped the country as well as important social and cultural movements. Often, certain dramatic themes and events recur, such as the rise and fall of empires, the flowering and decay of cultures, or the heroism and treachery of leaders. As well, in the history of most countries war, oppression, revolution, and deep social change feature prominently. Nonetheless, the details of such events vary greatly, as does their impact on the nation concerned. For example, England's "Glorious Revolution" of 1688 was a peaceful transfer of power that set the stage for the emergence of democratic institutions in that nation. On the other hand, in China, the overthrow of dynastic rule in 1912 led to years of chaos, civil war, and the eventual emergence of a Communist regime that used violence as a tool to root out opposition and quell popular protest. Readers of the Greenhaven Press History of Nations series will learn about the common challenges nations face and the different paths they take in response to such crises. However a nation's story may have developed, the series strives to present a clear and unbiased view of the country at hand.

The structure of each volume in the series is designed to help students deepen their understanding of the events, movements, and persons that define nations. First, a thematic introduction provides critical background material and helps orient the reader. The chapters themselves are designed to provide an accessible and engaging approach to the study of the history of that nation involved and are arranged either thematically or chronologically, as appropriate. The selections include both primary documents, which convey something of the flavor of the time and place concerned, and secondary material, which includes the wisdom of hindsight and scholarship. Finally, each book closes with a detailed chronology, a comprehensive bibliography of suggestions for further research, and a thorough index.

The countries explored within the series are as old as China and as young as Canada, as distinct in character as Spain and India, as large as Russia, and as compact as Japan. Some are based on ethnic nationalism, the belief in an ethnic group as a distinct people sharing a common destiny, whereas others emphasize civic nationalism, in which what defines citizenship is not ethnicity but commitment to a shared constitution and its values. As human societies become increasingly globalized, knowledge of other nations and of the diversity of their cultures, characteristics, and histories becomes ever more important. This series responds to the challenge by furnishing students with a solid and engaging introduction to the history of the world's nations.

INTRODUCTION

Until recently many historians regarded Spain as somewhat apart and different from the rest of Europe. The country was often viewed as abnormal and even backward, failing to acquire the attributes of other western European societies and maintaining itself in darkness and intolerance. It was not considered a flourishing and prosperous democratic nation. Its contributions to the world were largely overlooked or understated. In fact, despite the vast achievements of the Spanish empire, the country was often perceived as a second-class nation. Historians José Alvarez Junco and Adrian Shubert assert, "These negative portrayals became associated not only with Spanish policies but also with Spanish character and with the 'race' itself. The image of Spain as the epitome of absolutism and intolerance would remain fixed in the European collective mind for centuries."[1]

The view of Spain as exceptional is rooted in a number of aspects of the nation's history. The differences, however, may be less significant than previously assessed, and thus Spain may be less exceptional than once thought. In fact, Spanish history in many ways resembles the histories of other western European nations. Like most of the rest of Europe, Spain came under control of the Roman Empire. The Romans invaded Spain in 218 B.C. and finally secured control over the region in 19 B.C., after two centuries of resistance on the part of the natives. As a result of Roman influence, Spain shares much in terms of political, social, economic, and cultural heritage with the other nations of Europe. During the period of Roman control Christianity became the dominant religion in Spain, as it did all over Europe. In the fifth century Spain was invaded by a Germanic people, the Visigoths, who eventually dislodged Roman rule and established their own kingdom. Similarly, most of western Europe was overrun by Germanic tribes, which toppled the western Roman Empire.

In the early eighth century Spanish history began to diverge somewhat from the general European track when the country was invaded by Muslims from North Africa. The other nations of western Europe managed to avoid this fate and remain independent of Muslim control. The Christian population of Spain never fully accepted the Muslims of Spain, or Moors, as they were called, and rallied their forces against the Moors for over two centuries as part of the Christian "reconquest." It was not until the late fifteenth century, when the Christians of Spain were unified under one rule, that the Moors were completely defeated. Fear of religious diversity led the Spanish rulers to establish the Inquisition, a tribunal aimed at weeding out heretical beliefs, and to expel the Jews, as had been done in a number of other European countries.

During this period Spain, which was fast becoming one of the great powers of Europe, joined in the "Age of Discovery." Like other European nations it sent numerous explorers and conquerors around the world. Similarly, Spain embarked on a program of vast military buildup to support its interests, both on the Continent and in the New World. It possessed the most powerful naval fleet in the world, the famous Spanish armada. Yet Spanish ambitions often came into conflict with other European powers. Frequent military conflict, overextension in the Old and New Worlds, bad harvests, and economic troubles led the country into decline during the seventeenth and eighteenth centuries.

The nineteenth century of Spanish history shares many similarities with the development of other European nations as well. The French Revolution had a profound effect on Spain, as it did all over Europe. Spain struggled to industrialize and modernize like other nations of Europe, only to a lesser degree. And Spain was also influenced by liberalism and democracy in its political development, although it was often ruled by monarchs and military dictators. In the twentieth century socialism, communism, and fascism all had significant influence in Spain, as they did in the rest of Europe. Indeed, the Spanish Civil War of 1936–1939 was fought by forces with allegiances to these ideas.

Thus, Spanish history is less exceptional than many have proposed, and in fact, mirrors that of the rest of Europe in many ways. There are some significant differences that make Spain somewhat unique. These include the occupation of Spanish lands by the Moors, Spain's conservative brand of Catholicism and corresponding intolerance of different faiths, its seemingly slow economic growth and lack of democratic and bourgeois development, and the diversity of Spain's population, often interpreted as a lack of national unity. Spain's geographic position on the physical edge of Europe also lends to the perception that it is separate from other European nations. However, even these factors may make Spain less different than previously assumed.

The Legacy of the Moors

Perhaps the most important factor contributing to the image of Spain as exceptional is the legacy of the Moors. Their effect on the development of Spain was undeniably large, but the images of the Moors, as well as the interpretation of their influence on Spain, are diverse. Spain is the only western European nation to have been conquered and occupied by Muslims. According to José Alvarez Junco and Adrian Shubert, "The Moorish occupation has left an abiding legacy."[2] In fact, as philosopher and essayist Julián Marías comments, "The Moors have become affixed to the image of Spain to such a degree that there is a tendency to explain everything by their presence or absence."[3] There was even a common misconception held by some foreign observers that the Moors were the ancestors of the modern Spanish people. "This obsessive presence of the Moors has sufficed to segregate Spain from Europe, to consider Spain as something different,"[4] according to Marías.

The presence of the Moors has often been seen as a civilizing agent in Spanish development, as they brought with them the learning and culture of the ancient Arabs, including a high level of mathematical and scientific knowledge and a well-developed tradition of poetry and art. The influence of the Moors is especially significant when compared to much of the rest of Europe, which was in the depths of the Dark Ages. Peter Pierson, professor at Santa Clara University, states, "While the greater part of Europe was sunk in barbarism, Spain [with the Moorish conquest] had become part of the most dynamic civilization in western Eurasia."[5] The accumulation of great wealth in medieval Spain has also been attributed to the hardworking habits and agricultural skills of the Moors. The Moors introduced trade with North Africa and the Middle East, bringing in a wide variety of new products. Spain's economic decline has often been ascribed to the expulsion of the Moors in 1609, with the view that it was this population that maintained the great wealth of the nation.[6]

While there is no doubt that the Moors brought many advances to Spain, more careful historiography has demonstrated that the region had experienced significant development for at least one thousand, possibly two thousand, years prior to their arrival. This was accomplished through both native efforts and the advances brought by the Romans, who dominated the region from the second century B.C. to the fifth century A.D. In fact, the invasion and dominance of the Moors over Spain occurred so quickly there was not much time for deep cultural change to take effect. The Moorish occupation was never truly accepted by the Hispanic population. The result was that although the Moors were the rulers of much of the Spanish territory for many years, the population remained much the same as before the invasion. The influence of the Romans, as well as the Visigoths, the Germanic people who controlled Spain from the fifth to the eighth century, were more significant in this sense. "The Islamic Invasion caused absolutely no break with the Visigothic past,"[7] according to Ramón Menéndez Pidal, professor of romance philology at the University of Madrid. Christians as well as Jews were allowed to practice their respective religions without hindrance from their Muslim overlords. There were large numbers of conversions to Islam among the native Christian population of Spain. For the most part, such conversions were not coerced; rather, they were largely voluntary efforts by those wishing to advance themselves in a Muslim-dominated society. Later, after the reconquest had reestablished Christian dominion over Spain, many Muslims converted to Christianity. There was also much intermarriage among Muslims, Christians, and Jews, resulting in an intermingling of cultures.

The invasion and conquest of Spain by the Moors did have the effect of separating that country somewhat from the rest of Europe. With their origins in North Africa and the Middle East, Moorish attentions were naturally focused on these regions and centered around the Mediterranean. Trade and international economies flowed eastward rather than north or west. The result was that Spain was partially isolated from western Europe. However, this separation was incomplete and impermanent. There was still much contact with French and Germanic peoples, including a strong religious connection between Spanish and western European Christians. Cultural exchange and economic trade with western Europe continued as well.

It is also important to consider the fact that the Moors never succeeded in taking control over all of Spain. While they were able to quash all resistance in the areas they did dominate, namely in the southern regions of Spain, the Moors were never able to penetrate the northernmost part of the Iberian Peninsula. As a result, the Christians maintained a stronghold from which, eventually, they were able to launch the reconquest. In these regions the Islamic presence had barely registered. In sum, recent scholarship, which places the Moorish contribution within a larger context and in more reasonable proportions, allows for a more balanced and accurate view of the Moors' influence on Spanish development.

Catholicism and the Church

The role of the Catholic Church and religion has always been extremely important throughout the development of the Spanish nation. It has been a defining feature of Spanish identity, despite the large numbers of Muslims and Jews that have lived in Spain. In fact, many consider the "real" Spain to be an exclusively Christian Spain. Christianity became well established in the Spanish lands under the Romans in the fourth century. As stated by Rhea Marsh Smith, the author of *Spain: A Modern History*, "The most important event in ancient Iberian and Roman history, both for its immediate impact on the empire and for the future, was the conversion of the natives to Christianity."[8] The Visigoths, who invaded and conquered the Iberian Peninsula in A.D. 409 became Christians as well, and Christianity was the religion of the majority of the Hispano-Roman population. As a result, the peninsula was united and the population rallied around the Visigothic monarchy. From this time on, the Catholic Church flourished, and it eventually came to dominate in Spain, supported by the secular powers as well as the lay population.

Spanish Christianity acquired a reputation of being highly intolerant, both of any deviation from orthodoxy within the religion as well as of other faiths. This reputation is attributable to several aspects of Spanish history that demonstrate that Spain could be extremely intolerant and even cruel: the Inquisition, the expulsion of the Jews, and the expulsion of the Muslims. However, closer inspection also reveals that such actions were not unique to Spain, and there was, perhaps, more tolerance and less cruelty than once assumed.

The Inquisition

The establishment of the Inquisition in the fifteenth century by King Ferdinand and Queen Isabella contributed greatly to the conception of Spain as exceptional or abnormal. As author Fred

James Hill explains, it "has passed into history as one of the most notorious and ruthless institutions."[9] The Inquisition was a religious tribunal, established in an effort to eliminate heresy and create a uniformity of belief and practice among Catholics. Those accused of heresy were tortured and often forced to confess. Once found guilty, the victims were usually executed.

The extreme intolerance and religious persecution associated with the Inquisition have led many to surmise that these features permeated Spanish society at large and severed it from more liberal traditions developing elsewhere in Europe. This view was exaggerated after the sixteenth century, when the "Black Legend" arose to explain the devastating defeat of the Spanish armada by the English fleet in 1588. The legend attributed the defeat to Spain's backwardness, poverty, and weakness and presented Spain as a bastion of intolerance, ignorance, and bigotry, all of which were seen as a result of the Inquisition, which, detractors claimed, had cut Spain off from the intellectual and scientific developments occurring in other European states (such as England and Germany). Noted Spanish author Julián Juderías states, "In a word, we understand by black legend the legend of the inquisitorial, ignorant, fanatical Spain, incapable of figuring among civilized nations . . . always ready for violent repressions; enemy of progress and innovations."[10] The Inquisition was thus seen as the root of many of Spain's problems, including that of a declining population in the seventeenth and eighteenth centuries; the Black Legend asserted that the executions carried out in the Inquisition's name had eliminated many among Spain's best and brightest and left only the genetically inferior for breeding.

There is no denying that the Inquisition was a terrible institution that inflicted torture on numerous people. Yet it is inaccurate to portray it as the source of Spain's numerous difficulties. Simon Lemieux, head of the history department at Portsmouth Grammar School in England writes, "That the Spanish Inquisition was oppressive to some extent is beyond doubt; what is much more debatable is just how cruel and harsh it was. Historians have debated this topic considerably."[11] Much of recent scholarship has revised the view of the Inquisition and the extent of its effect on Spanish society. As a result of the work of a number of modern historians, a more moderate view of the Inquisition has emerged.

Moreover, the Inquisition was not a peculiar or exclusively

Spanish institution, despite the fact that its strongest association has always been with Spain. It was actually created by the pope in France in the thirteenth century. In form and function, the Spanish Inquisition was little different than other religious tribunals that existed all over Europe. Moreover, it was only placed into effect in the region of Aragon, not throughout all of the Spanish lands and, in fact, the total number of its victims was significantly less than those of religious struggles in countries such as Germany and England. As Simon Lemieux states, "Certainly Catholic Spain was intensely intolerant of those who did not share the faith, but few if any places in Europe could be described as religiously tolerant in this period. Execution for heresy was not purely a Spanish prerogative."[12]

Arguments that the Inquisition effectively cut Spain off from the enlightened development experienced in other European countries are relatively weak as well. The Inquisition was most prominent in Spain at the same time the country was undergoing a great cultural flowering, during the period that is most often referred to as the "Golden Age" of Spain. Less than 1 percent of Spanish writers came into conflict with the institution, and one of the greatest novels ever written, Miguel Cervantes' *Don Quixote*, was produced while the Inquisition was in existence. Spain contributed hugely to areas of learning such as navigation, natural history, and medicine. Furthermore, although Spain began to decline in the seventeenth century, the Inquisition was more of a symptom than a cause of this decline.

The Expulsion of the Jews and the Muslims

Religious intolerance, which emanated both from the Spanish leadership as well as the population, led ultimately to complete rejection of differences in faith. The Jewish community in Spain was the first to suffer as a result of this sentiment, and the Jews were expelled in 1492. While always a small minority of the population in Spain, Jewish people had lived in the Spanish lands for many centuries. They had arrived during Roman rule, with thousands more entering Spain during the Visigothic period. Although they prospered to some extent during this time, prejudices soon led to persecution, and many were forced to convert to Christianity. The situation actually improved for Spanish Jews under Moorish rule, as Islamic law recognized them as one of the "peo-

Districts of Spain

ples of the book" [those of the old testament of the Bible] and did not subject them to the persecution they had suffered at Christian hands. The three religions intermingled to produce the distinctive culture of medieval Spain. Initially, the Moors afforded the Jews many privileges and freedoms, and commerce and industry flourished in Jewish communities. The Jews engaged in business, diplomacy, and cultural activities, and with their prosperity, their numbers grew. There was some persecution of the Jews in the later years of Moorish rule, and some Jews were forced to convert to Islam. After the Christian reconquest, intolerance and prejudice against the Jews increased. There was much anti-Semitism among the Spanish population. In particular, after a plague in the fourteenth century, persecution increased as many blamed the Jews for the epidemic. Despite popular hatred toward the Jews official policies remained rather lenient. Spanish rulers often extended protection to the Jews and even relied on them for financial and civic support. Many Jews obtained positions of prominence in Spanish society and government.

Many cite the Inquisition as a prime example of Spanish intolerance and persecution of the Jews. The Inquisition, however, was not directed against the openly Jewish population, but rather against the *conversos* (those Jews who had converted to Christianity), many of whom were thought to be continuing to practice their original faith and thereby committing heretical acts in the eyes of the Church. Ultimately, under pressure from the Church, Queen Isabella agreed to expel the Jews, despite the benefits they had brought to the country. Scholars such as Jaime Vicens Vive, professor of history at the University of Barcelona, have surmised that this move was damaging to the development of Spain, as "it eliminated . . . the only social groups that might have responded to the stimulus of incipient capitalism; it undermined the prosperous economies of many municipalities," and it denied the Catholic monarchs "an enormous quantity of wealth."[13]

The Muslims of Spain suffered a similar fate under Christian rule. Muslims had been the dominant power in much of the Spanish lands since the Moors invaded in the eighth century. The reconquest, however, had slowly removed them from power as Christian kings and warriors defeated them in territory after territory, beginning in the eleventh century. Finally, the last remaining Muslim-held region, Granada, was taken by the forces of King Ferdinand and Queen Isabella at the end of the fifteenth century. The Spanish Muslims were finally forced to leave the country altogether in 1609.

While the persecution and expulsion of the Jews and Muslims seem to bolster the view of Spain as a society of extreme intolerance, these acts were little different from those carried out in many other European societies, including France, England, and Italy. The major differences in Spain were that the Muslim population was significantly larger than in any other European nation and that the Jews had previously found Spain to be a relatively tolerant society. Furthermore, the decisions to expel the Jews and the Muslims from Spain were as much politically driven as they were religious in motivation. King Ferdinand had attempted to dissuade his wife from issuing the edict of expulsion in 1492, as he believed that Jewish financial expertise was valuable, but ultimately consented after the fall of Granada and the strong desire to make Spain a unified Catholic entity. In fact, the expulsions may have made Spain more similar to rather than different from other western European nations by creating a more religiously homogeneous population.

Political and Social Development

The political history of Spain is certainly one that can be labeled conservative, even reactionary at times. The nation did not truly achieve democracy until late in the twentieth century. In fact, its political development was fraught with absolutism, aristocratic dominance, and military dictatorship. Yet once again, when compared with the political life of other western European nations, Spain does not appear to be exceptional. The main point of departure is that democracy was slower in coming to Spain than to nations such as England and France.

Much of the image of Spain as politically despotic comes from exaggeration or distortion of truth. For instance, King Philip II, who ruled Spain from 1556 to 1598, was often represented as a despotic monster, accused of secretly murdering two of his wives as well as his son and heir to the throne, Don Carlos. Despite the fact that England's Henry VIII had a much worse, and openly known, record of murdering his wives, and that the death of Don Carlos was most likely an accident, Philip came to be seen, as José Alvarez Junco and Adrian Shubert describe, as "the embodiment of the 'immorality' coursing through Spanish veins."[14] This distorted view of Philip arose largely as a result of Spain's conflict with England at the end of the sixteenth century, when Philip attempted to invade England but was roundly defeated in 1588. Therefore, it can be interpreted to some degree as wartime propaganda that was incorporated into the historical representation of Spain.

During the seventeenth and eighteenth centuries, when Spain experienced a long period of decline, the country again came under attack. Its decline was perceived by many observers as proof of the damaging consequences of despotism, decadence, and intolerance. Scholars attempting to explain the decline often view the Spanish royalty and aristocracy as an outdated caste, entrenched in old ideas, old attitudes, and old systems, and that had squandered vast fortunes. It is true that the ruling elite in Spain was notoriously fearful of new ideas and that the Spanish political system lacked true checks and balances. Many Spaniards rejected the thought of the Enlightenment, which promoted reason and science over faith and religion, and a "White Legend" arose among reactionary elements who believed that the ideas of the Enlightenment had poisoned the Catholic essence of Spain. There was some degree of stagnation in Spanish development resulting from this turning away from the Enlightenment. Yet it can also be said that the Spanish Bourbon king Charles III was a true model of an "enlightened" monarch, undertaking major reforms similar to those adopted in other western European nations. Moreover, the aristocracy of other western European nations was similarly conservative and often rejected new ideas.

Lack of Bourgeois Development and Revolution

For many scholars of European history, the development of a strong and influential bourgeoisie (middle class) and subsequent revolution in which this group became the dominating political and social class were obligatory rites of passage for western European nations. The classic model is that of England, where a strong middle class developed—a class of industrial capitalists, businessmen, and professionals, who soon came to be more prominent (wealthier and more influential) than the class of nobles whose wealth was based on land ownership. Since Spain did not experience this transition in a timely or traditional fashion, such scholars look at that country as an abnormality in western European historical development. Spain suffered repeated coups, civil wars, and military dictatorships and failed to develop a democratic system of government until the late twentieth century.

Some historians argue that Spain indeed experienced something resembling a bourgeois revolution, albeit an unsuccessful one. In the nineteenth century, the old feudal land system was effectively eliminated, but this did not lead to the development of a truly capitalist society. Instead, as Adrian Shubert argues, it "left the nobility relatively unscathed, left the structure of landholding unchanged and produced a new landed elite which appeared to have neglected agricultural improvements."[15] A constitutional government was erected, and economic growth did occur, but there was no real middle class, no significant number of capitalist entrepreneurs. Instead, the business elite, especially industrial capitalists, were assimilated into the nobility. As opposed to influencing the nobility with new ideas, they adopted the old mentality and values of the nobility, which was anything but democratic, and clung to the existing social order. Although in some areas, such as Catalonia, capitalism did develop and there was opportunity for the industrial bourgeoisie to become political leaders, these new members of the middle class were so afraid of class conflict that they preferred to ally themselves with the land-owning nobility and did not press for change. It became clear that they would never lead a democratic revolution. These conditions have led many scholars to argue that Spain was peculiar, since it did not, and seemingly could not, follow the model believed to have been successfully carried out in other western European nations.

More recent evaluation has allowed other historians to conclude that Spain did indeed experience significant, even radical social and legal change, constituting something akin to a democratic bourgeois revolution. In the years following the Napoleonic invasion of 1808, many of the features of the old regime, particularly legal aspects, were effectively dismantled and a new type of society was created. Rights and privileges were not automatically given to those merely born into the upper class. The Church was stripped of its lands and lost much of its power over society. People of lower classes were given the opportunity to own land. After 1834 Spain was definitely committed to some form of political liberalism, even if it was not democratic. And between 1812 and 1914, as Adrian Shubert asserts, Spain experienced more years of constitutional representative government than any other continental country.[16]

Economics

Like its political development into a democracy, Spain was late in entering the arena of modern capitalist societies. Because of its primarily agricultural economy, it was seen by many as a premodern society well into the twentieth century. Even Spanish scholars described the country's economy, particularly prior to World War I, as underdeveloped. During the eighteenth and nineteenth centuries, when other nations were experiencing rapid economic development, fueled largely by technological advancement and industrial growth, Spain's economy was perceived as "a picture of stagnation" and "an effort to industrialize that failed," according to economist Gabriel Tortella.[17]

Spain's poor agricultural output is central to the view of the Spanish economy as backward. Spain's methods of agricultural organization and production seem antiquated and unproductive when compared to more modern and progressive forms practiced in other western European nations. Yet much of Spain's agriculture has been determined by its geography and terrain. Only 10 percent of Spanish land is productive, containing good quality soil. Another 45 percent is moderately productive, but suffers scarcity of water and difficult topographical conditions. The rest of the land is either barren rock, or located at altitudes too high for agricultural production, or gets such sparse rainfall that it cannot support cultivation. Moreover, negative assessments of Spain's agricultural production, while containing some truth, seem to have been exaggerated. Spanish agriculture did grow during the modern period, although more slowly than that of its neighbors, and that growth was not altogether unimpressive.

In terms of industrial development it can be said that Spain's performance was slow and lagged behind other nations such as England and Germany. The Spanish economy remained largely agrarian in its base well into the twentieth century. Industrial exports accounted for a very small percentage of the national income. Yet the same can be said for other western European countries such as France. There were areas of concentrated industrialization in Spain, such as Catalonia, where the textile industry flourished. Furthermore, when only domestic consumption is considered, the gap between Spain and other European nations narrows considerably.

Another important factor in the Spanish economy was the income gained from the colonial territories in the New World. The loss of these colonies in the nineteenth century had a negative impact on the economy of Spain, especially in the short term. As historian Leandro Prados de la Escosura comments, "Trade in goods and services fell sharply and investment levels declined. Domestic industry lost a protected market and the government's fiscal difficulties worsened as it lost an important source of revenue."[18] Yet the effect of the loss of the colonies on the Spanish economy has been overestimated. As de la Escosura states, "The quantitative evidence available suggests that the loss of the colonies had a less profound and widespread impact on the Spanish economy than has generally been thought. The most competitive and flexible sectors of the economy eventually adapted to the new circumstances."[19] Furthermore, in the twentieth century, particularly the second half, the Spanish economy performed very well in comparison to other European nations, and even experienced a boom in the 1980s and 1990s.

The Diversity of Spain

Another factor that has contributed to the view of Spain as abnormal or exceptional is the idea that the country is not a homogeneous nation, but rather a collection of nationalities and groups living in the same geographical area who have little in common and little to do with each other. Some see this as a deficiency and a reason why Spain cannot properly be termed a nation. Indeed, Spain is made up of a number of territories within which different peoples, with different cultures and even different languages, reside.

Within the borders of Spain there are not only Castilians, who speak Spanish and are primarily associated with Spanish culture, but also Catalans, Basques, and Galicians. These "so-called 'historic nationalities' in Spain . . . have maintained a separate cultural identity from the more specific Castilian culture," as Spanish political expert Crispin Coates attests.[20] In addition to their own linguistic and cultural identities, each of these regional groups had their own traditions of distinct legal codes, customary laws, and even political organizations well into the nineteenth century. Such groups have maintained strong nationalist movements, which even today pressure the central Spanish government for greater autonomy in their regions. The Basques in particular have been fighting, literally, for control of their lands for decades, and some among the movement have taken on extreme measures, including the use of violent terrorist acts against the Spanish government as well as against civilians. In addition to these three historic nationalities, Spain also has other regionally diverse populations. These include the peoples of the Balearic Islands, Canary Islands, Andalusia, and Valencia. These groups are as diverse as the historic nationalities and exert considerable influence on the political system.

Yet this image of Spain as a fractured territory with competing regional identities is not completely accurate. It ignores the fact that Spain achieved a level of geographic and administrative unity much earlier than most of the other western European countries (in the late fifteenth century with the marriage of Ferdinand and Isabella and the conquering of Granada, uniting the various regions of Spain under their central rule). The issue of language is also less divisive than many would think. As Julián Marías argues, "Except for very small nations—and even in them we would have to examine things very closely—all the European nations, with the sole exception of France, represent a lesser linguistic unit than that of Spain, which is far from being a mosaic of small countries, but rather a nation made up of individuals who form part of it through regions with strong and energetic personalities."[21] Although the regionalist movements of Spain's different peoples are often seen as in conflict with general Spanish nationalism, this is not always the case. Many such movements (with the exception of Basque and Catalan regionalism) coexist in a complementary manner with Spanish nationalism and do not hinder its growth.

A Part of the European Mainstream

Various factors have played a significant role in making Spain unique. But they are not enough to reject Spain as a part of Europe. Every nation possesses such characteristics and such diversity. It is through the study of such diversity that one gains the most complete picture of the history of Spain. Modern scholars now reject the image of a Spain as exceptional and seek to include the nation in the course of general European history. Many, such as historian Raymond Carr of Oxford University, argue that Spanish history should be approached as "one would study the history of any other major European country."[22] There is no denying that, as Adrian Shubert asserts, "economically, socially and even politically Spain has been fully a part of the European mainstream."[23]

There are numerous aspects in Spain's historical development that are comparable to those of other western European nations. Like its neighbors, Spain was conquered and ruled by the Roman Empire for hundreds of years and experienced similar governing methods, cultural influences, and social development. Roman rule in Spain was ended by the invasion and domination of a Germanic people in the fifth century, an event that also occurred throughout the countries occupied by the Romans in western Europe. Once again, Spain underwent similar processes of change and influence under these new leaders similar to those of its neighbors. In the Christian kingdoms of Spain many factors of medieval life were quite comparable to those in France, England, and other western European nations. During the late medieval and early modern periods (roughly the fifteenth through the seventeenth centuries) Spain experienced a cultural revival and participated in the exploration and colonization of the New World, much as its fellow western European powers did. Spaniards were exposed to the ideas of the Enlightenment and the Scientific Revolution, as were the subjects of France and England. And by the end of the twentieth century Spain had a democratic government, a capitalist economic system, and a social structure dominated by the middle class, like most of western Europe. Thus, while Spanish history does possess unique elements, such as the period of Muslim domination, its turn away from many aspects of the Enlightenment, its slowness in industrialization and economic modernization, these are insufficient to characterize Spain as an exceptional case in western Europe.

Notes

1. José Alvarez Junco and Adrian Shubert, eds., *Spanish History Since 1808*. New York: Oxford University Press, 2000, p. 3.

2. Junco and Shubert, *Spanish History Since 1808*, p. 3.

3. Julián Marías, *Understanding Spain*, trans. Frances M. Lopez-Morillas. San Juan: University of Puerto Rico, 1990, p. 4.

4. Marías, *Understanding Spain*, p. 5.

5. Peter Pierson, *The History of Spain*. Westport, CT: Greenwood, 1999, p. 24.

6. A similar postulate exists concerning the expulsion of the Jews in 1492.

7. Quoted in Marías, *Understanding Spain*, p. 110.

8. Rhea Marsh Smith, *Spain: A Modern History.* Ann Arbor: University of Michigan Press, 1965, p. 11.

9. Fred James Hill, *Spain: An Illustrated History.* New York: Hippocrene, 2001, p. 62.

10. Quoted in Marías, *Understanding Spain*, p. 206.

11. Simon Lemieux, "The Spanish Inquisition," *History Review*, December 2002, p. 47.

12. Lemieux, "The Spanish Inquisition," p. 47.

13. Jaime Vicens Vive, *Approaches to the History of Spain*, trans. Joan Connelly Ullman. Berkeley and Los Angeles: University of California Press, 1970, p. 92.

14. Junco and Shubert, *Spanish History Since 1808*, p. 3.

15. Adrian Shubert, *A Social History of Modern Spain*, London: Routledge, 1990, p. 2.

16. Shubert, *A Social History of Modern Spain*, pp. 4–5.

17. Quoted in Junco and Shubert, *Spanish History Since 1808*, p. 179.

18. Leandro Prados de la Escosura, "Economic Growth and Backwardness, 1780–1930," in Junco and Shubert, p. 183.

19. Escosura, "Economic Growth and Backwardness, 1780–1930," p. 184.

20. Crispin Coates, "Spanish Regionalism and the European Union," *Parliamentary Affairs*, April 1998, p. 259.

21. Marías, *Understanding Spain*, p. 11.

22. Raymond Carr, ed., introduction to *Spain: A History*. Oxford: Oxford University Press, 2000, p. 1.

23. Shubert, *A Social History of Modern Spain*, p. 2.

THE HISTORY OF NATIONS
Chapter 1

Foundations

Prehistoric and Roman Spain

BY RHEA MARSH SMITH

Rhea Marsh Smith was a history professor at Rollins College from 1930 to 1972. His scholarly interest was in Latin American and Spanish studies. In this selection Smith details the earliest history of the Spanish lands, from their occupation by prehistoric nomads from Africa to Roman conquest and control. He maintains that it was not until Roman rule was firmly established that Spain gained any kind of political unity. Furthermore, it was under the Romans that the Christianization of the Iberian peoples occurred, which, Smith argues, was the most significant event in the early history of Spain.

The Iberian Peninsula, which from the Pyrenees to its southern coast bears on the map a false appearance of unity, was for centuries without any political cohesion whatever. The Greek name Iberia apparently referred at the outset only to a vague coastal strip. Not until Rome established an all-embracing authority did the prefiguring of a nation emerge, and this was centuries after the Phoenicians and Carthaginians had begun to mingle their blood with that of the people of the land.

The First Settlers

The tardiness with which the outlines of a separate and identifiable country appeared may be attributed in part to the character of the tribes which in prehistoric times had entered Spain from North Africa, coming across the Strait of Gibraltar between the two great rocks which Greek mariners were to call the Pillars of Hercules. These hardy, independent-spirited migrants—perhaps seeking refuge from the aridity that was turning so much African soil into a desert—planted well-fortified settlements on mountain tops, whence they regarded each other with the suspicion and instant readiness for war which stamp most primitive peoples. Although the thrusts of invaders—first the Carthaginians, then the Romans—drove them to form loose confederacies, they never united in a truly national war against their enemies. . . .

In the dim twilight of the past, twelve or thirteen centuries before the Christian era, Celts from Western Europe found their way through the passes of the Pyrenees and scattered across the northwestern and western parts of the peninsula. They also occupied the Ebro Valley alongside the Iberians and penetrated the central meseta, but they never spread into the eastern and southeastern parts, where the Iberians retained all their cultural and political independence. The Celts were not strong enough to give any real measure of unity in language, customs, and outlook to the whole peninsula, or any great part of it. The task had been made more difficult, when they arrived, by the fact that competing migrants from the Mediterranean basin were placing their own strong imprint on the eastern reaches.

Contact with the Near East

The first Near Eastern people to reach the peninsula by the sea lanes were the Phoenicians. Modern Spaniards proudly point to the foundations of the ancient Phoenician lighthouse at La Coruña as an historic monument established early in the twelfth century B.C. or thereabouts by hardy navigators from Sidon. This beacon served mariners cautiously following the coast northward to the British Isles in their quest for tin to be alloyed with copper in making bronze.

The sailors of another Phoenician city, Tyre, followed their compatriots to the west later in the twelfth century B.C. They not only found precious metals in Spain, but developed a flourishing commerce with the Iberians, planting trading posts in the Guadalquivir Valley and along the southern coast. The most important trade center was Gades, now Cádiz founded about 1100 B.C., from which Phoenician products were widely distributed among the people of the region. The Phoenicians never tried to colonize the peninsula, but their trading posts were kept prosperous by their merchants and seamen.

The Greeks did not penetrate the western Mediterranean until much later than the Phoenicians. Reports of the wealth of the so-called Tartessians—apparently the Iberians in the Guadalquivir Valley—and of the profitable commerce which the Phoenicians had developed finally attracted seamen and merchants from the Greek islands. The earliest Greek to reach Tartessos was Kolaeus of Samos, about 630 B.C., and the profits of his trade with the country stimulated Greeks from Phocaea to follow. Their enterprise and sagacity so impressed the Tartessian king, Arganthonius, that he urged them to settle in his realm. They called the peninsula either Hesperia or Iberia....

The Greeks introduced the olive and grape into Spain, used the first coined money at Emporion, and exercised a great influence on the improvement of Iberian ceramics.

After the Persians conquered Tyre in the sixth century, the place of leadership in the western Mediterranean was inherited from the Phoenicians by the kindred city of Carthage, whose strategic position on the North African coast enabled her rulers to dominate the other Phoenician colonies and to extend her control over nearly the entire Iberian Peninsula. According to the historian Polybius, Carthage by the fourth century B.C. had established a protectorate over all the Iberian tribes as far north as the Pyrenees and had incorporated Iberian volunteers in her armies. The Carthaginians adopted a militant policy, alternating between brutality and conciliation, which aimed at the conquest of the peninsula and the exploitation of its mineral resources and manpower. The ambition of Carthage to dominate the land was stimulated by the First Punic War (264–241 B.C.) with Rome.

Hamilcar Barca, the father of Hannibal, who had won fame in the stubborn but unsuccessful attempt of the Carthaginians to gain control of Sicily, led an army across the Strait of Gibraltar into Spain with the farsighted intention of bringing all the rich resources of the country under Carthaginian control (237 B.C.). He saw that this land could more than compensate Carthage for the loss of Sicily. The agricultural and mineral wealth, warlike tribesmen, and ports and fortresses would be invaluable if properly organized. And Hamilcar was sufficiently statesmanlike to use his army in a peaceable rather than a violent conquest of the land; he treated the people as allies, not subjects, encouraged the intermarriage of his soldiers with Spanish women—his own son Hannibal taking one as wife—and assisted the Spaniards in improving their economic position. Tradition credits him with the founding of Barcelona, which bears the family name, and it was he who developed New Carthage (Cartagena) as a splendid seaport.

By the time Hamilcar Barca died in 228 B.C., to be succeeded by his nephew, the equally statesmanlike Hasdrubal, the Carthaginians had established an ascendancy over the entire southern half of the peninsula. Their success aroused the jealous apprehension of the Romans, who were meanwhile fighting to extend their own sway over southern Gaul. In their alarm the Romans demanded from Hasdrubal an assurance that the Carthaginian advance would not be pushed northeast of the Ebro River, which flows to the Mediterranean south of the present city of Barcelona; they did not wish to be pushed entirely out of Spain.

When Hannibal succeeded Hasdrubal in 221 B.C., though not yet thirty, he recognized with the insight of genius that war with Rome was inevitable. He proceeded to reorganize the Carthaginian army—incorporating into it many Iberians as mercenaries—and to consolidate his power in Spain. The Romans had assumed the role of protector of the Greek colonies along the east coast, and one of these, Saguntum, a strong citadel, was the only obstacle to Carthaginian domination south of the Ebro River. Hannibal besieged and captured Saguntum while the Romans vainly protested and finally sent an ultimatum to Carthage. Thereupon the Carthaginians declared war on Rome (218 B.C.).

The Second Punic War (218–201 B.C.) was savagely contested in three theaters—Italy, Spain, and North Africa. The Romans prepared to dispute Carthaginian control of the Iberian Peninsula, but in one of the greatest offensive movements of history Hannibal, with his Carthaginians, Iberian mercenaries, Balearic slingers, and elephants, crossed the Alps and invaded Italy, annihilating a Roman army at Cannae. No match for Hannibal in pitched battle, the Romans adopted the Fabian policy of wearing down the Carthaginian army by attrition. Meanwhile, in Spain, the recklessly dashing Scipio Africanus revived the spirit of the Roman soldiers and gained the adherence of many Iberians. He carried the war into Carthaginian Spain, captured New Carthage by a sudden brilliant blow (210 B.C.), and forced the Carthaginians out of Gades into North Africa.

Roman Occupation

After the final defeat of the Carthaginians at the battle of Zama, the Romans under the able leadership of Scipio Africanus began to occupy the whole peninsula. By the end of the year 205 B.C. they had partly succeeded. An impressive new era in the history of the country began; indeed, one of the most impressive of all its eras, lasting more than six hundred years. The civilization of the Carthaginians, rich in commercial and military achievements though it was—its harsh power is graphically reflected in [French novelist Gustave] Flaubert's novel *Salammbô*—had been largely identical with the culture of the earlier comers, the Phoenicians. Now a much ampler and stronger authority had taken control, with one of the grandest civilizations of all history. Spain became the first great area assimilated by the Romans, and one of the most important overseas provinces of the empire. The country was soon divided into two great provinces, Farther Hispania west of the Ebro, and Hither Hispania east of that river, both governed by praetors. There was little homogeneity in either province, and neither of them was fully pacified for many decades. The Romans were forced to become conquerors of Spain by their eagerness to exploit all the values of its minerals and manpower, but at first they sadly underestimated the tenacity of native resistance. The conquest required nearly continuous warfare for two hundred years and exacted a heavy toll of Roman lives and treasure.

Although the Romans hoped—by developing the mineral resources and using the natives as mercenaries—to make the conquest of Spain pay for itself, they found this impossible. Profitable use of the mines required peace, which could be obtained only by the maintenance of standing armies. The disunity of the Iberians meant constant warfare, for their successive tribal defeats brought neither submission nor peace. While the Romans fought in massed array with heavy arms and elaborate equipment, the Iberians fought in small groups, surprising the invaders in sudden attacks, falling upon them from ambush, and taking full advantage of their familiarity with the terrain. As this guerrilla warfare was marked by savage desperation, service in the peninsula was dreaded by the Roman legionnaires.

A succession of violent and rapacious praetors excited a spirit of bitter resistance among the "Celtiberians." After 181 B.C. Rome belatedly adopted a more conciliatory policy and, through diplomacy and honest administration, induced numerous cities to submit, pay an annual tribute, and provide auxiliaries for the imperial forces. During the ensuing interlude of peace the Iberians accepted Roman authority and sought justice at the hands of Roman officials. But this happy period ended when Roman officials again abused their authority—pillaging villages, imposing excessive fines, and, in general, acting in the most arbitrary manner. The Celtiberians were goaded to rebellion in 153 B.C. by Roman treachery and withdrew to the settlement called Numantia, their principal stronghold near the river Douro, where they repeatedly repelled superior Roman armies until Scipio Aemilianus starved them into submission (132 B.C.). . . .

The Roman Empire

Within a short time a far greater figure appeared on the Spanish stage. Julius Caesar, who became praetor in Rome in 59 B.C., went to Spain the following year to suppress the remnants of guerrilla warfare. He was doubly successful, for he not only gained the sympathy of the Iberians by reducing the tribute, but he also restored his personal fortunes and relieved himself of his enormous debts. When Caesar, [Gnaeus Pompeius Magnus] Pompey, and [Marcus Licinius] Crassus as members of the First Triumvirate (60 B.C.) divided the territories under Roman jurisdiction, Pompey obtained control of Spain, which had become a more important source of wealth and manpower than ever, while Caesar held command in Gaul. In the ensuing struggle between Caesar and Pompey, Caesar first marched to Rome and then transferred his forces to Spain, where he quickly restored order. His decisive victories over the sons of Pompey, culminating in a great battle at Munda near present-day Córdoba in 45 B.C., made Caesar the master of the Roman world.

When the Roman Empire came into existence after the assassination of Caesar in 43 B.C., Octavian, as his heir, soon became its head, assuming the name of Augustus Caesar. He at once began to restore order in Spain, which was one of the most important parts of the empire, and completed its conquest; he crushed the last resistance to Roman arms in Cantabria and Asturias. The Iberian Peninsula then entered the longest period of calm and order ever enjoyed by its inhabitants. The process of romanization was already well advanced. Relations with the Roman legionnaires, both as friends and enemies, the use of Roman methods in developing mines, agriculture, and trade, and the tolerance of Roman colonies led the native tribes to accept Roman institutions and customs until they became as Latin as the Latins themselves. Abandoning the old intertribal wars, they devoted themselves to a great and healthy variety of pursuits. The population increased from some six millions under Augustus to nine millions by the year 400 A.D. The Iberians also adopted the conquerors' language, and Spain became a center of Latin culture.

As the romanization proceeded, new provinces were added in Betica and Gallecia. The Emperor Diocletian made Spain a part of the Prefecture of Gaul, and its five provinces—with Balearica and Mauretania—were placed under the direct control of the emperor. The extension of Roman political and civil rights was an important factor in the process of unification. Julius Caesar and Augustus Caesar labored to incorporate the mass of the natives into Roman life, to create new colonies, and to transform them and existing cities into Roman *municipia*. Several classes of cities evolved as the Romans erected distinctions between those which submitted and those which resisted. Thus, the Iberian centers were gradually transformed during six centuries of Roman rule into communities of Latin or Roman citizenship. The *municipia*, as free cities, enjoyed a large measure of autonomy and attained a skill in self-government that persisted into the Middle Ages.

In the Roman armies native components were organized as auxiliaries, largely independent and highly respected. After the peninsula was fully pacified, the Roman garrison in Spain was reduced to a single legion. While the armed forces were composed only of Roman citizens, the Spaniards could be recruited after the Emperor Caracalla admitted all provincials to citizenship. Special legions of Spaniards served as garrisons, and the cities where they were stationed became fertile markets for trade.

The southern part of the peninsula was more prosperous than other areas. In the fertile lands of the Guadalquivir Valley wheat, grapes, and olives flourished, and Spanish wheat and olive oil were highly esteemed in Rome. Although at first the Romans tried to restrict Spanish competition, later they encouraged the introduction of special varieties of grapes, and Spanish wines became celebrated.

The Iberians had little interest in commerce, but it flourished with Italy and Africa through the enterprise of Roman and oriental merchants. Internal commerce was facilitated by the construction of an excellent network of roads—undertaken for military purposes but utilized also for trade—which greatly accelerated the unification of the peninsula. A majority of the Spanish rivers were dry for part of the year, but some of them were navigable for considerable distances—the Guadalquivir as far as Seville. The Hispano-Romans also developed an excellent

merchant marine and ports, which were improved with light-
houses and docks.

Spanish Society Under the Romans

Two principal classes composed the society of Roman Spain, the
freemen and the slaves. Among the freemen the aristocracy consisted of a small group of wealthy and privileged officials, who
obtained title to extensive lands. As the conquest proceeded a
middle class gradually appeared, including romanized freemen of
mercantile and professional status and bureaucrats. The remaining freemen were manual workers in the cities and on farms, or
served as soldiers and sailors. Some urban workers were organized
into primitive cooperative societies (*collegia*). The burden of taxation fell most heavily on the lower and middle classes, and a majority of the rural workers were transformed into the *coloni* of the
landed estates, the latifundia. Some slavery existed in Spain under Roman domination, but slaves were fewer than in Rome and
less numerous than free workers.

Education was important as a means of diffusing Roman culture. While the Spaniards at first used Latin literary models, by
the Augustan Age they began to exert an influence of their own
on Roman literature. The list of Spaniards who attained prominent positions in the literary world in Rome is impressive. Julius
Higinius became palace librarian of Augustus, and Marcus Por-
cius Latrus was a teacher of Ovid. The most influential family of
Spanish origin in Rome was that of Seneca. Annaeus Seneca, the
rhetorician, migrated from Córdoba. His son Lucius Annaeus
Seneca, a versatile writer of verse and prose and a Stoic philosopher, was a principal adviser to Nero. Marcus Annaeus Lucanus,
a nephew, was a poet celebrated for felicity of expression and
original philosophical and political ideas. Also natives of Spain
who made contributions to Latin literature were Quintilian, the
rhetorician; Martial, composer of poetic epigrams; Columella,
who retired to his native Cádiz to write twelve books on agriculture; and Pomponius Mela, author of the most ancient geographical work in Latin.

The most important event in ancient Iberian and Roman history, both for its immediate impact on the empire and for the future, was the conversion of the natives to Christianity. The Roman gods and the imperial cults had been introduced into the
Iberian Peninsula largely as an exercise of patriotic duty. Then

Christianity gained strength as the empire declined. The Spanish Church has always claimed the dignity of an apostolic origin, although no historic facts support the tradition of the missionary activity of St. James (Santiago) in the peninsula. Nevertheless, a belief in his residence, his martyrdom, and the translation of his body to Campus Stellae (Santiago de Compostela) is deeply woven into the national tradition. It is more probable that St. Paul was in Spain, perhaps between 63 and 67 A.D., although no evidence of his missionary labors has survived. The principal obstacle to the expansion of Christianity was the persistence of the imperial cult. The Christian converts, zealous in their pacifism and their denial of the pagan gods, were angrily opposed by officials and even by more tolerant citizens. The Emperors Decius, Valerian, and Diocletian were especially active in the persecution of the subversive sect.

Heresy soon began to appear among the less stalwart Christians under the Decian persecution, for they held that it was better to retract their faith than to become martyrs. But many were heroic even to death, and under later persecutions, martyrdom became a common avenue of escape to eternal life. The Catholic Church was recognized as a legal institution on an equal footing with other religions in 312, but then Hispanic individualism found expression in heretical divergence from orthodox opinion. The ideas of the Priscillians, who had absorbed some of the Iberian religious ideas and emphasized ascetic chastity, appealed especially to the natives and spread rapidly. Despite ecclesiastical condemnation the Priscillians dominated the peninsular church for a time, especially in Galicia; after the martyrdom of the founder, Bishop Priscillian of Ávila (d.385), they persisted until the sixth century. Meanwhile, an order of the Council of Iliberis (306) required clerical celibacy in the Spanish Church, this being probably the first prohibition of the marriage of priests.

In many ways the Romans united Spain. They unified the Iberians politically and culturally and gave them economic prosperity. As the Iberians became romanized they were the more easily converted to Christianity, which provided still another bond of unity. The Hispano-Romans finally became one of the most stable of all the peoples controlled by Rome and contributed their full share to the prosperity and strength of the Empire.

Six hundred years of Roman rule (205 B.C.–410 A.D.) made an indelible imprint on the population of Iberia. After reducing the inhabitants to submission, the conquerors proceeded to "romanize" them by giving them political and civil rights, recruiting them into the army, integrating their agricultural products into the imperial economy, and educating them in classical culture. The most obvious indication that the people had truly become Hispano-Romans was their adoption of Latin as the common language.

Christianity was introduced to the peninsula through Roman culture. It proved to be one of the most cohesive forces in Spanish civilization. The organized Church outlived the empire under which it had grown and played a vital part in the subsequent history of Spain.

Spain Under the Visigoths

By Stanley G. Payne

Stanley G. Payne is a professor of modern European history at the University of Wisconsin in Madison. He specializes in the history of Spain, Portugal, and Italy. In this passage Payne outlines the conquest of Spanish lands by the Germanic Visigoths and the establishment of Visigothic rule in Spain from the fifth to the eighth centuries A.D. He assesses the degree of success of the Visigoths in creating a unified political entity and discusses their influence on the development of early Spanish society.

The dissolution of Roman authority and its replacement by that of a Visigothic monarchy was a long, slow process. There was no sudden Visigothic invasion or conquest. The small host of the Visigothic ruler Ataulf that crossed the Pyrenees into Hispania in 415 acted as a federated army of the feeble Roman state, charged with expelling Vandal invaders from southern Hispania and subduing the Germanic Suevi who had dominated the northwestern quarter of the peninsula for several years. From their principal base in southwestern France, Visigothic bands slowly began to extend their control over the more lightly inhabited central plateau of the peninsula, sometimes acting in the name of the emperor, sometimes merely advancing their own interests. The imperial government had broken down and the Hispanic population lacked the civil or military means to defend itself. The main body of Visigoths did not enter the peninsula until the reign of Alaric II (484–507), and then largely as a result of military pressure from the Franks to the north. They may have numbered no more than 300,000 in a peninsula with 4,000,000 inhabitants. The Visigoths were superior to the Hispani only in the application of armed force;

economically, socially, and culturally the Hispanic population was in most regions far more advanced.

Though before their entry into the peninsula the Visigoths were culturally more Romanized than any other Germanic group, they were an essentially pastoral people, unlike the Ostrogoths and Suevi, whose societies were agrarian. The Visigoths settled in greatest numbers in the more sparsely populated, largely pastoral north-central area of the peninsula, and were thereby isolated from the main social and economic centers of the Hispanic population.

The Visigothic monarchy as an independent state was first proclaimed by Euric in southwestern France in 476, after the deposition of the last emperor in Rome by the Ostrogoths. The political center of the monarchy was not moved to the peninsula, however, until the reign of Athanagild (551–567), when a new capital was established at the town of Toledo in the central plateau, moving the axis of Hispanic life from the coastal regions for the first time. Visigothic authority was slowly expanded throughout the entire peninsula with the conquest of the Suevi during the reign of Leovigild (568–586) and the expulsion of Byzantine forces from their last remaining toehold in the southeast by Swinthila (621–631).

The Heirs of Rome

Like other post-Roman rulers in different parts of the former empire, the Visigothic kings of Hispania considered themselves the heirs of Rome and adopted Roman insignia and symbols of authority. They viewed themselves as successors, rather than destroyers or even replacers, of the empire. The Visigothic monarchy accepted the Roman theory of the state as a public power resting upon essentially absolute authority, though the official conversion to Catholicism that occurred during the reign of Leovigild accepted a modification of royal sovereignty by the religious and ethical tutelage of the church.

At the top of Hispano-Visigothic society there emerged an elite of some two hundred leading aristocratic families associated with the court and a broader aristocratic class of perhaps ten thousand people who held possession of most of the best land. Under the Visigoths, the aristocracy did not form a closed caste but were steadily recruited from below on the strength of personal achievement or royal favor. Over a period of a century or more there occurred a partial fusion of the original Visigothic warrior aristocracy and the socioeconomic elite of Hispanic society.

The Visigothic monarchy remained an elective institution, each new king nominally chosen or ratified by the aristocracy. The crown was assisted in decisions and administration by *aula regia* or royal council, but until the next to the last generation of Visigothic rule broad assemblies of notables were called to ratify important decisions, a last residue of the earlier tribal assemblies of the Germanic peoples. Administratively, the Visigothic monarchy relied on much of Roman usage and employed Hispanic personnel in local administration. By the sixth century, however, the Roman administrative system had fallen into such decay that it could not be revived, and in place of the old provincial system there evolved a new pattern of regional and local overlordship based upon regional dukes (*duces*) and heads of smaller districts or *territoria* called counts (*comes*). The new ducal administrative regions tended to coincide with the old Roman provinces, and the territoria of the counts with the old civitas units. The old municipal system also fell into desuetude and was slowly replaced by a pattern of royal administration and local overlords nominally ratified by the crown. Most of the Hispanic population remained juridically free, but the process of commendatio continued, as peasants pledged parts of their land or services to local overlords for security, and the class of enserfed coloni grew larger. Yet there were still a number of relatively autonomous local rural communities that preserved their legal identity.

Spanish Society Under Visigothic Rule

The cultural and economic life of Visigothic Hispania was carried on almost exclusively by the native Hispani, to whom was due the relative prosperity of part of the sixth and seventh centuries. Roman law had to be relied upon in administering the affairs of the social and economic infrastructure, and over a period of two centuries there evolved a slow fusion of Visigothic custom and Roman common law. The general trend was away from the Roman system of explicit private property toward more communal, reciprocal, usufructural relations in the ownership and use of property. The Hispano-Visigothic modus vivendi found codified expression in the promulgation of the *Liber Iudiciorum* (later commonly known in Castilian as the *Fuero Juzgo*) in 654. This fusion of aspects of Visigothic personal codes with Latin

The Laws of the Visigoths

These statutes outlining the Visigothic laws concerning inheritance reveal that women had the legal right to inherit and possess property. Moreover, daughters received an equal share of the inheritance upon their parents' deaths, thereby indicating a degree of gender equality with sons.

I. Brothers and Sisters shall Share Equally in the Inheritance of their Parents. If the father or mother should die intestate, the sisters shall have the property equally with their brothers. . . .

IX. A Woman shall be entitled to a Share in an Entire Inheritance. A woman shall inherit, equally with her brothers, the property of their father or mother, of their grandparents, on the paternal and the maternal side, as well as of their brothers and sisters; and also any property which may be left by a paternal uncle, or a cousin, or a nephew, or a niece. For it is only just that those who are nearly related by blood, should enjoy the benefit of hereditary succession

X. As a Woman has a Right to a Share of an Entire Inheritance, so he who is next in Succession shall Inherit the Remainder of the Property. Women shall share all properly left by relatives on the maternal side, with those in the same degree of relationship whether they be uncles, aunts, or cousins. For those should have the inheritance who are the most nearly related to the deceased.

XI. Concerning the Inheritance of Husband and Wife, respectively. Husband and wife shall inherit from each other, respectively, when they leave no relatives nearer than the seventh degree.

The Visigothic Code (Forum Judicum), book 4, *Concerning Natural Lineage,*
Title II: Concerning the Laws of Inheritance. http://libro.uca.edu/vcode/
visigoths.htm.

civil and property law superseded several less complete codifications and provided an organized code on which to base property rights and civil administration for the Visigothic aristocracy and, to some extent, the Hispanic common people.

It has sometimes been maintained that under the Visigothic monarchy a mode of theocracy developed that thereafter characterized Hispanic religion and government. Such a notion is considerably exaggerated. Even during the Arian period of the Visigothic monarchy, when a great theological gulf existed between the rulers and organized Christianity, the Hispanic bishops proved themselves to be obedient to legally established authority. They rarely hesitated to uphold the power of the state in the secular realm, even to the extent of supporting one Arian king against his rebellious (but orthodox Catholic) son. When finally the monarchy accepted Catholicism in 589, it was made clear that this conversion was not forced upon the state by the church but was freely decided upon by the monarchy to promote its own interests. The church lost a significant measure of independence by recognizing the right of the crown to appoint the members of the ecclesiastical hierarchy. The king became the nominal head of church councils and took a formal responsibility to see that church affairs were properly run. The subsequent Councils of Toledo were organized along more or less Byzantine lines as mixed assemblies of high ecclesiastical and state officials, with the clerics responsible for church affairs and the secular officials bearing primary responsibility for state legislation.

Thus rather than theocracy there developed a church-state symbiosis in which the power of the crown was uppermost but in which the church played a major role in trying to stabilize public institutions and authority. After the Fourth Council of Toledo in 633, approval by the councils was required to legalize succession to the nonhereditary Visigothic throne, anathematize usurpers, and ratify amnesties. Church leaders were increasingly employed by the crown in administration because they were the primary source of educated, technically competent, and trustworthy personnel. Yet the crown did not intervene in the theological affairs of the church; religious councils were presided over by an archbishop, not the king. The Christian church became the only cohesive institution in Visigothic Hispania.

The early Hispanic church reached its cultural height during the era of Isidore of Seville (first third of the seventh century), shining briefly as the brightest center of learning in western Europe. For the common people it provided the only identity and hope which they knew during this period. Hispanic monasteries played a special role, becoming quite numerous, and the most active force in raising spiritual standards, expanding the influence of the church, and providing a spiritual leadership for the church.

Toward the end of the Visigothic period the church had become a major property holder, with almost every parish and monastery of note possessing lands or rights that provided it with income. The church had achieved a special legal status, developing a code of canon law and special tribunals for the clergy and their affairs. The Hispanic church thus came to constitute a fairly well ordered state of its own within the poorly structured Visigothic political framework.

Yet despite its outwardly imposing strength, the Hispanic church failed to incorporate all the population of the peninsula within its following even as late as the seventh century. The peoples of the northern hills remained vague in their religious identification, while the Basques were almost untouched by Christianity. Even among the more densely inhabited southern and eastern districts, conversion of much of the rural population remained nominal at best. Hispanic Christianity was still to a considerable degree an urban religion, and tended to become weaker the farther one moved from the principal centers of population.

This was the more significant because it may be roughly generalized that throughout the Visigothic era the urban economy and society of southern and eastern Hispania continued to decline. The failure of administration, which the Visigothic crown was unable to restore, the absence of monetary order, progressive disruption of trade routes, and the decline of economic opportunities all continued even after the disorders of the fifth and sixth centuries had ended. The rise of Muslim power in the east Mediterranean during the seventh century presaged new commercial and military challenges. By that time Hispanic urban society had lost most of the vigor and prosperity that it had known during the high Roman period.

Even at its height, Roman rule had been unable to eliminate the strong regional and ethnic differences that divided the peninsula, and these became more pronounced again under the Visigoths. Fusion between the Visigothic elite and the Hispani population was never complete. The northwestern corner of the peninsula, ruled for two hundred years by the Suevi monarchy, remained a distinctive, not thoroughly assimilated region. The southwestern tip of France, known as Septimania, remained under Visigothic rule and tended to link northeastern Hispania with France. The sophisticated eastern coastal region had long been interconnected with the commerce and culture of the Italian peninsula, while the equally sophisticated towns of the south were closely associated with northwest Africa and with Byzantine commerce. In the far north, Asturians and Cantabrians were at best only partly assimilated, and the Basques remained almost entirely apart. Finally, there was a significant Jewish minority in the southern and eastern towns that played a major role in manufacturing and commerce. Subjected to attempted conversion and sporadic persecution by the Visigothic crown in the seventh century, Hispanic Jews were a politically disaffected and potentially rebellious element in the major towns.

A Less-than-Unified Political Entity

The Visigothic monarchy never developed a cohesive polity. Visigothic aristocrats and military leaders deemed themselves part of a personal power association with the crown and resisted extension of juridical control. Royal succession remained elective, and the entire history of the monarchy was one of revolt, assassination, and internecine feuding. This insecurity placed a premium on military power, but the monarchy could not marshal resources to restore the independent standing army of Rome. Instead, a process of protofeudalization developed early and was expanded more rapidly in Visigothic Hispania than in Merovingian France. Decentralization was unavoidable, and power became a matter of personal relationship and example. The chief lieutenants of the crown were rewarded for their services by salaries or *stipendia* in the form of overlordship of land or temporary assignment of income from land held *in precarium*, that is, on a nominally revocable basis. This system was actually first used by the church to support local establishments, and by the seventh century was widely employed by the crown and also by the *magnates* (the high aristocracy) to pay their chief supporters and military retainers. The process of protofeudalization inevitably carried with it a splintering of juridical and economic sovereignty that further weakened political unity.

If the Visigothic aristocracy was unable to develop a unified, viable political system, it was nevertheless itself the beginning of the historic Hispanic master class. In this Visigothic caste the military aristocracy of the peninsula had its roots, creating a style and a psychology of the warrior nobleman that provided the dominant leadership for Hispanic society for more than a thousand years; this psychology ultimately managed to superimpose its values and attitudes on much of the society as a whole. Yet the success of the aristocratic ethos was a consequence of the experience of medieval Hispania, not of the rule of the Visigothic oligarchy, which largely proved an historic failure.

In the seventh century the caste relationship between the ruling group and much of the peasantry was little better than that of master to serf. A large proportion of the peasantry had been reduced to a kind of serfdom, and as the economy declined, economic exactions very likely increased. Evidence indicates that many Hispanic serfs and even many free peasants did not consider the protection and leadership they received worth the service demanded of them. During the last Visigothic century there were a number of peasant revolts and urban riots in protest against economic conditions.

In sum, the political and social structure of Visigothic Hispania was brittle and incohesive. It survived only until the first major challenge from without, then collapsed much more rapidly than it had been built.

Islamic Conquest and Rule

By Will Durant

In 712 an army of Moors and Berbers invaded Spain and defeated a Visigoth army. Within five years, Muslims had seized most of Spain and had established a flourishing civilization. In the following selection Will Durant describes the Muslim invasion and the characteristics of Muslim society and culture in Spain, including the construction of ornate mansions and mosques and the development of the arts and education. Durant was a journalist and a professor of Latin, French, and philosophy. With his wife, Ariel Durant, he coauthored the multivolume work The Story of Civilization.

It was at first the Moors,[1] not the Arabs, who conquered Spain. Tariq was a Berber, and his army had 7000 Berbers to 300 Arabs. His name is embedded in the rock at whose foot his forces landed; the Moors came to call it Gebel al-Tariq, the Mountain of Tariq, which Europe compressed into Gibraltar. Tariq had been sent to Spain by Musa ibn Nusayr, Arab governor of North Africa. In 712 Musa crossed with 10,000 Arabs and 8000 Moors; besieged and captured Seville and Merida; rebuked Tariq for exceeding orders, struck him with a whip, and cast him into prison. The Caliph Walid recalled Musa and freed Tariq, who resumed his conquests. . . .

Islam Fails to Move Beyond Spain

The victors treated the conquered leniently, confiscated the lands only of those who had actively resisted, exacted no greater tax than had been levied by the Visigothic[2] kings, and gave to reli-

1. northern African Muslims of Arab and Berber descent; Berbers were tribes from North Africa.   2. Western Goths who invaded the Roman Empire and established a monarchy lasting from the fourth to the eighth century

Will Durant, *The Story of Civilization: The Age of Faith.* New York: Simon & Schuster, 1950. Copyright © 1950 by Will Durant. Reproduced by permission.

gious worship a freedom rare in Spain. Having established their position in the peninsula, the Moslems scaled the Pyrenees and entered Gaul,[3] intent upon making Europe a province of Damascus. Between Tours and Poitiers, a thousand miles north of Gibraltar, they were met by the united forces of Eudes, Duke of Aquitaine, and Charles, Duke of Austrasia. After seven days of fighting, the Moslems were defeated in one of the most crucial battles of history (732); again the faith of countless millions was determined by the chances of war. . . .

The caliphs of Damascus undervalued Spain; till 756 it was merely "the district of Andalusia," and was governed from Qairwan. But in 755 a romantic figure landed in Spain, armed only with royal blood, and destined to establish a dynasty that would rival in wealth and glory the caliphs of Baghdad. When, in 750, the triumphant Abbasids ordered all princes of the Umayyad family slain, Abd-er-Rahman, grandson of the Caliph Hisham, was the only Umayyad who escaped. Hunted from village to village, he swam the broad Euphrates, crossed into Palestine, Egypt and Africa, and finally reached Morocco. News of the Abbasid revolution had intensified the factional rivalry of Arabs, Syrians, Persians, and Moors in Spain; an Arab group loyal to the Umayyads, fearing that the Abbasid caliph might question their titles to lands given them by Umayyad governors, invited Abd-er-Rahman to join and lead them. He came, and was made emir of Cordova (756). He defeated an army commissioned by the Caliph al-Mansur to unseat him, and sent the head of its general to be hung before a palace in Mecca.

Perhaps it was these events that saved Europe from worshiping Mohammed: Moslem Spain, weakened with civil war and deprived of external aid, ceased to conquer, and withdrew even from northern Spain. From the ninth to the eleventh century the peninsula was divided into Moslem and Christian by a line running from Coimbra through Saragossa and along the Ebro River. The Moslem south, finally pacified by Abd-er-Rahman I and his successors, blossomed into riches, poetry, and art. Abd-er-Rahman II (822–52) enjoyed the fruits of this prosperity. Amid border wars with the Christians, rebellions among his subjects, and Norman raids on his coasts, he found time to beautify Cordova with palaces and mosques, rewarded poets handsomely, and

3. an ancient region comprising modern-day France

The Iberian Peninsula
At the Beginning of
the Tenth Century

Kingdoms/Counties	4 Condado de Ribagorza	8 Condado de Gerona
1 Reino de Pamplona	5 Condado de Pallares	9 Condado de Barcelona
2 Condado de Arragon	6 Condado de Rosellon	10 Condado de Ausona
3 Condado de Sobrarbe	7 Condado de Ampurias	11 Condado de Urgel

forgave offenders with an amiable lenience that may have shared in producing the social disorder that followed his reign.

Abd-er-Rahman III (912–61) is the culminating figure of this Umayyad dynasty in Spain. Coming to power at twenty-one, he found "Andaluz" torn by racial faction, religious animosity, sporadic brigandage, and the efforts of Seville and Toledo to establish their independence of Cordova. Though a man of refinement, famous for generosity and courtesy, he laid a firm hand upon the situation, quelled the rebellious cities, and subdued the Arab aristocrats who wished, like their French contemporaries, to enjoy a feudal sovereignty on their rich estates. He invited to his councils men of diverse faiths, adjusted his alliances to maintain a balance of power among his neighbors and his enemies, and administered the government with Napoleonic industry and attention to detail. He planned the campaigns of his generals, often took the field in person, repulsed the invasions of Sancho of Navarre, captured and destroyed Sancho's capital, and discouraged further Christian forays during his reign. In 929, knowing himself as powerful as any ruler of his time, and realizing that the caliph of Baghdad had become a puppet of Turkish guards, he assumed the caliphal title—Commander of the Faithful and Defender of the Faith. When he died he left behind him, in his own handwriting, a modest estimate of human life:

> I have now reigned above fifty [Mohammedan] years in victory or peace. . . . Riches and honors, powers and pleasures, have waited on my call; nor does any earthly blessing appear to have been wanting to my felicity. In this situation I have diligently numbered the days of

Tarik's Address to His Soldiers

Tarik was the Muslim leader who led the conquest of Spain. In this passage he addresses his soldiers during their invasion of Spain, urging them to be courageous in the face of the counterattack by the Spanish forces. He promises them great rewards for their efforts, including glory and treasure.

Oh my warriors, whither would you flee? Behind you is the sea, before you, the enemy. You have left now only the hope of your courage and your constancy. Remember that in this country you are more unfortunate than the orphan seated at the table of the avaricious master. Your enemy is before you, protected by an innumerable army; he has men in abundance, but you, as your only aid, have your own swords, and, as your only chance for life, such chance as you can snatch from the hands of your enemy. If the absolute want to which you are reduced is prolonged ever so little, if you delay to seize immediate success, your good fortune will vanish, and your enemies, whom your very presence has filled with fear, will take courage. Put far from you the disgrace from which you flee in dreams, and attack this monarch who has left his strongly fortified city to meet you. Here is a splendid opportunity to

pure and genuine happiness which have fallen to my lot. They amount to fourteen. O man! place not thy confidence in this present world!

Cordova Under Moslem Rule

... Gleaming cupolas and gilded minarets marked the thousand cities or towns that made Moslem Spain in the tenth century the most urban country in Europe, probably in the world. Cordova under al-Mansur was a civilized city, second only to Baghdad and Constantinople. Here, says al-Maqqari [in *History of Mohammedan Dynasties in Spain*], were 200,077 houses, 60,300 palaces, 600 mosques, and 700 public baths; the statistics are slightly Oriental. Visitors marveled at the wealth of the upper classes, and at what

defeat him, if you will consent to expose yourselves freely to death. Do not believe that I desire to incite you to face dangers which I shall refuse to share with you. In the attack I myself will be in the fore, where the chance of life is always least.

Remember that if you suffer a few moments in patience, you will afterward enjoy supreme delight. Do not imagine that your fate can be separated from mine, and rest assured that if you fall, I shall perish with you, or avenge you. You have heard that in this country there are a large number of ravishingly beautiful Greek maidens, their graceful forms are draped in sumptuous gowns on which gleam pearls, coral, and purest gold, and they live in the palaces of royal kings. The Commander of Trus Believers, Alwalid, son of Abdalmelik, has chosen you for this attack from among all his Arab warriors; and he promises that you shall become his comrades and shall hold the rank of kings in this country. Such is his confidence in your intrepidity. The one fruit which he desires to obtain from your bravery is that the word of God shall be exalted in this country, and that the true religion shall be established here. The spoils will belong to yourselves.

Charles F. Horne, ed., *The Sacred Books and Early Literature of the East*, vol. 6, *Medieval Arabia*. New York: Parke, Austin, and Lipscomb, 1917.

seemed to them an extraordinary general prosperity; every family could afford a donkey; only beggars could not ride. Streets
were paved, had raised sidewalks, and were lighted at night; one
could travel for ten miles by the light of street lamps, and along
an uninterrupted series of buildings. Over the quiet Guadalquivir
Arab engineers threw a great stone bridge of seventeen arches,
each fifty spans [an English unit of measure equal to 9 inches] in
width. One of the earliest undertakings of Abd-er-Rahman I
was an aqueduct that brought to Cordova an abundance of fresh
water for homes, gardens, fountains, and baths. The city was famous for its pleasure gardens and promenades.

Abd-er-Rahman I, lonesome for his boyhood haunts, planted
in Cordova a great garden like that of the villa in which he had
spent his boyhood near Damascus, and built in it his "Palace of
the Rissafah." Later caliphs added other structures, to which
Moslem fancy gave florid names: Palace of the Flowers . . . of the
Lovers . . . of Contentment . . . of the Diadem. Cordova, like later
Seville, had its Alcazar (al-qasr, castle, from the Latin castrum), a
combination of palace and fortress. Moslem historians describe
these mansions as equaling in luxury and beauty those of Nero's
Rome: majestic portals, marble columns, mosaic floors, gilded
ceilings, and such refined decoration as only Moslem art could
give. The palaces of the royal family, the lords and magnates of
land and trade, lined for miles the banks of the stately stream. A
concubine of Abd-er-Rahman III left him a large fortune; he
proposed to spend it ransoming such of his soldiers as had been
captured in war; proud searchers claimed they could find none;
whereupon the Caliph's favorite wife, Zahra, proposed that he
build a suburb and palace to commemorate her name. For
twenty-five years (936–61) 10,000 workmen and 1500 beasts
toiled to realize her dream. The royal palace of al-Zahra that rose
three miles southwest of Cordova was lavishly designed and
equipped; 1200 marble columns sustained it; its harem could ac-
commodate 6000 women; its hall of audience had ceiling and
walls of marble and gold, eight doors inlaid with ebony, ivory, and
precious stones, and a basin of quicksilver whose undulating surface reflected the dancing rays of the sun. Al-Zahra became the
residential center of an aristocracy renowned for the grace and
polish of its manners, the refinement of its tastes, and the breadth
of its intellectual interests. At the opposite end of the city al-
Mansur constructed (978) a rival palace, al-Zahira, which also

gathered about it a suburb of lords, servants, minstrels, poets, and courtesans. Both suburbs were burned to the ground in the revolution of 1010.

The Blue Mosque

Normally the people forgave the luxury of their princes if these would raise to Allah shrines exceeding their palaces in splendor and scope. The Romans had built in Cordova a temple to Janus; the Christians had replaced it with a cathedral; Abd-er-Rahman I paid the Christians for the site, demolished the church, and replaced it with the Blue Mosque; in 1238 the *reconquista*[4] would turn the mosque into a cathedral; so the good, the true, and the beautiful fluctuate with the fortunes of war. The project became the consolation of Abd-er-Rahman's troubled years; he left his suburban for his city home to superintend the operations, and hoped that he might before his death lead the congregation in grateful prayer in this new and majestic mosque. He died in 788, two years after laying the foundation; his son al-Hisham continued the work; each caliph, for two centuries, added a part, till in al-Mansur's time it covered an area 742 by 472 feet. The exterior showed a battlemented wall of brick and stone, with irregular towers, and a massive minaret that surpassed in size and beauty all the minarets of the time, so that it too was numbered among the innumerable "wonders of the world." Nineteen portals, surmounted by horseshoe arches elegantly carved with floral and geometrical decoration in stone, led into the Court of Ablutions, now the Patio de los Naranjos, or Court of Oranges. In this rectangle, paved with colored tiles, stood four fountains, each cut from a block of solid marble so large that seventy oxen had been needed to haul it from the quarry to the site. The mosque proper was a forest of 1290 columns, dividing the interior into eleven naves and twenty-one aisles. From the column capitals sprang a variety of arches—some semicircular, some pointed, some in horseshoe form, most of them with voussoirs, or wedge stones, alternately red or white. The columns of jasper, porphyry, alabaster, or marble, snatched from the ruins of Roman or Visigothic Spain, gave by their number the impression of limitless and bewildering space. The wooden ceiling was carved into cartouches[5] bearing Koranic and other

4. reconquering   5. an oval shield or oblong scroll used as an architectural ornament to bear an inscription

inscriptions. From it hung 200 chandeliers holding 7000 cups of scented oil, fed from reservoirs of oil in inverted Christian bells also suspended from the roof. Floor and walls were adorned with mosaics; some of these were of enameled glass, baked in rich colors, and often containing silver or gold; after a thousand years of wear these dados[6] still sparkle like jewels in the cathedral walls. One section was marked off as a sanctuary; it was paved with silver and enameled tiles, guarded with ornate doors, decorated with mosaics, roofed with three domes, and marked off with a wooden screen of exquisite design. Within this sanctuary were built the mihrab and *minbar,* upon which the artists lavished their maturest skill. The mihrab itself was an heptagonal recess walled with gold; brilliantly ornamented with enameled mosaics, marble tracery,[7] and gold inscriptions on a ground of crimson and blue; and crowned by a tier of slender columns and trefoil[8] arches as lovely as anything in Gothic art. The pulpit was considered the finest of its kind; it consisted of 37,000 little panels of ivory and precious woods—ebony, citron, aloe, red and yellow sandal, all joined by gold or silver nails, and inlaid with gems. On this *minbar,* in a jeweled box covered with gold-threaded crimson silk, rested a copy of the Koran written by the Caliph Othman and stained with his dying blood. To us, who prefer to adorn our theaters with gilt and brass rather than clothe our cathedrals in jewelry and gold, the decoration of the Blue Mosque seems extravagant; the walls encrusted with the blood of exploited generations, the columns confusingly numerous, the horseshoe arch as structurally weak and aesthetically offensive as obesity on bow legs. Others, however, have judged differently: al-Maqqari (1591–1632) thought this mosque "unequaled in size, or beauty of design, or tasteful arrangement of its ornaments, or boldness of execution"; and even its diminished Christian form is ranked as "by universal consent the most beautiful Moslem temple in the world."

Scholarship and Education in Moslem Spain

It was a common saying in Moorish Spain that "when a musician dies at Cordova, and his instruments are to be sold, they are

---

6. lower portion of a wall, decorated differently from the upper part   7. ornamental work of interlaced and branching lines   8. an architectural form appearing like a leaf

sent to Seville; when a rich man dies at Seville, and his library is
to be sold, it is sent to Cordova" [according to A.F. Calvert in
Cordova]. For Cordova in the tenth century was the focus and
summit of Spanish intellectual life, though Toledo, Granada, and
Seville shared actively in the mental exhilaration of the time.
Moslem historians picture the Moorish cities as beehives of poets, scholars, jurists, physicians, and scientists; al-Maqqari fills sixty
pages with their names. Primary schools were numerous, but
charged tuition; Hakam II added twenty-seven schools for the
free instruction of the poor. Girls as well as boys went to school;
several Moorish ladies became prominent in literature or art.
Higher education was provided by independent lecturers in the
mosques; their courses constituted the loosely organized University of Cordova, which in the tenth and eleventh centuries
was second in renown only to similar institutions in Cairo and
Baghdad. Colleges were established also at Granada, Toledo,
Seville, Murcia, Almeria, Valencia, Cadiz. The technique of paper making was brought in from Baghdad, and books increased
and multiplied. Moslem Spain had seventy libraries; rich men displayed their Morocco bindings, and bibliophiles collected rare or
beautifully illuminated books. The scholar al-Hadram, at an auc-
tion in Cordova, found himself persistently outbid for a book he
desired, until the price offered far exceeded the value of the volume. The successful bidder explained that there was a vacant
place in his library, into which this book would precisely fit. "I
was so vexed," adds al-Hadram, "that I could not help saying to
him, 'He gets the nut who has no teeth.'"

Scholars were held in awesome repute in Moslem Spain, and
were consulted in simple faith that learning and wisdom are one.
Theologians and grammarians could be had by the hundred;
rhetoricians, philologists, lexicographers, anthologists, historians,
biographers, were legion. Abu Muhammad Ali ibn Hazm
(994–1064), besides serving as vizier to the last Umayyads, was a
theologian and historian of great erudition. His *Book of Religions
and Sects,* discussing Judaism, Zoroastrianism, Christianity, and the
principal varieties of Mohammedanism, is one of the world's earliest essays in comparative religion. If we wish to know what an
educated Moslem thought of medieval Christianity we need only
read one of his paragraphs:

> Human superstition need never excite our astonish-
> ment. The most numerous and civilized nations are

thralls to it. . . . So great is the multitude of Christians that God alone can number them, and they can boast of sagacious princes and illustrious philosophers. Nevertheless they believe that one is three and three are one; that one of the three is the Father, the other the Son, and the third the Spirit; that the Father is the Son and is not the Son; that a man is God and not God; that the Messiah has existed from all eternity, and yet was created. A sect of theirs, the Monophysites, numbered by hundreds of thousands, believes that the Creator was scourged, buffeted, crucified, and that for three days the universe was without a ruler.

Ibn Hazm, for his part, believed that every word of the Koran was literally true. Science and philosophy, in Moslem Spain, were largely frustrated by the fear that they would damage the people's faith.

Late Medieval and Early Modern Spain

Christian Reconquest

By Fred James Hill

Fred James Hill is a writer and editor who has spent many years living and traveling in Spain. In this piece Hill describes the centuries-long process of consolidation of the Christian kingdoms of Spain and efforts by Christians to reconquer lands that had been taken by the Muslims during the eighth and ninth centuries. Eventually, the Christians were able to re-establish control over nearly all of the Spanish territories, with the exception of the kingdom of Granada, which remained an Islamic stronghold until the end of the fifteenth century.

In the early 11th century, there were four Christian Kingdoms in Spain—Castilla, León, Navarra, Aragón—and the counties of Catalonia. But there was little unity between them as they fought not only the Muslims but also each other. Yet, very gradually these kingdoms were to forge alliances and unions and present a united front to the Muslims, rallying behind the banner of Christianity. By the year 1230, these had merged into the two main kingdoms of León-Castilla and Aragón-Catalonia. However, it was not until the joint reign of the Catholic Monarchs, Isabella and Fernando, that these two kingdoms would invite and finally conquer the last Muslim stronghold of Granada in 1492.

Fernando I and the Union of Castilla-León

The 11th-century Castilian king, Fernando I, went some way to forging Christian unity by successfully, albeit temporarily, merging the kingdoms of Castilla and León in 1037. The new power created a formidable challenge to the Muslim *taifas* [independent kingdoms]. Yet Fernando I was careful not to upset the status quo when it came to the Muslims. There were great profits to be made from the tributes extracted by the Muslim kingdoms of Zaragoza, Toledo, Sevilla and Badajoz, in return for which Castilla-León guaranteed protection from attacks by Christians or other Muslim *taifas*.

It was a practice that became firmly rooted in the peninsula and amounted to a protection racket on a massive scale. The Christian kings, taking advantage of the weakened and fragmented Muslim kingdoms, demanded tribute payment—principally in gold—from various leaders in return for military aid and a guarantee to leave them in peace. These payments, known as *parias*, became a major source revenue for the kings. In the complex politics of the time, it became the norm for Christians to make (and break) alliances with Muslims against other Muslims, depending on where the best rewards lay.

Alfonso VI

If Al-Mansur had been the scourge of the Christians, Alfonso VI, during his rule as king of León-Castilla from 1072 to 1109, was likewise the bane of the Muslims. Like his father Fernando I before him, he extracted high payments from the *taifa* kingdoms, including Granada. Yet Alfonso VI had territorial designs on the non-Christian territories to the south. In 1085, he delivered a serious blow to the Muslims when he attacked Toledo. As it turned out, the city was fortunate. Since it had surrendered without a struggle, the inhabitants were spared the horrors of execution or enslavement and the terms of peace were conciliatory. Alfonso VI showed the same tolerance that the Muslims were known for, and upon payment of taxes, permitted the inhabitants of the city to continue to practice their religion, keep their possessions, and come and go as they pleased. He appointed a *mozárabe* (the name given to Arabized Christians) as governor. The loss of Toledo appalled the Muslim kings of Granada, Sevilla and Badajoz, who saw the development as the possible beginning of a wider pattern of Castilian expansion. They called on the help of the fanatical North African Muslim group, the Almoravids, who subsequently launched an aggressive religious war to restore Muslim rule in Spain. In a confrontation with the Almoravids, Alfonso VI was delivered a series of blows, yet managed to hold on to Toledo. After his death in 1108, his kingdom was divided amongst his children and a long period of civil war began, temporarily putting an end to the unity of Castilla-León.

The Legend of *El Cid*

The reconquest of Spain is a period in Spanish history that has given rise to countless legends and tales of bravery in the war against the Muslims. One Castilian nobleman whose life inspired one of the most enduring myths in Spanish history was Rodrigo Díaz de Vivar, better known as *El Cid*, from the Arabic *Al-Sayyid* meaning "The Lord." Rodrigo had fallen out with Alfonso VI, after making the king swear in public that he had played no part in his own brother's murder, and was rewarded for his troubles by being exiled in 1081. He then embarked on a career as a daring warrior who was just as likely to attack Christian strongholds as Muslim ones. Before long he threw himself into the task of pillaging the countryside and exacting tribute from the various *taifas*, growing exceedingly rich in the process. Certainly capable of extreme ruthlessness against Muslim and Christian adversaries alike, he was rich enough to have his own private army and ended up seizing Valencia, which he ruled until his death in 1099. His legend was immortalized in the *Poem of the Cid*, the earliest and greatest surviving literary epic of Castilla, composed

The Iberian Peninsula
During the Thirteenth Century

several decades after his death. In the process, Rodrigo the man was transformed into a hero whose exploits against the Muslims symbolized the spirit of the age.

Territorial Expansion of Castilla and Aragón

The 13th century was a key period in the rise of Christian Spain. At first, the Christian expansion was checked first by the invasion of the Almoravids, and then again in 1146 by the invasion of another fundamentalist group, the Almohad Berbers, based in Morocco. However, a new powerful Christian alliance—formed by Castilla, Aragón, and Navarra—closed ranks and decisively beat the Almohad army at the Battle of Las Navas de Tolosa, in 1212. It was a major turning point for the Christian kingdoms, which now launched a major thrust into Muslim-held territories. Within forty years practically the whole of the Iberian Peninsula was under the rule of Christian kings.

Jaime I of Aragón and Fernando III of Castilla-León were the principal players in the territorial expansion of the 13th century. Under Jaime I, the *taifas* to the east suffered a major blow, beginning with the Muslim-held Balearic Islands in the Mediterranean. In 1229, Jaime I's Aragonese fleet set sail to conquer the islands, and within a few years all of them—except Minorca which agreed to pay tribute to Aragón in return for its independence—were absorbed into the Aragonese kingdom. Jaime I then turned his attention southwards to the important Muslim city of Valencia. Having taken control of all the key towns on the way, he then blockaded the city by sea. Valencia endured two years of siege before finally surrendering in 1238. Five years later, Murcia was also conquered.

Meanwhile Fernando III, king of the recently reunited kingom of Castilla-León, marched south and laid siege to Córdoba, once the city that had been the crowning glory of Islamic civilization in Spain, but which had now fallen into decline. It fell in 1236, and as soon as the Great Mosque was ritually cleansed and consecrated as a cathedral, Fernando III entered the city and heard mass. It was a landmark event for Christian Spain, which had reclaimed a city that for so long had been the seat of Islamic authority in the Iberian Peninsula. In another highly symbolic act, the bells that had been seized by Al-Mansur in 997 and had hung in the Great Mosque of Córdoba ever since were finally returned to the Cathedral of Santiago in Galicia.

Fernando III did not stop there, but marched on to Sevilla, now the greatest city in Muslim Spain, and laid a long and grueling siege to it. After two years, conditions in the beleaguered city were utterly miserable. There was little food and water, and disease was rampant. When the city finally surrendered, all Muslims were ordered to leave the city with only the possessions they could carry. When the Christians finally entered in 1248, they

DAILY LIFE IN THE SPANISH RECONQUEST: SCENES FROM TENTH-CENTURY LEÓN

Historian Claudio Sánchez Albornoz paints a picture of life during the tenth century in the city of León, the most important Christian settlement in Spain at this time. He depicts the social structure of the inhabitants and their major concerns, which centered around the Catholic Church.

During the tenth century, León was the most important settlement in Christian Spain. Readers should not imagine, however, that it was a large city. Its boundaries were very small.... Girded about by the old Roman wall, it was accessible by four gates....

Inside the walls, the city was criss-crossed by many roads, streets, alleys and tracks. The old public baths were turned into the site of the episcopal see by Ordoño II, who moved the royal seat to a palace next to the Market Gate, henceforth known as King's Gate, and in the course of the century we are studying, various churches and a number of monasteries were built both outside and inside the city walls. Some housed monks, some housed nuns, and some housed both. ... The clerics of the episcopal church also followed a monastic rule. This sketch of the inhabitants of León may be completed by noblemen and various non-noble commoners. Of these, some were knights and others were workers; all had specific professions or worked the land, cultivat-

found a ghost town of empty streets and houses.

After centuries of political turmoil and expansion, and with these recent landmark gains, Spain emerged with four distinct Christian kingdoms that hemmed in Granada, the last Muslim stronghold. These were Castilla, Aragón, Navarra, and the newly independent kingdom of Portugal. After incorporating León, Asturia, Galicia, and huge territorial gains in the south, Castilla was the largest of the kingdoms. It also imposed the conditions of

ing their own plots of land or the properties of others, sometimes with agrarian contracts.

The process of settling the land had brought a multitude of small and middle-sized properties on the high plateaus of León, creating a society of free men, sometimes enjoying the *benefactoría* or *behetría* (patronage) of a superior lord. It is also true, however, that on the middling and large properties there was a large mass of rent-paying peasants, who still retained their freedom of movement but who were tied by poverty to the lord's lands. There was, in addition, a class of young landless people, children of the rent-paying peasants, together with serfs in the fields and a variety of personal serfs who worked as servants in the households of the richest men of León. . . .

The people of León lived close to the land, driven purely by sensuality and by a deep and burning spiritual devotion. Mystical and sensual, militaristic and rural, the whole city divided its hours between prayer and agriculture, love and war. Laymen grasped their sword to fight the infidel, or the plough to work the land, a spade to dig the garden, or a quill to copy the Old or New Testament, the works of the leading Church Fathers or the current liturgical books. Almost all loved and prayed; but only a chosen few kept alive the dying flame of classical culture, reading and occasionally copying the beautiful verses of Horace and Virgil.

Claudio Sánchez Albornoz, "Daily Life in the Spanish Reconquest: Scenes from Tenth-Century León," trans. Simon Doubleday, 1999, American Academy of Research Historians of Medieval Spain. www.uca.edu.

peace upon the kingdom of Granada, which was required to pay tribute and lend military assitance when required.

The Dark Years of the Fourteenth Century

After the heady days of the Christian conquests, the 14th century brought with it economic decline, wars, and social unrest. Added to this was the appalling loss of life suffered at the hands of the Black Death that swept across Europe and into the Iberian Peninsula.

Nobody was safe from the dreadful plague—not even royal households, as the death of King Alfonso XI of Castilla in 1350 was to prove. The disease was truly horrific with the victims being struck first by boils, followed by prolonged bouts of vomiting blood and, mercifully, death, usually within three days. Highly contagious, it spread rapidly throughout Europe and hit northeastern Spain particularly hard. Although death statistics are not known, it decimated entire populations, leaving farmland untended for want of laborers and villages emptied of their inhabitants.

No longer absorbed by military expansionism into Muslim territories, the attention of the kings now turned inwardly to the thorny issue of how to control an increasingly unruly nobility. As it attempted to keep its privileges, the intrigues and plots on the part of the nobility became so complex that it drew in members of the royal families themselves, leading to murderous rifts and disputes over succession.

This was exemplified by the notorious rule of Pedro I, the king of Castilla-León, whose ruthless and bloody reign from 1350 to 1369 earned him the nickname of the *El Cruel*. During his rule, rivalry between members of the Spanish royalty reached its murderous pinnacle as he fought his half-brother, Enrique de Trastámara, the bastard son of Alfonso XI and his lover Leonor de Guzmán. Like his predecessors, Pedro faced an unruly nobility that was determined to resist any attempts by the monarch to reduce its power. There was a great deal of discontent amongst the nobility at this time. Its members were experiencing serious economic losses owing to the shortage of farmhands to work their fields. Seeking to undermine Pedro's authority, a group of noblemen allied themselves with Enrique who managed to depose his half-brother. But Pedro was quick to regain his throne. The struggle reached its bitter conclusion as the two finally engaged in savage hand-to-hand combat—Pedro *El Cruel* was slain, stabbed in the chest by his half-brother.

Enrique II ascended to the throne, and so began the reign of the Trastámara dynasty. This was not the end of the troubles for Castilla, which descended into a long period of royal infighting and clashes with the nobility.

Enrique II was heavily indebted to his allies for his successful bid for the throne. He had called on France, which was ready to help on account of its displeasure over Pedro's desertion of his French wife, Princess Blanche; and also on Aragón, which was keen to exploit its neighbor's weakness. These allies, in addition to the nobility that supported him, needed to be rewarded generously.

All in all, it was a constant struggle for the royalty to keep the nobility loyal. A content nobility, if indeed this was possible, was an expensive business that could cost the monarchy well over half of its income. It normally fell on the populace to shoulder the financial burden through increased taxation.

The Nobility, Townsfolk, and Peasants

For the peasants, life under the nobility was harsh. Noblemen and ecclesiastical orders held vast areas of land, granted by the monarchs, and were a law unto themselves. The civil and church lords took full administrative control over their estates, which included collecting taxes, appointing officials, and dispensing justice. Amongst their privileges was the right to demand services and payment of dues from their vassals. In Castilla, from the 13th century onwards, the nobles adopted the practice of passing property and land, called *señoríos*, to the first-born son, which prevented the land being divided amongst the different members of the family. Castilla now saw a considerable part of its territory concentrated in the hands of a few extremely powerful families who were not scared to challenge the authority of the king.

The relationship between the landed nobility and towns was similarly strained. A large number of towns were given special privileges and encouraged to develop a cooperative spirit. These towns formed the backbone of the reconquest and, for many years, remained like fortresses, braced for the likelihood of Muslim attacks. Merchants and artisans flourished, and craftsmen belonged to guilds that had a great degree of self-regulation. Around the towns were public lands, including woods, lakes, and rivers that the townsfolk had the right to use.

Predictably, given their strength, there was much abuse of power on the part of the nobility which attempted to exert its influence over the surrounding towns. Soon the situation deteriorated. In response, towns began to organize themselves into *hermandades*, meaning "brotherhoods," to defend themselves against the nobles' excesses. Amongst other measures, the *hermandades* developed their own police force and, acquiring weapons, on occasion went so far as to engage in limited wars against the nobility. The *hermandades* were not unpopular with the monarchs, who were always happy to see overambitious aristocratic noses bloodied.

The 15th century brought with it a continuation of indiscipline on the part of the nobility, as well as bitter royal feuding over rights of succession to the throne. It was to take the efforts of two monarchs, Isabella I of Castilla and Fernando II of Aragón, to impose the absolute power of the monarchy over the nobility, and to unite the two kingdoms of Castilla and Aragón. Theirs was a rule of tremendous political change that heralded in a new age. It was from this point that the foundations of the modern Spanish nation state were laid.

The History of El Cid

By Anonymous

This anonymous text, originally written in Latin, details the life of Don Rodrigo Díaz de Vivar, known to posterity as El Cid, an independent warrior who waged numerous campaigns against both Muslim and Christian kings in medieval Spain. His feats became legendary even during his own lifetime, and his national-hero status is firmly established in Spanish culture. This account of his life is considered to be the first biography of a layman and is the primary source of information about his historical career. The author writes favorably about Díaz de Vivar, praising his great feats in battle and lauding his honor and loyalty.

T he anonymous Latin work known to historians of Spain as the *Historia Roderici* or 'History of Rodrigo' (henceforward *HR*) has a claim to be regarded as one of the earliest biographies of a layman who was not a king, like Charlemagne, nor a saint, like Gerald of Aurillac, to have been composed in medieval Christendom. The Rodrigo whom it commemorates was an eleventh-century Castilian nobleman who enjoyed a strikingly successful career as a military adventurer. He is better known to posterity as El Cid.

Rodrigo was born near Burgos *c.* 1045. As a young man who showed promise as a soldier he was attached to the household of King Sancho II of Castile (1065–72). After Sancho's murder he transferred to the service of his brother, Alfonso VI (1065–1109). In the mid-1070s he married Jimena, reputedly a member of an aristocratic family from Asturias. After several years of profitable service to the king, Rodrigo fell from favour, partly by undertaking an unauthorised military campaign, partly owing to the calumnies of enemies he had made at the royal court. In 1081 he was sent into exile by the king, a not infrequent occurrence in

Simon Barton and Richard Fletcher, *The World of El Cid: Chronicles of the Spanish Reconquest*, translated and annotated by Simon Barton and Richard Fletcher. Manchester, UK: Manchester University Press, 2000. Copyright © 2000 by Simon Barton and Richard Fletcher. Reproduced by permission.

the career of a warrior-aristocrat of that epoch. During the following five years Rodrigo took service as a mercenary captain with the Muslim dynasty of the Banū Hūd, rulers of the Taifa principality of Zaragoza in the valley of the River Ebro. Reinstated in Alfonso's favour when the king was desperate for troops after the Almoravid invasion and the defeat at Sagrajas in 1086, Rodrigo remained in his service for the ensuing three years. A further breach with the king occurred in 1089. For the remainder of his life Rodrigo acted as an independent commander in the eastern parts of Spain. Skilful exploitation by diplomacy and force of the fractious Taifa principalities enabled him to become a tribute-taker on a princely scale. His greatest prize was secured in 1094 when he captured Valencia, the main city of the Spanish Levante. For the last five years of his life Rodrigo defended his vulnerable principality. He died in Valencia, peacefully, in July 1099. Rodrigo's truly remarkable career was made possible by the distinctive circumstances of his age: the instability of the Taifa principalities; the acceptability of tribute-taking as the primary mode of Christian-Islamic relationship in Spain; the ease of crossing cultural frontiers; the absence of any ideology of crusade; the availability of mercenary knights. Roughly comparable circumstances made possible the approximations to his career that we can see in other frontier zones of contemporary Christendom; for example, among the Normans who adventured in southern Italy and Sicily and in the Byzantine Empire. Yet his fame was more than that of a particularly talented and fortunate *condottiere* in the coastlands of the Spanish Levante. His Muslim enemies respected and admired him even as they hated him; his death was noted by a French chronicler writing hundreds of miles from Valencia, in Poitou. Rodrigo had become a hero in his own lifetime. This heroic aspect would be developed obscurely after his death until it yielded the portrait, or vision, that we find in Spain's greatest medieval epic, the *Poema de Mio Cid*, composed perhaps in the last quarter of the twelfth century, certainly in existence by 1207. A legendary Cid had been launched upon the world, to be further elaborated and celebrated as the centuries passed in chronicle, ballad, drama, painting, sculpture and film. . . .

Chapter 28

In the Era 1127 (= A.D. 1089), at that season at which kings were accustomed to set out with their army to wage war or to subdue land in revolt against them, King Alfonso departed from the city of Toledo and set out on campaign with his army. Rodrigo the Campeador, however, remained then in Castile, handing out payment to his troops.

Chapter 29

Having distributed wages and assembled a multitude of his army in Castile—7000 fully-armed men—Rodrigo went to the frontier region adjoining the River Duero, and crossing by the middle ford he ordered his camp to be made at the place called Fresno. Proceeding from there with his army he came to the place called Calamocha. There he encamped and celebrated the feast of Pentecost. Envoys from the king of Albarracín came to him there, requesting a face-to-face meeting. After this meeting had taken place the king of Albarracín became a tributary of King Alfonso and remained at peace with him.

Chapter 30

Rodrigo left that region behind and went on into the territory of Valencia. He set up camp in the valley called Torres, which is near Murviedro. Now at that time the count of Barcelona, Berenguer by name, was encamped with all his army near Valencia. He was attacking the city, and was building [the castles of] Cebolla and Liria against it. When Count Berenguer heard that Rodrigo the Campeador was approaching him with hostile intent, he trembled with great fear: for the two were mutual enemies. But Count Berenguer's knights began to boast, and to utter many curses against Rodrigo, and to scorn him with much mockery. They threatened him with many threats of capture and imprisonment and death—which afterwards they were unable to fulfil. This talk came to Rodrigo's ears. However, he was unwilling to fight against the count: for he respected his lord King Alfonso, whose relative the count was. Count Berenguer, shaken with fear, left Valencia in peace and speedily returned to Requena; from there he went to Zaragoza, and at length returned to his own land with his followers.

Chapter 31

Rodrigo, however, remained at the place where he had fixed his tents, attacking his enemies on all sides. Moving on from there he approached Valencia, and pitched camp. At that time al-Qādir was ruling as king of Valencia. He at once sent his envoys with innumerable and very valuable presents to Rodrigo. He became a tributary, and so did the commander of Murviedro. Afterwards Rodrigo the Campeador arose and entered the mountains of Alpuente. He fought fiercely there and mastered and laid waste the country, and remained there for not a few days. Then he left the region and established his camp at Requena, where he stayed for many days.

Chapter 32

While he was there he learned that Yūsuf the king of the Ishmaelites and many other Saracen kings of Spain had come with the Moabites to lay siege to the castle of Aledo which was then in the hands of the Christians. Then these aforesaid Saracen kings besieged that castle of Aledo and invested it so closely that those who were inside defending the castle ran seriously short of water. When King Alfonso heard this he sent a letter to Rodrigo ordering him to join him at once to relieve the castle of Aledo and bring help to its defenders by attacking Yūsuf and all the other Saracens who were fiercely besieging it. Rodrigo gave this reply to the king's messengers who delivered this letter to him: 'Let my lord the King come as he promised. According to his command I am ready with good heart and will to succour that castle. When he is pleased that I should set out with him, I request his majesty that he should deign to inform me of his coming.'

Chapter 33

Rodrigo the Campeador at once left Requena and went to Játiva. There a messenger from King Alfonso found him, and told him that the king was in Toledo with a very large army—an infinite multitude of horsemen and footsoldiers. On hearing this Rodrigo went up to Onteniente and waited there for tidings of the king's coming. For the king had ordered Rodrigo by messengers beforehand to wait for him at Villena, through which place he had stated that he would certainly pass. Meanwhile Rodrigo remained at Onteniente so that his army should not lack for provisions, awaiting the king. He sent out scouts from there to Villena and to the region of Chinchilla, who were under orders to inform him as soon as they should hear of the king's approach. While the scouts were thus confidently awaiting the royal arrival, the king took a different route and reached Hellín. When

Rodrigo heard that the king had already accomplished the journey and arrived before him, he was deeply dismayed. He set out with his army for Hellín, and went ahead of his troops in his eagerness to discover the truth about the king's movements. When he knew for certain that the king had completed his journey he left his army which was coming along after him and went on with a few companions as far as Molina. Yūsuf king of the Saracens, however, and all the other Ishmaelite kings of Spain and all the other Moabites who were there, learning of King Alfonso's arrival, left the fortress of Aledo in peace. They turned in flight at once, terrified by fear of the king even before his arrival, and fled before his face in confusion. When Rodrigo reached Molina the king, seeing that he could not possibly pursue the Saracens, had already set out with his army on the return journey to Toledo. Rodrigo, greatly sorrowing, returned to his camp which was at Elche. There he allowed certain of his knights whom he had brought with him from Castile to return to their homes.

Chapter 34

Then the Castilians, jealous of him in all things, accused Rodrigo before the king. They told Alfonso that Rodrigo was not a faithful vassal but an evil man and a traitor. They falsely and lyingly claimed that Rodrigo had been unwilling to go to the assistance of the king, in order that the king and all who were with him should be killed by the Saracens. When the king heard this false accusation he was possessed and fired by very great rage. He at once gave orders that the castles, estates and all the honour which Rodrigo held from him should be confiscated. In addition he ordered [his men] to enter upon Rodrigo's own hereditary lands and, what was still worse, he ordered his wife and children, arrested by trickery, to be cruelly retained in custody. The king also ordered [his men] to take charge of all Rodrigo's goods—gold and silver and everything that could be found of his possessions. Rodrigo considered the matter carefully and fully understood that the king had thus been roused to anger against him by the crafty tales and false accusations of his enemies; that this monstrous injury and unheard-of dishonour had been thus wickedly inflicted on him by their manoeuvres. Forthwith he sent one of his most distinguished knights to the king, to defend him firmly against the unjust charge and the false accusation of treason, and completely to clear his name. On being shown into the lord king's presence, this man spoke as follows: 'O renowned and ever-worshipful king, my lord Rodrigo, your most faithful vassal, has sent me to you to kiss your hands on his behalf and request that you accept in court his defence against and clearance of the charge which his enemies have falsely laid against him in your presence. My lord himself will fight in person in your court against another equal and similar to him; or his champion will fight on his behalf against another equal and similar to him. All those who proclaimed to you that Rodrigo was guilty of any deceit or any treachery towards you in the course of your journey to relieve Aledo such that the Saracens might kill you and your troops, have lied as false and evil men and lack good faith. Rodrigo intended to participate in that campaign. There is no count nor magnate nor knight faithful to assist you among all those who accompanied you to the relief of that castle, of greater fidelity in your aid against those Saracens and against all your enemies, than he, so far as lies within his power.' However the king, strongly enraged against them, would not only not accept his defence, although it was most just—he would not even give it a fair hearing. He did, however, permit Rodrigo's wife and children to return to him.

Chapter 35

When Rodrigo saw that the king did not deign to accept his defence, he personally drafted his own pleas of defence and innocence and then sent them to the king in proper written form.

'This is the plea which I Rodrigo submit concerning the accusation with which I am charged before King Alfonso. My lord the king was holding me in such love and honour as beforehand he was wont to hold me. I will fight in his court against one equal and similar to me, or my champion will fight against one equal and similar to him, stating as follows: "I Rodrigo swear to you who wishes to fight with me and who accuses me in connection with that expedition which King Alfonso made to Aledo to fight the Saracens, that the fact that I was not with him sprang from no other cause but this, that I did not know of his route, and could have learned it from no man. This is the very truth of the reason why I was not with him. On that campaign I was guilty of no lie, but obeyed the king's commands transmitted by his messenger and by letter: no mandate of his did I disregard. During that campaign, whatever the king intended to do against the Saracens who were besieging the aforesaid castle, I was guilty of no deceit towards him, no conspiracy, emphatically no treachery, and no evil thing for which my body stands dishonoured or deserves to stand dishonoured. No-one among the counts or magnates or knights, who ever were in the army which accompanied the king, had greater fidelity towards the king to assist him to fight the aforesaid Saracens than I, as far as lies within my power. I swear this to you, that what ever I say to you is entirely true. If I lie, may God deliver me into your hands to do your will upon me. If not, may God who judges justly deliver me from a false accusation." A similar oath will be sworn by my champion against the knight who wishes to fight with him over this charge.'...

But the king did not wish to accept this plea submitted by Rodrigo himself, nor his defence and innocence.

Chapter 36

After the king returned to Toledo, Rodrigo camped at Elche: there he celebrated Christmas Day. After the feast he departed from there and made his way along the coast until he reached Polop where there was a great cave full of treasure. He laid siege to it and invested it closely; after a few days he overcame its defenders and boldly entered it. He found inside it much gold and silver and silk and innumerable precious stuffs. Loaded thus with the riches he needed from what he had found, he left Polop and moved on until he came to *Portum Tarvani*, and outside the city of Denia, at Ondara, he restored and strengthened a castle. He fasted there for the holy season of Lent and celebrated at the same place the Easter of the Resurrection of Jesus Christ our Lord. While he was there al-Hāyib, who at that time was king of that land and reigned over it, sent an embassy to discuss terms of peace with him. When peace had been agreed and firmly established between them the Saracen envoys returned to al-Hāyib. Rodrigo left Ondara with his army and moved towards Valencia. King al-Hāyib left the region of Lérida and Tortosa and made his way to Murviedro. When al-Qādir, who was then king of Valencia, heard that King al-Hāyib had made peace with Rodrigo he was greatly terrified and extremely apprehensive. After taking counsel with his advisers he sent messengers to Rodrigo with very great and innumerable gifts of money. They heaped the many, the innumerable presents which they bore upon Rodrigo, and thus amicably brought about peace between him and the king of Valencia. In the same fashion, from all the castles which were rebelling against the king of Valencia in an attempt to throw off his rule, Rodrigo accepted many and innumerable tributes and gifts. When King al-Hāyib heard that al-Qādir king of Valencia had made peace with Rodrigo he was struck with great fear and retreated from Murviedro by night; thus, terrified, he fled from that region.

An Evaluation of the Catholic Monarchs

By Geoffrey Woodward

Geoffrey Woodward is the head of history at Wellington School, Somerset, England, and the author of Philip II *(1992),* The Development of Early Modern Europe *(1997), and* Spain in the Reigns of Isabella and Ferdinand *(1997). In this article Woodward examines the reign of King Ferdinand and Queen Isabella. He finds that although the Catholic monarchs indeed deserve much of the praise that has been afforded them by contemporaries and historians, aspects of their reign deserve resounding criticism. In particular, Woodward claims that the incompetence of Isabella's predecessor, Henry IV, has been exaggerated in order to boost Isabella's image. In addition, Ferdinand played a much greater role in the monarchy than he has been credited with. Finally, Woodward concludes that Isabella created political problems in her country.*

Historians have long admired the achievements of the Catholic Monarchs, Isabella, Queen of Castile (1474–1504), and Ferdinand, King of Aragon (1479–1516). 'The most glorious epoch in the annals of Spain', wrote W.H. Prescott in 1837. 'The monarchy was falling apart at every joint; the Catholic Sovereigns restored it on a new plan', claimed J.H. Mariejol in 1892. 'It was a happy golden age', declared Ramon Menendez Pidal in 1962. And it was the verdict of John Lynch, writing in 1981, that their reigns produced 'the makings of a nation state, united, peaceful beyond any in Europe'. Recent biographers of Isabella, notably Joseph Perez (1988) and Peggy Liss (1992), have been similarly fulsome in their praises. Contemporary writers had a near unanimous verdict on Isabella. She was

Geoffrey Woodward, "Isabella and Ferdinand of Spain, 1474–1516: A Re-Assessment," *History Review,* December 1998, p. 11. Copyright © 1998 by History Today, Ltd. Reproduced by permission.

the ideal monarch who brought greatness to their country. She was El Encubierto (the hidden one), who saved her people from anarchy and heresy, slayed the infidel and re-established order in a war-torn land. In the words of one of her chroniclers: 'It can be said in truth that just as our Lord wished that our glorious Lady might be born in this world because from her would proceed the Universal Redeemer of the human lineage, so he determined that you, My Lady, would be born to reform and restore these kingdoms and lead them from the tyrannical government under which they have been for so long.'

In an age when female rulers were a rarity, Isabella was certainly an exceptional woman. She introduced the Inquisition, assisted Ferdinand in the reconquest of Granada, and purged her country of heretics. Her reign saw the end of civil war and the restoration of royal justice, and, together with her husband, she unified the Spanish kingdoms and established an overseas empire. Any one of these accomplishments would be a major triumph, and to be successful in so many fields may well justify the view that this was a 'golden age'. The aim of this article is not to restate these achievements but to consider some of them in a wider context. Three questions will be asked. Firstly, what was the legacy of Henry IV, King of Castile, in 1474? Secondly, was the role of Ferdinand deliberately played down by Castilian chroniclers? And thirdly, and more controversially, did Isabella actually solve her country's political problems?

The Legacy of Henry IV (1454–1474)

Most chroniclers claimed that Henry was impotent, incompetent and unfit to rule. In the 1480s a Castilian chronicler, Andres Bernaldez, looked back upon his reign and stated:

> At this juncture envy and covetousness were awakened and avarice was nourished; justice became moribund and force ruled; greed reigned and decadent sensuality spread, and the cruel temptation of sovereignty overcame the humble persuasion of obedience; the customs were mostly dissolute and corrupt. . . . And Our Lord, who sometimes permits evils to exist on the earth in order that each malefactor should be punished according to the extent of his errors, allowed so many wars to break out in the kingdom, that nobody could say that

they were exempt from the ills that ensue from them.
. . . These wars lasted for the final ten years for which
this King reigned. Peaceful men suffered much violence
at the hands of new men who rose up and wrought
great havoc.

. . . Henry ruled Castile for 20 years and historians now ac-
knowledge that, in the first half of his reign, he administered his
country effectively, commanding widespread respect and obedience. In the absence of a central administration, the Crown depended upon the support of the principal nobles, clergy and
towns. Political tension was always near the surface and any attempts by the Crown to interfere in local affairs by, for example,
appointing corregidores (royal governors), were resented by town
councils. The Crown was also restricted financially and militarily. Neither the nobles nor the clergy paid direct taxation and, as
the King could not afford a standing army, he depended upon
them for loans, troops and cooperation. In effect, his position was
very vulnerable. Though most subjects recognised the advantages
of strong kingship, there were always elements in society that
were ready to put their own interests first.

In 1464 certain aristocratic factions, like the Enriquez and
Manrique families and the archbishops of Toledo and Seville,
who resented Henry's autocratic style of kingship, were joined
by the Marquis of Villena when he was dismissed as the King's
principal adviser. They declared that Henry was unfit to rule and
impotent—despite the alleged birth of a daughter, Joanna, in
1462—and called for his deposition and replacement by his step-
brother. Civil disturbances occurred between 1465 and 1468, and
Henry was fortunate to survive. When his step-brother unexpectedly died of plague, Henry convinced his nobles that peace
was preferable to war and agreed that Isabella, his step-sister,
should succeed him. He even blessed her marriage to Ferdinand,
heir to the Aragonese throne, in 1469. The king's Achilles' heel,
however, was Joanna. He appears to have genuinely hoped that
she would inherit his throne and consistently claimed that she
was his legitimate daughter. Nevertheless, several aristocratic families were willing to take sides. Some, like Villena, exploited
Henry's vulnerable position and received extensive gifts; others,
like the Mendozas and Enriquez, rallied to Isabella's cause.
Though there was little fighting between rival supporters in the

rest of Henry's reign, the country remained politically unstable.

How incompetent, then, was Henry IV? In many respects, he was a victim of powerful nobles and his own misjudgement. Much of the Crown's estate and wealth—worth some 30 million maravedis—was given away to his nobles in lands, pensions and grants in an attempt to win their support for Joanna's succession; but, in the early years of his reign, he had also developed the foundations of an effective administration. The hermandades or cavalry militia were revived to deal with rural disorder; the King-in-Council often heard judicial cases, a practice Isabella would continue, and a court of appeal operated in Valladolid. And, corregidores, who had existed since the fourteenth century, increased in number and became more permanent royal officers. Modern historians now believe that his reign was not an unmitigated failure. Indeed, it is the view of William Phillips that 'Enrique [Henry] left a set of policies and programs that his successors took over and preserved. Fernando and Isabel were merely successful in implementing them.' Henry resolutely denied the allegations that he was impotent and that Joanna was not his daughter, and modern research suggests that he was right. It suited disgruntled nobles and Isabella's chroniclers to damn him and to stress the poor condition of Castile at her accession. He was contrasted with the honourable Isabella, his weaknesses with her strengths, his daughter's spurious claim with Isabella's legitimacy. In their biased and retrospective view, her succession in 1474 marked the beginning of a new era.

The Role of King Ferdinand

Castilian writers were understandably biased in favour of Isabella. They courted royal patronage and were not averse to writing partisan accounts, even against her husband. 'If anything worthy of praise was accomplished in Andalucia', wrote Alonso de Palencia, 'it seemed to be due to the Queen's initiative.' 'It was certainly a marvellous thing', declared Fernando del Pulgar in 1485, 'that what many men and great lords could not agree to effect in many years, one lone woman carried out in a little time.' Ferdinand was thus portrayed as indecisive, weak, and subordinate to a dominant Queen. Yet this is a historical travesty since, without his help, she might never have secured her throne.

Within weeks of her accession, several nobles and towns declared their support for Joanna, revolts occurred throughout the kingdom, and, most seriously, the King of Portugal invaded Castile with the intention of marrying the princess. Ferdinand assumed command of Isabella's army and directed military operations. Between 1475 and 1476, he travelled from Burgos to Zamora, fought the battle of Toro, and stopped the Portuguese; two years later, he was on hand to repel a second invasion. There can be little doubt that if Alfonso, King of Portugal, had not been defeated, resistance to Isabella would have been much greater. Alfonso's subsequent acknowledgment that Isabella was the legitimate Queen, and his agreement to keep Joanna in Portugal, ended the War of Succession in 1479.

That same year, Ferdinand succeeded his father as King of Aragon. Like Castile, the kingdom was slowly recovering from civil war and foreign invasions. Royal finances were poor, trade and commerce had declined, and social conflict between landlords and peasants and between towns and nobles was endemic. Ferdinand spent very little time in Aragon—only eight out of 37 years—leaving the administration to viceroys and a council. Instead, he lived with his wife in Castile, the largest and most prosperous of their lands. From the outset of Isabella's reign, she directed Castilian domestic affairs and Ferdinand was responsible for the foreign relations of both Castile and Aragon. Historians have long acknowledged the Queen's religious zeal and especially her crusade against the Moors in Granada (1482–92), but of equal, if not greater significance, was Ferdinand's role in this holy war of reconquest. He led the combined Aragonese and Castilian army, was present at the sieges of Ronda, Malaga, Baza and Almeria, and accompanied the Queen on their triumphal entry into Granada in 1492. The war had been much harder, far longer and more costly than the monarchs had expected; but these lessons were not lost on Ferdinand who, at the same time, had been skilfully constructing a network of European alliances in preparation for his next war.

We have already seen his role in the War of Succession in Castile (1475–79) and the Granada War (1482–92); but he also went to war with France over Brittany (1488–93), Naples (1495–1504), and Milan (1509–16). Ferdinand's skill lay in his balancing different yet connected objectives; harmonising Castilian and Aragonese resources; and achieving his aims with the minimum of inconvenience. He concluded marriage alliances with the royal houses of Portugal, Burgundy, England and Austria to secure Castile and Aragon's political position, and, after the death of Isabella, he married Germaine de Foix to strengthen his claim to Navarre. He joined Holy Leagues in 1495 and 1509 to safeguard his interests in Naples and Milan; and he made treaties with any enemy of France—with Henry VII of England in 1489, for instance, in order to recover Rousillon and Cerdagne for Aragon, and with Henry VIII in 1512 to seize Navarre and drive the French out of Milan. Under pretence of fighting defensively to expel an aggressor, he emerged on numerous occasions with more territorial gains than anyone else. In an era when no country was strong enough to force its will upon another, Ferdinand recognised the importance of combining diplomacy with aggression, of building up allies and never being isolated, and thus of outmanoeuvring his enemies. Machiavelli, a Florentine diplomat, admired his statesmanship rather than his probity, claiming that 'if he had ever honoured either of them [peace and good faith], he would have lost either his standing or his state many times over'.

Some of Ferdinand's finest successes in foreign affairs, particularly resulting from his wars with Islam, occurred after the death of his wife. A plan to attack the north African coastline between Melilla and Oran, devised in the 1490s, was put into operation and seven settlements were seized between 1505 and 1510. The sea routes between Sicily, Sardinia and Tunisia were thus secured and the way was opened to advance into the interior of north Africa. Antonio de Nebrija, court poet and historian, was convinced that the Catholic Monarchs' reputation rested on their foreign achievements. Ferdinand agreed but believed that the credit should be attributed to him. Writing in 1514, he declared: 'For over 700 years the Crown of Spain has not been as great or as resplendent as it is now, both in the west and the east, and all, after God, by my work and labour.' Even allowing for his proud boast, there can be little doubt that Ferdinand was the power behind Isabella's throne.

Did Isabella Solve Her Country's Political Problems?

The Queen faced two serious problems at her accession: firstly, insubordinate nobles undermined the government's authority and flouted royal justice; secondly, the succession was disputed and civil war beckoned. Though she inherited other difficulties— economic, social and religious, for instance—it was the political problems which would test the mettle of the young monarch. Thirty years later, in her will written shortly before her death, she reviewed her reign and expressed concern for the future.

She acknowledged that the Castilian nobility were far from politically subdued. She had secured her throne with their assistance but in so doing had compromised her authority. In 1470 the Crown certainly recovered much property lost in the recent civil wars, but by allowing the nobility to keep former Crown lands, and in confirming their grants of nobility and their right to collect financial annuities awarded by Henry IV, she had relinquished far more. Indeed, she not only confirmed that the nobility would be exempt from paying direct taxation, she also granted them control of the assessment and collection of the principal indirect tax, the alcabala. In effect, these measures guaranteed their economic and social supremacy and went a long way towards securing their political independence.

The condition of the Crown's finances had also suffered. Difficulties were already evident in 1489 when the Crown could only balance its budget by borrowing from the aristocracy and offering them high interest bonds known as juros. Some nobles negotiated very favourable deals. The Duke of Cadiz, for example, was given the Granadan village of Casares in exchange for a loan of 10 million maravedis. Already the foundations of royal indebtedness had been laid and possible solutions—for instance, making the nobility pay direct taxation, eliminating some of the corruption in tax administration, and expanding the Crown's estates to make rents the basis of its revenue—had been compromised. By 1516 the Crown was paying out in juros one-third of its annual revenue and, in the opinion of the historian Stephen Haliczer, the treasury was in a 'state of extreme disorganisation and confusion, with frauds of unprecedented dimensions'.

The nobility also retained control of regional politics. Vizcaya, for instance, was dominated by the courts of Haro and Trevino, and Leon by the Court of Luna. Some nobles continued to threaten the freedom of nearby towns: the Court of Benavente controlled Valladoid, and Medina Sidonia the port of Gibraltar. Indeed, nothing better illustrates the nobles' power in the country than the number of castles built during Isabella's reign. In spite of royal orders to destroy rebel fortresses, apparently only 84 had been demolished by 1504, and at least 265 fortifications had been rebuilt or repaired. Given these conditions, the Crown appears to have conceded to the nobility its social dominance in local administration in order to retain its control of central government.

The major casualty in this political bear garden was justice. Intermittent civil war had left deep scars and the restoration of royal justice would be a slow process. Most nobles kept retainers whereas the Crown had no standing army, only a small number of Hermandad troops, which was never sufficient to challenge a disobedient noble. Both Isabella and Ferdinand took an active part in upholding law and order. In her early years the Queen attended public hearings every Friday in the alcazar, and twice a week the royal council acted as a supreme court of justice. Occasionally it was necessary for the monarchs to deal with a problem personally. In a celebrated case in 1486, the Count of Lemos, having ignored repeated warnings, was visited by the monarchs in the north-west of Castile and ordered to return disputed lands and pay compensation to his victims.

By visiting every town in Castile, the Catholic Monarchs confirmed their resolve to restore justice and impart effective government but they could not be everywhere at once and had to prioritise their time. The Queen's frequent pregnancies restricted her journeys and, in the years following the Granada war, the nobility reasserted itself in the face of royal justice. In the 1490s Constable Velasco threatened villagers in Old Castile, the Count of Burgos seized property near the town, the Cabrera family illegally claimed lands in Segovia, and the Duke of Najera terrorised people in Leniz. It is a myth that the aristocracy had been tamed by the Crown. They remained hungry for land and broke the law with impunity. Many townspeople, who petitioned the Crown to impart justice for all, were of the opinion that the judicial system was corrupt and that royal administration was breaking down.

Indeed, any misgivings Isabella may have had in 1504 seem to have been borne out after her death. Between 1506 and 1508, the Duke of Medina Sidonia tried to regain control of Gibraltar, the Marquis of Priego and the Count of Cabra stirred up trouble in Andalucia, and that inveterate trouble-maker the Count of Lemos overran the town of Ponferrada in Galicia. Political anarchy and domestic strife had not been suppressed, and public confidence in the Castilian government appears to have been justifiably low—and in sharp contrast with official propaganda. Ferdinand did little to remedy the situation. In 1512 the

Cortes was still complaining that the judiciary was biased and officials corrupt: the Crown was either unable or unwilling to restrain the rich and powerful. And further disturbances accompanied news of Ferdinand's death in 1516: the Mendoza, Enriquez, Velasco and Guzman families rebelled against the new government and revolts broke out in Navarre, Leon and Andalucia.

The Succession

The second serious problem facing Isabella in 1474 was how best to secure her throne for her family, the Trastamaras, having spent the early years of her reign fighting off a rival claimant. For much of their married life, Isabella and Ferdinand had laboured to secure their dynasty by producing as many children as possible, marrying them into powerful royal families, and acquiring a fist of claims to European thrones. Though they produced four daughters, only one son reached adulthood, and he predeceased his mother in 1497. Since he had no heirs, the Castilian succession passed to Isabella's eldest surviving daughter, Joanna, and to her husband, Philip Habsburg, Archduke of Burgundy. Isabella knew that Joanna's mental condition was very unstable and that her husband was likely to assert himself. She therefore declared in her will that, if Joanna was 'unwilling or unable to govern', Ferdinand would become regent until Joanna's son, Charles (who was four at the time), came of age. Since Ferdinand had no constitutional right to rule Castile, he was obliged to give up his title of King. Though these instructions made sense to Isabella, they caused confusion, resentment and civil war.

Upon the Queen's death and the ensuing deterioration in Joanna's health, the nobility and city councils split into rival camps. Some, like the Admiral and Constable of Castile and the archbishops of Toledo and Seville, supported Joanna; a second group, led by Mendoza and Villena, backed Philip; and a third faction, dominated by Alba and Tendilla, gathered round Ferdinand. No wonder an Italian diplomat commented: 'The nobles sharpen their teeth like wild boars with the hope of a great change.' The death of Philip in September 1506 may have removed one contender but it also provoked civil disturbances, and the political crisis only ended when Ferdinand intervened with an army. By 1508 he regained control and was recognised as regent but the Castilian succession was still far from settled. He accepted that Charles would succeed to both Castile and Aragon but, as the prince was still a minor and currently ruling and living in the Low Countries, arguments soon broke out between rival councillors and Ferdinand as to who should head the administration. Cardinal Cisneros, the Archbishop of Toledo, opposed Ferdinand's nominee, the Duke of Alba; there was support in some circles for the insane Joanna, now incarcerated in Tordesillas castle, and another faction viewed her younger son, Ferdinand, who had been born and brought up in Spain, as an alternative claimant. All these tensions surfaced at the death of King Ferdinand in 1516 and received varying support in the revolt of the Comuneros in 1519. If the main aim of the Catholic Monarchs had been to continue the Trastamara dynasty and to secure an undisputed throne free from the nobles' interference, then they failed on all counts.

The triumphs of the Catholic Monarchs were far-reaching and, in many respects, unprecedented. Isabella and Ferdinand were remarkable rulers and merited many of the plaudits heaped upon them. Many, but not all. This article has sought to set their reigns in a wider context beyond the blinkered vision of Castilian chroniclers. It has suggested that the reign of Henry IV was not an unmitigated failure, that Ferdinand played a vital part in laying the foundations of Castile's 'golden age', and that Isabella bequeathed serious political and dynastic problems, not altogether dissimilar to those which she had inherited. The political achievements of the Catholic Monarchs in general, and Isabella in particular, have been exaggerated by court propagandists and by historians—propagandists by a desire to look at the past nostalgically and historians by a readiness to accept such accounts all too uncritically.

The Inquisition and the Expulsion of the Jews

By Norman Roth

Norman Roth is a professor of Jewish history and studies at the University of Wisconsin, Madison. His specialty is the history of Jewish culture in medieval Spain, and he is the author of Jews, Visigoths, and Muslims in Medieval Spain *as well as a number of other books and articles on related topics. Here he outlines the history of Jews in Spain, their relations with Christians, and the events and circumstances that led to the expulsion of the Jews in 1492. Of primary importance, Roth contends, was the hostility between Old Christians, as well as Jews, and the conversos, or former Jews who had converted to Christianity. He refutes the commonly held view that Spain was a hotbed of anti-Semitism and that the Spanish government, particularly King Ferdinand and Queen Isabella, were violently intolerant of Jews.*

S pain was home to Jews longer than any other country, including even the Jewish homeland of ancient Palestine. Although it is not known when Jews first arrived in Spain, there is definite proof of significant Jewish settlement by at least 300 C.E. and undoubtedly much earlier. Documentary sources from that time already demonstrate that cordial interaction existed between Jews and Christians. However, that situation soon changed when invading Visigoths established their theocratic government. Following their conversion to Roman Christianity (Catholicism), they began to impose ever more severe restrictions on Jews aimed at their compulsory baptism.

The possible end of the Jewish presence on the Iberian Peninsula was prevented by the Muslim invasion of North African

Berber tribes in 711. The Jews, used by the small invading Muslim forces to garrison conquered cities, soon became integrated into Muslim society. Increased immigration of both Muslims and Jews from Islamic lands rapidly built Spain into a major political and cultural center, from Andalusia in the south to Barcelona in the north. Muslims established an independent caliphate at Córdoba, where Jews played a key role in the cultural renaissance that followed. From government service to the marketplace, Jews and Muslims interacted with little or no tension.

The situation took a turn for the worse with the Almohad invasion of Andalusia at the end of the twelfth century, although claims by modern historians of the total liquidation of Jewish settlements and the compulsory conversion of all Jews and Christians to Islam are greatly exaggerated. Nevertheless, many Jews and Christians were converted to Islam. . . .

As the Reconquest of Muslim Spain by the Christians began in earnest in the twelfth century and continued throughout the thirteenth, Jews served not only in administrative and diplomatic positions, but in large numbers as soldiers fighting in both Muslim and Christian armies. Along with Christians, Jews were rewarded with substantial grants of lands and houses in reconquered areas such as Seville, Jerez, and elsewhere.

The law codes (fueros) enacted by towns and cities, as well as privileges of settlement throughout the lands of Christian Spain, demonstrate a total equality of all citizens—Jews, Christians, and often Muslims. Frequently, Jews attained a favored subject status, marked by special exemptions from taxes and from service to overlord or king. In civil cases between Christians and Jews, both Jewish and Christian witnesses were required and judges from both communities were required to hear the case. Christian law granted full judicial rights to Jews, including the ability to testify and even serve as attorneys on behalf of Christians as well as Jews. Even kings, in their capacity as court of final appeal, were required to know Jewish law or to be informed by Jewish advisors.

With the completion of the Reconquest of all but the Muslim kingdom of Granada, Christian Spain was firmly established in its various if somewhat confusing and complicated kingdoms. Jews lived not only in the major cities but in literally every village and town in Spain, with sometimes as few as two or three families living in a village populated by Christians. There were no separate Jewish quarters, although in larger cities Jews often lived together in specific neighborhoods, which testifies more to the neccesity to live within walking distance of a synagogue on the Sabbath than to any tension with Christians.

Jewish-Christian Relations

Although it is impossible to detail the complex history of Jewish-Christian relations in medieval Spain, to say nothing of Jewish contributions to political life or the developments of Jewish culture, relations between Christians and Jews remained generally cordial. . . .

Jewish culture in Spain flourished. There was a profoundly important renaissance of the Hebrew language. The result was the first development of a secular literature of Hebrew poetry and novels that were added to legal sources and commentaries on the Talmud as Spain's Jewish scholars became the most prominent in the world. Hardly less significant were Jewish contributions to Spanish culture; the first examples of written Spanish were early translations of the Bible that Jewish scholars did for Christians.

The Jewish role in science and medicine continued to grow in importance. Physicians served not only the royal and noble families, but frequently appeared on city payrolls as official physicians treating the general population. There is a vast amount of documentation on this subject that serves as important source material for the historian. Jewish government officials played an increasingly important role in the administration of the government, but not only or even chiefly in the farming of taxes. . . .

Uninformed scholars mistakenly believe that what caused the break in *convivencia* [cultural interdependence and good relations between Jews and Christians] was the attack on Jews in 1391. The laws promulgated by Alfonso XI (b. 1311–d. 1350) in Alcalá in 1348, which culminated earlier attempts to restrict Jews, were the most serious signs of impending trouble. Europe's Black Death had little impact in Castile, but more in Aragón and Catalonia. The Jews in Spain were not blamed for causing the plague nor were they subject to attacks as was the case in Europe generally.

The increasing role of the missionary campaign of the Dominican and Franciscan orders was also important. From the early thirteenth century, these friars intensified efforts to convert Muslims and Jews by preaching and through writing polemical works. The friars' incorporation even of some Muslim ideas attacking the Jewish faith was strengthened by the hostility of Jewish converts to Christianity. Polemics were not confined to Christians, but Jewish polemics against Christianity have received practically no attention. . . .

Jewish conversion to Christianity became a flood in the late fourteenth century. In the summer of 1391, inspired by the anti-Jewish propaganda of a minor archdeacon in Seville, mobs of lower-class peasants attacked and robbed Jews throughout Spain. Few Jews were actually killed: in many communities they were protected by their Christian neighbors and by officials; the kings severely punished all perpetrators. Nevertheless, immense damage had been done. Frightened and demoralized, thousands of Jews spontaneously converted and in a few cases were forcibly baptized. Compulsory baptism had been prohibited by Pope Gregory I (b. 540–d. 604) and that prohibition was an official part of canon law. Nevertheless, once baptized, a convert had to remain a Christian. However, secular authorities were seldom bound by canon law, especially in Spain. The kings indicated their willingness to ignore such compulsory baptisms, but few converted Jews—forced or otherwise—returned to their former faith. . . .

A massive population of Jews who had converted to Christianity (*conversos*) had been created by the middle of the fifteenth century. Weakened by the decline in numbers, demoralized by the conversion of relatives and friends, and intimidated by the religious fervor of the age, the remaining Jews saw themselves for the first time as embattled. The most important rabbinical leaders fled Spain for North Africa after the events of 1391. Although they continued to direct responses to the legal and social problems of various Jewish communities in Spain, the Jews were in effect left leaderless.

Nevertheless, there is no evidence of increased hostility toward Jews on the part of ordinary Christians throughout the fifteenth century. Life went on as before. Jews continued to play an important role in business and trade, but to a lesser extent in agriculture, medicine, and government service (again probably due to the loss of Jewish population). Churches, convents, and monasteries continued to rely on Jewish administrators of estates, as did the nobility. Jews still collected various taxes and borrowed and loaned money on a regular basis. From king to commoner, substantial personal friendships prevailed between Jews and Christians, including bishops and archbishops. . . .

Conversos in Spain

The nature of the *conversos* in Spain is important to understanding the events that led to the Expulsion of the Jews in 1492. The prevailing myth has long been, and continues to be, that *conversos* were crypto-Jews, that is, their conversion was insincere and that they secretly professed Jewish beliefs. In the 1960s, a prominent Jewish historian wrote a book that successfully demolished this myth. Jewish and other sources clearly demonstrate that the *conversos* in fifteenth-century Spain converted of their own free will, not under any compulsion, and that most *conversos* were the descendants of those who had already converted. In any case, *conversos* were complete and willing Christians.

Jews saw *conversos* not merely as having changed their faith, but as having changed their identity. In the telling words of rabbinical authorities, the *conversos* had "gone out of the peoplehood of Israel and become another people." Thus, there was no hope of their return to Judaism. It was frequently noted that *conversos* had every opportunity to leave Spain and go to Muslim Granada, North Africa, or Portugal, where they could live as Jews if they so desired, since there was never any prohibition against *conversos* leaving the country, but they chose not to do so. . . . Jewish hostility toward the *conversos* was already prevalent by the fourteenth century.

Not all Jews who converted did so purely from religious motivations. Many Jews converted to Christianity as a result of the anti-Jewish polemics of *converso* writers, the preaching of the Franciscans or Dominicans, or their own doubts about the ever-increasing duration of the exile and the apparent failure of the messiah to appear. But more Jews converted to Christianity to enhance their social and economic standing. By the middle of the fifteenth century, a substantial *converso* class had been created. All doors were open to them as Christians, including those of the Church. . . .

This aroused increasing resentment and hostility among elements of the general Christian population. As early as the 1430s, there were repeated petitions to the papacy by *conversos* to redress their grievances arising from mistreatment and attempts to bar them from obtaining further ecclesiastical and secular offices. The popes responded vigorously to what they rightly saw as unwarranted discrimination among Christians. . . .

AN ACCOUNT OF THE JEWISH EXPULSION FROM SPAIN

In this account, written in 1495, an Italian Jew gives an accurate and detailed picture of the expulsion of the Jews from Spain in 1492 as well as the immediate consequences of the expulsion for Spanish Jewry.

And in the year 5252 [1492], in the days of King Ferdinand, the Lord visited the remnant of his people ... and exiled them. After the King had captured the city of Granada from the Moors, and it had surrendered to him on the 7th [2d] of January of the year just mentioned, he ordered the expulsion of all the Jews in all parts of his kingdom—in the kingdoms of Castile, Catalonia, Aragon, Galicia, Majorca, Minorca, the Basque provinces, the islands of Sardinia and Sicily, and the kingdom of Valencia. Even before that the Queen had expelled them from the kingdom of Andalusia [1483].

The King gave them three months' time in which to leave.... About their number there is no agreement, but, after many inquiries, I found that the most generally accepted estimate is 50,000 families, or, as others say, 53,000. [This would be about 250,000 persons. Other estimates run from 100,000 to 800,000.] They had houses, fields, vineyards, and cattle, and most of them were artisans....

One hundred and twenty thousand of them went to Portugal, according to a compact which a prominent man, Don Vidal bar Benveniste del Cavalleria, had made with the King of Portugal, and they paid one ducat for every soul, and the fourth part of all the merchandise they had carried thither; and he allowed them to stay in his country six months. This King acted much worse toward them than the King of Spain, and after the six months had elapsed he made slaves of all those that remained in his country, and banished seven hundred children to a remote island to settle it, and all of them died. Some say that there were double as many....

Many of the exiled Spaniards went to Mohammedan

countries, to Fez, Tlemçen, and the Berber provinces, under the King of Tunis. [These North African lands are across the Mediterranean from Spain.] On account of their large numbers the Moors did not allow them into their cities, and many of them died in the fields from hunger, thirst, and lack of everything. The lions and bears, which are numerous in this country, killed some of them while they lay starving outside of the cities. . . .

When the edict of expulsion became known in the other countries, vessels came from Genoa to the Spanish harbors to carry away the Jews. The crews of these vessels, too, acted maliciously and meanly toward the Jews, robbed them, and delivered some of them to the famous pirate of that time who was called the Corsair of Genoa. To those who escaped and arrived at Genoa the people of the city showed themselves merciless, and oppressed and robbed them, and the cruelty of their wicked hearts went so far that they took the infants from the mothers' breasts.

Many ships with Jews, especially from Sicily, went to the city of Naples on the coast. The King of this country was friendly to the Jews, received them all, and was merciful towards them, and he helped them with money. The Jews that were at Naples supplied them with food as much as they could, and sent around to the other parts of Italy to collect money to sustain them. . . . On account of their very large number, all this was not enough. Some of them died by famine, others sold their children to Christians to sustain their life. Finally, a plague broke out among them, spread to Naples, and very many of them died, so that the living wearied of burying the dead.

Part of the exiled Spaniards went over sea to Turkey. Some of them were thrown into the sea and drowned, but those who arrived there the King of Turkey received kindly, as they were artisans. He lent them money and settled many of them on an island, and gave them fields and estates.

"The Expulsion from Spain," in *The Jew in the Medieval World: A Source Book: 315–1791*, ed. Jacob Rader Marcus. Cincinnati: Hebrew Union College Press, 1999.

On the other side was the animosity of those who feared the growing power of the *conversos*.

Failing in their efforts to enforce a legal distinction between old and new Christians, *converso*-phobes evolved the first medieval example of true anti-Semitism, as opposed to anti-Jewish sentiment based on objections to Jewish religious tradition. According to the notorious doctrine of *limpieza de sangre* (purity of blood), Jews and Jewish converts to Christianity constituted a race. Jewish blood irreconcilably corrupted its possessor down to the fourth generation, despite intermarriage with old Christians. This doctrine removed the sincerity of converts and their descendents from consideration and made opposition to Jews a biological issue. Since "Jewish blood" remained to the fourth generation, such people were to be barred from holding public or ecclesiastical office or from studying in universities. . . .

There was a clear obsession with purity in fifteenth-century Spain that is evident in how the word was used in chronicles, biographies, and literary works. It was a short step from this doctrine to the belief that it was necessary to purify any Christian tainted by heresy, especially the hated *conversos* themselves. To achieve this end the Inquisition was instituted in Spain. . . .

The Inquisition

From the outset, the Pope made it clear that the Inquisition was to be under the supervision of bishops; no more than two or three Inquisitors, masters of canon law, were to be appointed. The Inquisition was to follow strict rules of procedure. None of this was followed because of Tomás de Torquemada (b. 1420–d. 1498), the confessor of the young Isabel who had enormous influence over her. Under Torquemada an enormous, independent bureaucracy appeared without any semblance of episcopal control. Although sermons were preached and an opportunity for heretics to recant was given, secret accusations were actually solicited and the accused were simply thrown into prison to await trial. In the meantime, they were expected not only to confess their own crimes but to implicate others in turn. The Inquisition began in Seville, spread quickly throughout Andalusia and finally all of Castile into Aragón and Catalonia. Its activities cannot be detailed here except to note the paucity of scholarly studies and that most of the important sources have been ignored.

Contrary to yet another popular myth, the Inquisition had authority only over Christian heretics, not Jews. Thus, its activities are of no importance to Jewish history except as they relate to the question of Jewish conflicts with *conversos*. By the time of the establishment of the Inquisition in Spain, there were third- or fourth-generation *conversos* who, with the exception of a few recent converts, had been born and reared as Christians. Most were no better or no worse than old Christians. Why, therefore, were they accused of heresy?

The answer lies in the intense hostility of many old Christians toward *conversos*. Under the guise of purifying, the opportunity existed to eradicate them. For this purpose, the truth or falseness of the charges against the *conversos* was hardly of concern. Manuals were drawn up for the Inquisition, usually by trustworthy *conversos*, to present a litany of charges to be used. These included such obvious absurdities as the failure to light a fire in the house on the

The torture wheel was of the instruments used to extract confessions during the Spanish Inquisition.

Jewish Sabbath in a climate so warm that a fire would be unbear-
able, or the failure to recite the Trinitarian formula before reading
the Psalms aloud. Such charges can be found in the Inquisition
records as proof of the supposed "crypto-Judaism" of the accused.
Rarely was there any originality in the claimed observances.

The entire purpose of the Inquisition was to arrest, to intimi-
date by imprisonment or torture, and to kill as many *conversos* as
possible, but this goal was secondary to what many regard as its
chief motive, the seizure of property. Indeed, property was confiscated and, as the implication of this source of wealth became increasingly apparent, blanket preventive seizures were made whereby
all the property of *conversos* was taken on the general supposition
of heresy even before they were accused. Nevertheless, far more
important was the burning of thousands of the despised *conversos.*

Although Jews were not the subject of Inquisitional activity,
they did testify in substantial numbers against accused *conversos*,
often against members of their own family. They did this knowing that their testimony was false and knowing what fate awaited
the accused. In instances where the king and queen had proof of
such false testimony, the Jewish witnesses were punished. Jews
willingly gave such testimony because they, too, saw *conversos* as
their worst enemies. Not only had the increasingly sharp anti-
Jewish polemics written by *conversos* become a major problem,
but the continued apostasy and abandonment of their people by
the *conversos* made them the target of any abuse, including murder when possible, by the Jews. Not one Jewish source discussing
the Inquisition shows any particular horror and expresses real
criticism of this. Historians should not write, as some have, of
cordiality between Jews and *conversos* throughout Castile, although in Aragón there were still some exceptions.

Of all the cases tried by the Inquisition, only one appears to
have possibly involved Jews—the notorious ritual murder case of
the "holy child of La Guardian" in 1490. Among those arrested
and accused of the supposed murder, including old Christians
and *conversos*, was at least one person who appears to have been
Jewish. . . . Under torture, the accused confessed. All were burned
at the stake. As to the murder, no such child was ever reported
missing and no body was ever found. Although this case did de-
moralize both *converso* and Jewish communities, its almost total
lack of repercussions for the Spanish Jews does not justify the
hysterical reporting that has taken place in modern histories. . . .

Once the Inquisition was established and under way, further conversion of Jews came virtually to a halt. Whatever incentives may earlier have attracted such converts were now far outweighed by the obvious danger. Another motivation for the Inquisition may have been to halt further conversion of Jews to Christianity.

Contrary to popular mythology, reinforced by ill-informed Jewish historians who refer to one or the other of the monarchs as fanatics, and ferocious, Fernando and Isabel were universally received with great joy and ceremony by Jews wherever they appeared. Very little throughout their reign shows unjust treatment, much less hostility, to the Jews. One exception was the Cortes of Madrigal (1476), its restrictions being enacted mostly against usury. These were no different than similar laws enacted by Cortes of previous rulers. . . .

Throughout this period, the monarchs continued to extend their protection to Jewish communities and to individual Jews whenever there were signs of disturbances or acts against them. Fernando and Isabel showed repeated, scrupulous concern for the just treatment of Jews and for redressing their grievances.

Life continued normally for Jews in the last decades of the fifteenth century. . . . At the same time certain danger signs began to manifest themselves. In such cities as Plasencia and Ávila, some knights and others attacked Jews and Jewish property. . . . Although there are isolated examples of some friars stirring up trouble in Zamora and Segovia, church officials appear to have played no role in arousing anti-Jewish sentiment.

Another unrecognized but important factor is the major role *converso* writers played in the growing eschatological fervor of a united Christian Spain. *Conversos* saw the monarchs, especially Isabel, whom they glorified as a reincarnation of the Virgin Mary, as model Christian rulers. Spain, under the glorious rule of Fernando and Isabel, was to have a role unparalleled in Christian history that was to include perhaps the defeat of the entire Muslim world. That campaign had to begin with the conquest of the last Muslim stronghold in Spain itself, the kingdom of Granada. This was part of the general campaign being urged by the real fanatics in the kingdom, such as Torquemada. . . .

The edict [of Expulsion] was proclaimed in Granada on 31 March 1492, giving the Jews three months from the date of the edict to leave Spain. Within a month, Jews, who had not yet received word of this, continued to buy and sell property and conduct normal business relations with Christians. In an important letter by the monarchs on the date the Edict was proclaimed, the Inquisitors were specified as the ones who had decided to expel Jews. In fact, it was Torquemada himself who demanded this. However, Fernando and Isabel continued their policy of scrupulous justice with regard to the rights of Jews. . . .

Despite the myths concerning the fanaticism of the Catholic monarchs, Jews were not banned from taking money and personal property with them, nor was their property seized as was the case in the expulsion of Jews from England and in their repeated expulsions from France. Spanish Jews were also permitted to sell all personal real property. These sales were legitimate, with the payment of just prices. Fernando issued an order in May that the Jews of Aragón-Catalonia were under his personal protection and that they and their goods were under royal protection when they left the kingdom. He ordered officials to provide troops to guard the Jews and their property. Yet, the Inquisitors of Zaragoza countermanded Fernando's orders there, prohibiting Jews from taking goods with them. That prohibition was ultimately rescinded. Only such communal property as schools, synagogues, cemeteries, and hospitals could not be sold and was acquired by the Crown. Many of these properties were later sold to cities or individuals. . . .

Following the Expulsion, the monarchs continued to ensure that fair treatment had been accorded to the Jews in repayment of debts and sales of property. Commissions were appointed in July to conduct local investigations into these matters. Since there were cases of Jews engaged in complicated business partnerships and other affairs that could not be quickly liquidated, officials were chosen to handle these matters and make payment to Jews *after* the Expulsion. Many Jews chose baptism rather than face expulsion from their homeland. Most of the large Jewish population of Ávila converted.

Many expelled Jews returned to Spain and were baptized, unable or unwilling to face the perils of an uncertain destiny abroad. However, most of the Jews of Castile who left simply went by foot across the border into Portugal and upon payment of bribes and "entry fees," lived there for a short period in peace until they were again compelled to convert or face another exile. The evidence points to the overwhelming majority of Jews still in Spain in 1492 choosing conversion rather than exile.

Contrary to myth, the economy of Spain was neither bankrupted nor even slightly affected by the Expulsion of the Jews. Spain was culturally diminished, however, and its reputation tarnished for centuries to come. The glorious history of tolerance and of harmonious cultural and social symbiosis that characterized Spain for nine centuries had come to an end.

The Muslim Expulsion from Spain

By Roger Boase

Roger Boase is an honorary research fellow in Hispanic studies at the Centre for Medieval and Renaissance Studies at Queen Mary College, University of London. He examines the policies and attitudes toward Muslims in medieval Spain and explains the impetus behind their final expulsion in 1609. Although, prior to 1492 Muslims by and large enjoyed the status of a protected minority, much like the Jews of Spain, the reconquest of Granada by Ferdinand's army signaled a turning point in their treatment by the Christians. Subsequent rulers increased restrictions and persecution of Muslims in Spain, under strong pressure from the church, until ultimately, their expulsion was ordered in 1609. Anti-Muslim attitudes were fueled by a number of misconceptions and stereotypes, including myths of Islamic licentiousness, fears that the Muslim population would surpass that of Christians, and general mistrust and misunderstanding of their differing cultural and religious practices.

'Everything declines after reaching perfection . . .

The tap of the white ablution fount weeps in despair, like a passionate lover weeping at the departure of the beloved.

Over dwellings emptied of Islam, vacated, whose inhabitants now live in unbelief.

Where the mosques have become churches in which only bells and crosses are found . . .

O who will redress the humiliation of a people who

were once powerful, a people whose condition injustice and tyrants have changed?

Yesterday they were kings in their own homes, but today they are slaves in the land of the infidel!

Were you to see them bewildered, with no one to guide them, wearing the cloth of shame in its different shades.

And were you to behold their weeping when they are sold, it would strike fear into your heart, and sorrow would seize you.

Alas, many a maiden as fair as the sun when it rises, as though she were rubies and pearls,

Is led off to abomination by a barbarian against her will, while her eve is in tears and her heart is stunned.

The heart melts with sorrow at such sights, if there is any Islam or faith in that heart!'

These words were written by the poet ar-Rundi after Seville fell to Ferdinand III of Castile (1199–1252) in December 1248. By that date many other cities, including Valencia, Murcia, Jaén and Córdoba, had been captured and it seemed that the end of Muslim Spain was imminent. However, it was not until 1492 that the Moorish Kingdom of Granada surrendered to Ferdinand V and Isabella, and the final Muslim expulsion did not take place until over a century later, between 1609 and 1614. This means that there was a large Moorish population in Spain half a millennium after the high point of Andalusian culture in the eleventh century.

Ar-Rundi might well have been responding to the plight of his co-religionists after the fall of Granada or at the time of the expulsion when many similar atrocities were committed: homes were destroyed and abandoned, mosques were converted into churches, mothers were separated from their children, people were stripped of their wealth and humiliated, armed rebels were reduced to slavery. But by the seventeenth century the Moors had become Spanish citizens; some were genuine Christian converts; indeed many, like Sancho Panza's neighbour Ricote in [Miguel de] Cervantes' novel *Don Quixote* (1605–15), were deeply patriotic and considered themselves to be '*más cristiano que moro*'. Yet all were the victims of a state policy, based on racist theological arguments, which had the backing of both the Royal Council and the Church, for which the expulsion of the Jews in 1492 provided an immediate legal precedent.

According to the terms of the treaty drawn up in 1492, the new subjects of the Crown were to be allowed to preserve their mosques and religious institutions, to retain the use of their language and to continue to abide by their own laws and customs. But within seven years these terms had been broken. When the moderate missionary approach of the archbishop of Granada, Hernando de Talavera (1428–1507), was replaced by the fanaticism of Cardinal Cisneros (c.1436–1518), who organised mass conversions and the burning of all religious texts in Arabic, these events resulted in the First Rebellion of the Alpujarras (1499–1500) and the assassination of one of the Cardinal's agents. This in turn gave the Catholic monarchs an excuse to revoke their promises. In 1499 the Muslim religious leaders of Granada were persuaded to hand over more than 5,000 priceless books with ornamental bindings, which were then consigned to the flames; only some books on medicine were spared. In Andalusia after 1502, and in Valencia, Catalonia and Aragon after 1526, the Moors were given a choice between baptism and exile. For the majority, baptism was the only practical option. Henceforward the Spanish Moors became theoretically New Christians and, as such, subject to the jurisdiction of the Inquisition, which had been authorised by Pope Sixtus IV in 1478.

For the most part, conversion was nominal: the Moors paid lip-service to Christianity, but continued to practise Islam in secret. For example, after a child was baptised, he might be taken home and washed with hot water to annul the sacrament of baptism. . . .

The fall of Granada marked a new phase in Muslim-Christian relations. In medieval times the status of Muslims under Christian rule was similar to that of Christians under Muslim rule: they belonged to a protected minority which preserved its own laws and customs in return for tribute. But there was no Scriptural basis for the legal status of Jews and Muslims under Christian rule; they were subject to the whims of rulers, the prejudices of the populace and the objections of the clergy. Before the completion of the Reconquest it was in the interests of the kings of Aragon and Castile to respect such laws and contracts. Now, however, Spain not only became, at least in theory, an entirely Christian nation but purity of faith came to be identified with purity of blood so that all New Christians or *conversos*, whether of Jewish or Muslim origin, were branded as potential heretics.

As a member of a vanquished minority with an alien culture, the *moro* became a *morisco*, a 'little Moor'. Every aspect of his way of life—including his language, dress and social customs—was condemned as uncivilised and pagan. A person who refused to drink wine or eat pork might be denounced as a Muslim to the Inquisition. In the eyes of the Inquisition and popular opinion, even practices such as eating couscous, using henna, throwing sweets at a wedding and dancing to the sound of Berber music, were un-Christian activities for which a person might be obliged to do penance. Moriscos who were sincere Christians were also bound to remain second-class citizens, and might be exposed to criticism from Muslims and Christians alike. Although *morisco* is a derogatory term, historians find it a useful label for those Arabs or Moors who remained in Spain after the fall of Granada.

In 1567 Philip II renewed an edict which had never been strictly enforced, making the use of Arabic illegal and prohibiting Islamic religion, dress and customs. This edict resulted in the Second Rebellion of the Alpujarras (1568–70), which seemed to corroborate evidence of a secret conspiracy with the Turks. The uprising was brutally suppressed by Don John of Austria. One of his worst atrocities was to raze the town of Galera, to the east of Granada, and sprinkle it with salt, having slaughtered 2,500 people including 400 women and children. Some 80,000 Moriscos in Granada were dispersed to other parts of Spain and Old Christians from northern Spain were settled on their lands.

By 1582 expulsion was proposed by Philip II's Council of State as the only solution to the conflict between the communities, despite some concern about the harmful economic repercussions—the loss of Moorish craftsmanship and the shortage of agricultural manpower and expertise. But as there was opposition from some noblemen and the King was preoccupied by international events, no action was taken until 1609–10 when Philip III (r. 1598–1621) issued edicts of expulsion.

Royal legislation concerning the Moriscos was dictated at every stage by the Church. Juan de Ribera (1542–1611), the aging Archbishop of Valencia, who had initially been a firm believer in the efficacy of missionary work, became in his declining years the chief partisan of expulsion. In a sermon preached on September 27th, 1609, he said that the land would not become fertile again until these heretics had been expelled. The Duke of Lerma (Philip III's first minister, 1598–1618) also underwent a change of heart when it was agreed that the lords of Valencia would be given the lands of the expelled Moriscos in compensation for the loss of their vassals.

The decision to proceed with the expulsion was approved unanimously by the Council of State on January 30th, 1608, although the actual decree was not signed by the King until April 4th, 1609. Galleons of the Spanish fleet were secretly prepared, and they were later joined by many foreign merchant ships, including several from England. On September 11th, the expulsion order was announced by town criers in the Kingdom of Valencia, and the first convoy departed from Denia at nightfall on October 2nd, and arrived in Oran less than three days later. The Moriscos of Aragon, Castile, Andalusia and Extremadura received expulsion orders during the course of the following year. The majority of the forced emigrants settled in the Maghrib or Barbary Coast, especially in Oran, Tunis, Tlemcen, Tetuán, Rabat and Salé. Many travelled overland to France, but after the assassination of Henry of Navarre by [French assassin François] Ravaillac in May 1610, they were forced to emigrate to Italy, Sicily or Constantinople.

There is much disagreement about the size of the Morisco population. The French demographer Henri Lapeyre estimated from census reports and embarkation lists that approximately 275,000 Spanish Moriscos emigrated in the years 1609–14, out of a total of 300,000. This conservative estimate is not consistent with many of the contemporary accounts that give a figure of 600,000. Bearing in mind that the total population of Spain at that time was only about seven and a half million, this must have constituted a serious deficit in terms of productive manpower and tax revenue. In the Kingdom of Valencia, which lost a third of its population, nearly half the villages were deserted in 1638.

There is equal disagreement about the number of Moriscos who perished in armed rebellion or on the journey into exile. Pedro Aznar Cardona, whose treatise justifying the expulsion was published in 1612, stated that between October 1609 and July 1611 over 50,000 died resisting expulsion, while over 60,000 died during their passage abroad either by land or sea or at the hands of their co-religionists after disembarking on the North African coast. If these figures are correct, then more than one in six of the Moorish population perished in the space of two years. [Historian] Henry Charles Lea, drawing on many contemporary sources, puts the mortality figure at between two-thirds and three-quarters.

The demographic factor was one of the decisive arguments employed in favour of expulsion by Juan de Ribera in 1602. He warned Philip III that, unless he took swift action, Christian Spaniards would soon find themselves outnumbered by Muslims, as all Moriscos married and had large families, whereas a third or a quarter of all Christians remained celibate after taking holy orders or entering military service. The Moriscos, Ribera said, think only of reproducing and saving their skins, while their temperance in food and drink gives them a high life expectancy. Ribera's fears were prompted by a census of the Valencian population that he himself had supervised that same year, which revealed that the Morisco population had increased by one-third.

At a meeting of the State Council in January 1608 the Comendador de León attributed the decline of the Old Christian population to their reluctance to shoulder the financial burden of marriage at a time of rising costs. He warned that soon the Moriscos would be able to achieve their objective simply by means of their population growth, without either taking up arms or receiving help from abroad. With Turkey distracted by war and with Persia and North Africa weakened by plague, drought and civil war, it was an opportune moment to take firm action....

In the minds of many, the fertility of the Morisco population was associated with the myth of Islamic sensuality and licentiousness. The failure of the Church in its missionary efforts was attributed to this alleged aspect of Islam that offered—so they said—carnal delights both here and in the hereafter. The Moriscos came to personify the sins of the flesh, later romanticised in visions of oriental harems. But they were considered equally susceptible to 'the sins of the superego', such as pride, hypocrisy, cunning, avarice and grasping ambition, all features traditionally ascribed to the Jews. Prejudiced people will not hesitate to use mutually exclusive stereotypes to justify their dislike, and this is certainly true of many Spanish writers in the seventeenth century: the Moriscos are lazy, yet industrious; abstemious, yet lascivious; miserly, yet extravagant; cowardly, yet belligerent;

ignorant, yet anxious to acquire learning in order to rise above their station.

There were, as we have seen, some genuine grounds for fearing and envying the Moriscos: their numbers were increasing rapidly; some had become successful merchants and shopkeepers, despite attempts to exclude them from these occupations; they exemplified in their conduct the virtues of thrift, frugality and hard work; the majority outwardly conformed to the religious requirements imposed on them, but by subterfuge continued to celebrate their own festivals and practise the basic rituals of Islam. It was this refusal to renounce their religious and cultural identity that many Old Christians found offensive. There was no serious attempt to understand Morisco culture and religion. Any slanderous anecdote, any insulting remark, any distortion of the truth was acceptable if it served what these Christians considered to be the laudable aim of denigrating Islam. Cultural diversity was an alien concept and assimilation was equally unacceptable.

The experience of the Moriscos varied enormously from one region to another. In some parts of Spain there were exceptionally good relations between Old and New Christians. A detailed study of Villarubia in La Mancha where the Moriscos comprised 20 per cent of the population, owned the best farmland and were well integrated within the community, has shown that they were protected by their Old Christian neighbours from unwelcome visits from government inspectors. Many of those expelled managed to slip back into Spain and travelled hundreds of miles to reach their homes.

The full tale of the sufferings endured by the Moriscos has never fully been told: how those who survived the journey arrived at their destination starving and destitute because the bare necessities and money that they were permitted to take with them had been extorted from them by thieves and swindlers; how those travelling overland to France were forced by farmers to pay whenever they drank from a river or sat in the shade of a tree; how thousands of those who resisted and survived ended their days as galley-slaves; how those waiting to board ship were starved so that they would agree to sell their children in exchange for bread; how it was the official policy of the Church to separate Morisco children from their parents.

It was Juan de Ribera's original intention, approved by the Council of State on September 1st, 1609, that all children aged ten or under should remain in Spain to be educated by priests or trustworthy persons whom they would serve until the age of twenty-five or thirty in return for lodging, food and clothing, and that sucking babes should be given to Old Christian wet-nurses on the same conditions. Later in the month the age limit was reduced from ten to five years or under. The policy was at least partially executed, though it proved impossible to implement in full. Among the Moriscos who embarked at Alicante in Andalusia between October 6th, and November 7th, 1609, there seem to have been nearly 14,000 children missing (conservatively assuming an average 2.5 children per family). According to a document dated April 17th, 1610, there were 1,832 Morisco boys and girls aged seven or under in the Kingdom of Valencia, all of whom, against the wishes of their guardians, were to be sent to Castile to serve the prelates and other notables of the realm. In July 1610 the Church recommended that all Morisco children above the age of seven in the Kingdom of Valencia should be sold as perpetual slaves to Old Christians. These included the orphans of rebels, children seized by soldiers and others concealed and cared for by people who believed they were doing an act of charity. The theologians who signed this document argued that slavery was not only morally justifiable but spiritually beneficial: these children would be less likely to become apostates, since their masters would ensure that they remained Roman Catholics and, as slaves rarely married, this would be another method of ridding Spain of 'this evil race'.

What was the significance of the age limit? It was thought that above the age of six or seven a child begins to lose his innocence and becomes more difficult to indoctrinate, whereas a younger child would have no real knowledge of his origins. The policy was justified on the grounds that innocent children baptised as Christians should not be punished for the sins of their fathers, although, paradoxically, the principle of hereditary guilt was found acceptable as a justification for expelling all adults, whether or not they were practising Christians. Furthermore, it was said that to banish children with their infidel parents would be to guarantee their confirmation as Muslims and their consignment to hellfire in the hereafter. But young Morisco children should not be educated above their proper station: apart from pupils preparing for the priesthood, they were to be brought up by artisans and farm labourers, and they should certainly not be allowed to study literature. In this way it was hoped that all memories of Islam in Spain would be wiped out forever. This point was much appreciated by Philip III.

Much has been written about the exodus of the Spanish Jews in 1492 and the plight of the many Jewish *conversos* who suffered at the hands of the Inquisition, but the Spanish Arabs or Moors have not received the same attention. In most people's minds, the Spanish Inquisition is associated with the persecution of Jews. It is not so widely known that Muslims were terrorised by this institution and that they too were the victims of an anti-Semitic ideology. About 12,000 Moriscos were charged with apostasy by the Inquisition, 50 per cent of them in the last thirty years before the expulsion.

Racial and religious intolerance is nowhere more evident than in the reports of some of the meetings of Philip III's Council of State and in works written to justify the need for a policy of expulsion. In these works, most of them by frustrated Dominican missionaries, one finds a highly unorthodox racist theology, supported by biblical precedents: there was an attempt to judaise Islam and to depict Christian Spaniards of old Christian stock as the new Chosen Race engaged in a crusade to recover their Promised Land from the Antichrist Muhammad. . . .

It is ironic that those same Old Testament passages which have been used to support the theory that Palestine is the Jewish promised land were not only cited by apologists for a policy of mass expulsion for the Moriscos but were cited by anti-Jewish theologians in advocating the need for statutes of purity of blood. These authors regarded the Spanish Old Christians as the spiritual heirs of the Children of Israel and compared Philip III with Abraham, Moses or King David. They called him a second Abraham because, they said, he was obliged to banish his illegitimate son, that is to say the Moriscos, the descendants of Hagar, the Egyptian slave-girl. . . .

The Portuguese Dominican Damián Fonseca even suggested that God expected a burnt offering from His Catholic Majesty to appease His divine wrath. The phrase he used in 1611 was *el agradable holocausto* ('the agreeable holocaust').

To these antisemites, the Jews were descended from Judas, who betrayed Christ, not Judah, son of Jacob. They would not have admitted that Jesus was a Jew sent by God to preach to the 'lost sheep of the House of Israel'. As a result of the role that

God had predestined for them, the Jews ceased to be God's chosen people and inherited the sin of deicide for which they were condemned to wander the earth.

The simplest method of vilifying the last remnants of Arab Spain was to depict Islam as a form of pseudo-Jewish heresy. Jaime Bleda, the royal chaplain and chief anti-Morisco polemicist, even suggested that the Moorish invasion of Spain was a divine punishment for the pro-Semitic policies of the Visigothic King Wittiza (698–710), who had revoked the decrees of his father by liberating the Jews from slavery and restoring to them their lands and privileges. This was cited as a legal precedent applicable to the Moriscos at the Council of State held on January 30th, 1608. However, the immediate historical precedent was the expulsion of the Jews in 1492. In April 1605, Bleda urged Philip III to follow the example of his royal predecessors Ferdinand and Isabella, who had been persuaded by Fray Thomás de Torquemada to banish the Jews from their realms and would have done the same to the Moors had they refused baptism. God, he said, rewarded the Catholic monarchs for their Christian zeal by giving them the New World.

Much of the vituperation that Bleda and other polemicists levelled against the Moriscos had previously been levelled against the Jews. Of both peoples it was said that they were inherently sinful and inferior, that they were incorrigible in their obstinate infidelity, and that their heretical depravity was a contagion which would have to be removed. Philip III is even described as a Catholic Galen, charged with the task of purging the poison and corruption of heresy from the mystical body of Christian Spain.

The Golden Age of Spain and Its Decline

Conquest and Settlement of the New World

By Richard C. Harris

Richard C. Harris was a colonel who served as an attaché under the U.S. ambassador to Spain, Stanton Griffis, during the early 1950s. He describes the exploration of the New World by Christopher Columbus, Hernán Cortés, Francisco Pizarro, Hernando de Soto, and other conquistadores as they discovered new routes and lands, conquered native peoples, and established new settlements. The Spanish government largely viewed these new conquests as resources to enrich the mother country and increase its power and dominance in Europe. Had the Spanish leaders focused on expanding their control of the New World rather than the Old, Harris argues, Spain could have created a truly great and enduring empire.

On August 3, 1492, Columbus set sail from the small Spanish port of Palos with three tiny caravels. With this miniature fleet, manned by a total crew of only ninety officers and men, Columbus sailed to the Canary Islands, where provisions were restocked. On September 6th the small band of courageous adventurers, not at all sure that they would ever see land again, set sail into the unknown.

By October 10th., having sailed for thirty-four days without seeing a single sign which would indicate land ahead, nerves were on edge and many of the sailors wanted to turn back. Some accounts have it that there was a near mutiny and that Columbus was forced to promise that he would give up the expedition if land were not sighted within three more days. At any rate, before

Richard C. Harris, *Highlights of Spanish History*. Zaragoza, Spain: El Noticiero de Zaragoza, 1955.

dawn on the morning of the 12th, a lookout on the *Pinta* gave an exultant shout—and Spain had discovered America.

The island upon which Columbus first planted the Spanish flag was probably Watlings Island of the Bahama group. From there he went on to Santo Domingo, where he left a small number of men to form the nucleus of the first Spanish colony in the Americas, and then sailed to Cuba. The explorer was convinced that the islands he had seen were part of the Japanese group of which Marco Polo had written so glowingly; but instead of palaces with golden roofs and floors he found miles of unbroken jungle inhabited by strange animals, rare birds, and curious ruddy colored men who, although friendly enough, had obviously never advanced much beyond the Stone Age. But most interesting of all was the fact that many of those naked savages wore ornaments fashioned from little chunks of gold which they picked from stream beds. That, more than anything else, served to strengthen Columbus's conviction that he had discovered the outskirts to the fabulously rich lands of the Orient.

Columbus made three more voyages to the New World during the next twelve years and partially explored a number of the Caribbean islands plus a strip of the mainland from Honduras south to Panama. During the course of his four voyages he planted three colonies. Of those only the colony of Santo Domingo was to endure; and even in that colony there were rebellions which caused Columbus, the hero of all Europe, to be accused of mal-administration and to be deprived of the governorship of the new lands he had discovered. The colonies had not yielded the immediate riches expected of them, and Columbus had failed to find a passage through the Central American mainland to the Indies, which he was convinced lay inmediately beyond. Furthermore, the belief was rapidly gaining popularity that the newly discovered lands were not Asiatic at all, but of a new continent.

Columbus died in the year 1506, an unhappy and somewhat disillusioned man but still firmly convinced that he had found the sea route to Asia. There was no way for Columbus to realize that the New World he had actually discovered was to have far greater effect on the history of Europe than was the real sea route to Asia—a route which the Portuguese explorer Vasco de Gama discovered a few years later by sailing around the southern tip of Africa.

The Conquistadors

The next fifty years following the discovery of America constitute an era of exploration, discovery and conquest which has never before nor since been equaled in the history of the world. Undoubtedly one of the greatest driving forces behind this enormous zeal for conquest and expansion was the unprecedented opportunity to convert hundreds of thousands of savages to Christianity. The zest with which this wholesale conversion was carried out was a direct carry-over from the Holy Crusades and, although the methods employed were frequently brutal, the motives were entirely sincere. Even the bloodiest and most disreputable plunderer who ever waved a sword in one hand and a crucifix in the other solemnly believed it to be God's will that he forcibly convert pagans, wherever encountered, to Christianity. The loot that might fall into his hands while he was so engaged was considered to be legitimate plunder—and besides, a good portion of it would be divided with King and Church.

Although the discovery of America is frequently cited as marking the end of the Middle Ages, the medieval cruelty which characterized that period throughout Europe—in England, France and Germany as much as in Spain and Italy—was far from extinct (and a review of atrocities committed in nazi and communist prison camps during World War II and the Korean conflict would indicate that it is *still* far from extinct). Religious tolerance was incompatible with the times and the torture and murder of an unrepenting heretic was considered to be as natural and as blameless a procedure as was the employment of torture by the legal courts of the times to obtain confessions from civil offenders. That this intolerance and cruelty should be so characteristic of a period in history which is also known as the Age of Chivalry and Gallantry—a period which produced some of the noblest and most daring exploits the world has ever seen—is a riddle for the psychologists. The important fact, from the historical standpoint, is that the conquerors of America were neither more nor less cruel, nor more nor less gallant, than was the average European adventurer, soldier or missionary of that day and age.

Not all *conquistadores*, of course, were cruel; and some of those who were the most cruel were also, at times, the most generous and gallant. In all fairness it must be noted that it was the priests, who fully shared with the soldiers-of-fortune their incredible hardships and privations, who fought most incessantly for humane treatment of the Indians and the abolition of slavery. It was these men of God, fanatic and intolerant though they may have been, who built universities and who brought the learning of Europe to the wilderness of the Americas. From the very first the cross was fully as powerful a force as was the sword in molding the new world; and its conquests were far more permanent.

A second great driving power behind the conquest of the Americas was the quest for wealth and power. In consonance with the frailties of mankind this quest soon came to be a much more powerful incentive for enduring the hardships and perils of the New World than was the religious motive. New fortunes

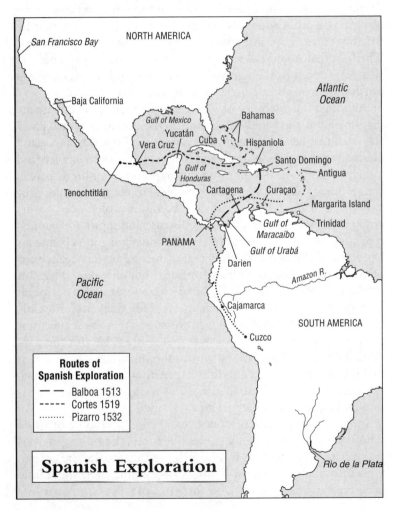

Spanish Exploration

were to be made by boldness and by toughness, and the foundation was laid for a new aristocracy based on achievement rather than on lineage. The conquistadors who followed Columbus were more often of the hardy lower classes than of the nobility, and it was their hardihood and imperviousness to the hardships and privations they endured which made possible the conquest of the Americas.

Within fifty years of the first voyage of Columbus the greatest part of the extensive territory now known as Spanish America had been traversed by Spanish conquistadors, and most of the millions of inhabitants of those lands had acknowledged fealty to the Christian God and to the Spanish sovereigns. There is no more romantic or adventurous chapter in the history of the world than that dealing with those far-reaching conquests and the men who led them.

There was Vasco Núñez de Balboa, who hid himself in an empty cask to become a stowaway on a vessel bound for Santo Domingo and who, by an unscrupulous bit of treachery, later became ruler of the small settlement of Santa María del Darien. It was at Darien that the son of a neighboring Indian chieftain contemptuously watched Balboa and his men quarrel over a bit of gold they had discovered and, to rid his land of those greedy invaders, concocted a story of a land farther on where the natives ate and drank from dishes and cups of gold. This story provided the incentive for Balboa, with a hundred and ninety men, to set out on his famous march across the Isthmus. Upon reaching the Pacific coast he splashed into the water and took possession of the ocean in the name of the King of Spain—and immediately after him splashed a young priest bearing aloft a crucifix to take possession of the ocean in the name of Jesus Christ. Curiously enough, Balboa also found gold and pearls in sufficient quantity to make every member of his little expedition rich for life. But Balboa himself was beheaded by the Spanish governor of the Isthmus as recompense for the treachery by which he had originally siezed command of his expedition—and thus ended the career of one of the most promising of the conquistadors.

Hernando Cortes missed his first chance to sail to the New World. A devil-may-care lad of eighteen, Cortes was the son of an Andalusian family of noble blood but of little wealth. The night before he was to sail for Santo Domingo with an expedition financed by a family friend, young Cortes attempted to scale the wall of a respected home in Seville to reach the window of an attractive young lady's boudoir. A piece of masonry gave way and the young cavalier landed in an ungainly heap at the bottom of the wall, covered with bits of masonry and crippled with a broken ankle.

Eventually, however, Cortes made his way to Cuba and there became a planter. Despite numerous adventures and escapades he soon amassed fortune enough to outfit an expedition to Mexico. With 11 small ships, 110 sailors and 530 soldiers, plus 16 horses and a small number of Indian slaves, Cortes set out to conquer tens of thousands of Aztec warriors and a territory many times the size of his native Spain. From time to time he received reinforcements but never, during his entire campaign, did his Spanish soldiers number more than fifteen hundred men.

Like most of his compatriots, Cortes was deeply religious and sincerely believed himself to be a crusader. He felt that any means he might employ to spread the faith would be more than justified by the successful accomplishment of that mission. He was generous and honorable in his dealings with the Indians so long as his authority was not imperiled thereby, but ruthless and merciless when he found himself and his men in jeopardy. The epic of his march against Mexico City and his dealings, through his devoted Indian mistress and interpreter Malinche, with the mighty Aztec monarch, Montezuma, is easily the most fabulous in the annals of the entire history of fabulous exploits which made possible the conquest of the Americas.

Francisco Pizarro, conqueror of Peru, was an illiterate swineherd from Trujillo in Extremadura. One day when he was about sixteen years old one of the pigs he was charged with watching ran away and Pizarro, fearful of the wrath of his employer, followed the little pig's example. Somehow, he made his way to Italy and from there to the New World. He was a member of the expedition which Balboa led across the Isthmus and was one of the first Spaniards to view the Pacific Ocean. Later, by sheer brawn and brute courage, Pizarro fought his way into a position of leadership among the Spanish settlers on the Isthmus. It was this illiterate soldier-of-fortune who organized and led the conquest of the Peruvian Inca empire and who found more gold and treasure than Columbus had ever dreamed of. It was Pizarro who demanded and received, as ransom for the Inca Emperor whom he had made captive, gold trinkets and ornaments of a sufficient quantity to fill an eighteen by twenty foot room to a mark on the wall placed as high as the tall Inca could reach—plus an equal amount of silver.

Pizarro was as treacherous as he was courageous, but despite his many villainous acts of treachery and cruelty he was an inspired leader of men and a valiant soldier. Although avaricious and greedy, he also considered himself to be a crusader and some of his worst atrocities were committed in the name of Christianity. It was Pizarro's custom, before closing in battle with the Incas, to have his priest exort them to renounce their false gods and to accept Jesus Christ as the Son of the one true God.

It was Hernando de Soto, one of Pizarro's lieutenants, who discovered and explored the Mississippi River. Pedro de Valdivia, another of Pizarro's lieutenants, endured almost incredible hardships and privations to found the city of Santiago, Chile—only to be killed at last by the Araucano Indians.

Magellan followed the coast of South America to the straits which bear his name. He traversed those treacherous straits and found, at last, the westward passage to Asia. He took the Philippines for Spain but was killed in a skirmish with the natives. One of his ships, however, continued the journey westward to Spain and thus completed the first circumnavigation of the globe.

And there was [Pedro de] Mendoza, who founded the city of Buenos Aires; [Gonzalo Jiménez de] Quesada, who fought his way through five hundred miles of swamps and mountains to found the capital of Colombia; and, [Francisco de] Orellana, who crossed the precipitous Andes and traveled three thousand miles down the Amazon to become the first man to traverse the continent of South America from coast to coast, and almost at its widest point. [Álvar Núñez] Cabeza de Vaca made a ten thousand mile march across the United States and south to Mexico City, and then sailed to South America to cut his way through a thousand miles of Brazilian jungle to Paraguay. Many others performed similar heroic feats. And with them always went the priests, the spreaders of Christianity and European learning.

Few of the great conquistadors returned to Spain to spend the fortunes they acquired; those who survived their conquests for the most part remained to develop colonies in the New World. Thus, along with the zeal for converting pagans to Christianity and the lust for wealth and power, a third great driving force behind the conquest of the Americas must be listed—that pioneering spirit which is vested in a few hard-bitten men of high courage and gambling instincts, the empire builders of the world. Those were the men who faced odds of thousands to one against the Indians, who struggled for months and even years through swamps, jungles, deserts and over mountains, who suffered from extremes of heat and cold, insects and disease—those are the men to whom the Americas owe a debt that can never be repaid, nor even adequately summed up.

There is little doubt that Spain would have become and remained, for centuries yet to come, the most powerful empire in the world had her wealth and efforts been devoted to the colonization and development of the Americas rather than to imperialistic schemes in Europe. But the untold riches which flowed from the Americas into the coffers of Spain during this period and during the succeeding generations were not reinvested in the profitable new colonies but instead were dissipated in supporting long and costly military efforts to dominate Europe. The Spanish leaders were unable to realize that Spain's most promising future lay in the New World rather than in the Old.

Correspondence Between Christopher Columbus, King Ferdinand, and Queen Isabella

PART I: KING FERDINAND AND QUEEN ISABELLA;
PART II: CHRISTOPHER COLUMBUS

Christopher Columbus was an explorer from Genoa, Italy, contracted by Queen Isabella and King Ferdinand of Spain to sail on a voyage to discover a sea route to the Indies in 1492. In the process, he discovered America. The first document, Part I, was drafted by the king and queen conferring a number of privileges and prerogatives on Christopher Columbus for his service to them as an explorer. Part II is a correspondence from Columbus to his employers, written after his discovery of the islands of the Caribbean. In it, he attempts to establish rules and regulations for the colony being settled there. He is particularly concerned with the gold found by the colonists.

I

FERDINAND and ELIZABETH [Isabella], by the Grace of God, King and Queen of *Castile*, of *Leon*, of *Arragon*, of *Sicily*, of *Granada*, of *Toledo*, of *Valencia*, of *Galicia*, of *Majorca*, of *Minorca*, of *Sevil*, of *Sardinia*, of *Jaen*, of *Algarve*, of *Algezira*, of *Gibraltar*, of the *Canary Islands*, Count and Countess of

Part I: King Ferdinand and Queen Isabella, "Privileges and Prerogatives Granted by Their Catholic Majesties to Christopher Columbus: 1492," The Avalon Project, www.yale.edu/lawweb/avalon, 1997. Part II: Christopher Columbus, letter to the King and Queen of Spain, 1494.

Barcelona, Lord and Lady of *Biscay* and *Molina*, Duke and Duchess of *Athens* and *Neopatria*. Count and Countess of *Rousillion* and *Cerdaigne*, Marquess and Marchioness of *Oristan* and *Gociano*, &c.

For as much of you, *Christopher Columbus*, are going by our command, with some of our vessels and men, to discover and subdue some Islands and Continent in the ocean, and it is hoped that by God's assistance, some of the said Islands and Continent in the ocean will be discovered and conquered by your means and conduct, therefore it is but just and reasonable, that since you expose yourself to such danger to serve us, you should be rewarded for it. And we being willing to honour and favour You for the reasons aforesaid: Our will is, That you, *Christopher Columbus*, after discovering and conquering the said Islands and Continent in the said ocean, or any of them, shall be our Admiral of the said Islands and Continent you shall so discover and conquer; and that you be our Admiral, Vice-Roy, and Governour in them, and that for the future, you may call and stile yourself, D. *Christopher Columbus*, and that your sons and successors in the said employment, may call themselves Dons, Admirals, Vice-Roys, and Governours of them; and that you may exercise the office of Admiral, with the charge of Vice-Roy and Governour of the said Islands and Continent, which you and your Lieutenants shall conquer, and freely decide all causes, civil and criminal, appertaining to the said employment of Admiral, Vice-Roy, and Governour, as you shall think fit in justice, and as the Admirals of our kingdoms use to do; and that you have power to punish offenders; and you and your Lieutenants exercise the employments of Admiral, Vice-Roy, and Governour, in all things belonging to the said offices, or any of them; and that you enjoy the perquisites and salaries belonging to the said employments, and to each of them, in the same manner as the High Admiral of our kingdoms does. And by this our letter, or a copy of it signed by a *Public Notary*; We command Prince *John*, our most dearly beloved Son, the Infants, Dukes, Prelates, Marquesses, Great Masters and Military Orders, Priors. Commendaries, our Counsellors, Judges, and other Officers of Justice whatsoever, belonging Courts, and Chancery, and Constables of Castles, Strong Houses, and others; and all Corporations, Bayliffs, Governours, Judges, Commanders, Sea Officers; and the Aldermen, Common Council, Officers, and Good People of all Cities, Lands, and Places in our Kingdoms and Dominions, and in those you shall conquer and subdue, and the captains masters, mates, and other officers and sailors, our natural subjects now being, or that shall be for the time to come, and any of them that when you shall have discovered the said Islands and Continent in the ocean; and you, or any that shall have your commission, shall have taken the usual oath in such cases, that they for the future, look upon you as long as you live, and after you, your son and heir, and so from one heir to another forever, as our Admiral on our said Ocean, and as Vice-Roy and Governour of the said Islands and Continent, by you, *Christopher Columbus*, discovered and conquered; and that they treat you and your Lieutenants, by you appointed, for executing the employments of Admiral, Vice-Roy, and Governour, as such in all respects, and give you all the perquisites and other things belonging and appertaining to the said offices; and allow, and cause to be allowed you, all the honours, graces, concessions, preeminences, prerogatives, immunities, and other things, or any of them which are due to you, by virtue of your commands of Admiral, Vice-Roy, and Governour, and to be observed completely, so that nothing be diminished; and that they make no objection to this, or any part of it, nor suffer it to be made; forasmuch as we from this time forward, by this our letter, bestow on you the employments of Admiral, Vice-Roy, and perpetual Governour forever; and we put you into possession of the said offices, and of every of them, and full power to use and exercise them, and to receive the perquisites and salaries belonging to them, or any of them, as was said above. Concerning all which things, if it be requisite, and you shall desire it, We command our Chancellour, Notaries, and other Officers, to pass, seal, and deliver to you, our Letter of Privilege, in such form and legal manner, as you shall require or stand in need of. And that none of them presume to do any thing to the contrary, upon pain of our displeasure, and forfeiture of 30 ducats for each offence. And we command him, who shall show them this our Letter, that he summon them to appear before us at our Court, where we shall then be, within fifteen days after such summons, under the said penalty. Under which same, we also command any Public Notary whatsoever, that he give to him that shows it him, a certificate under his seal, that we may know how our command is obeyed.

GIVEN at *Granada*, on the 30th of April, in the year of our Lord, 1492.

II

Most High and Mighty Sovereigns,

In obedience to your Highnesses' commands, and with submission to superior judgment, I will say whatever occurs to me in reference to the colonization and commerce of the Island of Espanola, and of the other islands, both those already discovered and those that may be discovered hereafter.

In the first place, as regards the Island of Espanola: Inasmuch as the number of colonists who desire to go thither amounts to two thousand, owing to the land being safer and better for farming and trading, and because it will serve as a place to which they can return and from which they can carry on trade with the neighboring islands:

1. That in the said island there shall be founded three or four towns, situated in the most convenient places, and that the settlers who are there be assigned to the aforesaid places and towns.

2. That for the better and more speedy colonization of the said island, no one shall have liberty to collect gold in it except those who have taken out colonists' papers, and have built houses for their abode, in the town in which they are, that they may live united and in greater safety.

3. That each town shall have its alcalde [Mayor] . . . and its notary public, as is the use and custom in Castile.

4. That there shall be a church, and parish priests or friars to administer the sacraments, to perform divine worship, and for the conversion of the Indians.

5. That none of the colonists shall go to seek gold without a license from the governor or alcalde of the town where he lives; and that he must first take oath to return to the place whence he sets out, for the purpose of registering faithfully all the gold he may have found, and to return once a month, or once a week, as the time may have been set for him, to render account and show the quantity of said gold; and that this shall be written down by the notary before the alcalde, or, if it seems better, that a friar or priest, deputed for the purpose, shall be also present.

6. That all the gold thus brought in shall be smelted immediately, and stamped with some mark that shall distinguish each town; and that the portion which belongs to your Highnesses shall be weighed, and given and consigned to

each alcalde in his own town, and registered by the above-mentioned priest or friar, so that it shall not pass through the hands of only one person, and there shall be no opportunity to conceal the truth.

7. That all gold that may be found without the mark of one of the said towns in the possession of any one who has once registered in accordance with the above order shall be taken as forfeited, and that the accuser shall have one portion of it and your Highnesses the other.

8. That one per centum of all the gold that may be found shall be set aside for building churches and adorning the same, and for the support of the priests or friars belong-

Christopher Columbus explains his discovery of America to King Ferdinand and Queen Isabella.

ing to them; and, if it should be thought proper to pay any thing to the alcaldes or notaries for their services, or for ensuring the faithful perforce of their duties, that this amount shall be sent to the governor or treasurer who may be appointed there by your Highnesses.

9. As regards the division of the gold, and the share that ought to be reserved for your Highnesses, this, in my opinion, must be left to the aforesaid governor and treasurer, because it will have to be greater or less according to the quantity of gold that may be found. Or, should it seem preferable, your Highnesses might, for the space of one year, take one half, and the collector the other, and a better arrangement for the division be made afterward.

10. That if the said alcaldes or notaries shall commit or be privy to any fraud, punishment shall be provided, and the same for the colonists who shall not have declared all the gold they have.

11. That in the said island there shall be a treasurer, with a clerk to assist him, who shall receive all the gold belonging to your Highnesses, and the alcaldes and notaries of the towns shall each keep a record of what they deliver to the said treasurer.

12. As, in the eagerness to get gold, every one will wish, naturally, to engage in its search in preference to any other employment, it seems to me that the privilege of going to look for gold ought to be withheld during some portion of each year, that there may be opportunity to have the other business necessary for the island performed.

13. In regard to the discovery of new countries, I think permission should be granted to all that wish to go, and more liberality used in the matter of the fifth, making the tax easier, in some fair way, in order that many may be disposed to go on voyages.

I will now give my opinion about ships going to the said Island of Espanola, and the order that should be maintained; and that is, that the said ships should only be allowed to discharge in one or two ports designated for the purpose, and should register there whatever cargo they bring or unload; and when the time for their departure comes, that they should sail from these same ports, and register all the cargo they take in, that nothing may be concealed.

- In reference to the transportation of gold from the island to Castile, that all of it should be taken on board the ship, both that belonging to your Highnesses and the property of every one else; that it should all be placed in one chest with two locks, with their keys, and that the master of the vessel keep one key and some person selected by the governor and treasurer the other; that there should come with the gold, for a testimony, a list of all that has been put into the said chest, properly marked, so that each owner may receive his own; and that, for the faithful performance of this duty, if any gold whatsoever is found outside of the said chest in any way, be it little or much, it shall be forfeited to your Highnesses.
- That all the ships that come from the said island shall be obliged to make their proper discharge in the port of Cadiz, and that no person shall disembark or other person be permitted to go on board until the ship has been visited by the person or persons deputed for that purpose, in the said city, by your Highnesses, to whom the master shall show all that he carries, and exhibit the manifest of all the cargo, it may be seen and examined if the said ship brings any thing hidden and not known at the time of lading.
- That the chest in which the said gold has been carried shall be opened in the presence of the magistrates of the said city of Cadiz, and of the person deputed for that purpose by your Highnesses, and his own property be given to each owner.

I beg your Highnesses to hold me in your protection; and I remain, praying our Lord God for your Highnesses' lives and the increase of much greater States.

Philip II and the Spanish Catholic Church

By David McKinnon-Bell

David McKinnon-Bell is the head of history at King Edward VI College in Stourbridge, England. He is the author of the Access to History: In Depth *volume on Philip II, published in 2001. In the following excerpt McKinnon-Bell discusses the extent to which Philip II, king of Spain from 1556 to 1608, was a "champion of Catholicism." He examines Philip's attempts to reform the church, to attack "heresy" through the Inquisition, and to subdue the Moriscos. He also looks at the significance of religious principles in Philip's foreign policy. He finds that although many of Philip's efforts were indeed motivated by his faith, his reforms were often less than successful, especially in terms of elevating the level of religious practice among his subjects. Furthermore, McKinnon-Bell asserts, Catholicism was not the primary force behind Philip's decisions in foreign affairs, although it did become more important as his reign progressed.*

Unquestionably Philip II was a loyal son of the Catholic Church. He famously told Pope Pius V in 1566 that, 'rather than suffer the least damage to religion and the service of God, I would lose all my states and a hundred lives if I had them; for I do not propose or desire to be the ruler of heretics'. Philip also attempted to improve the quality of the Spanish Church. He enforced the decrees of the Council of Trent in Spain and employed the Spanish Inquisition to eradicate heresy and monitor the progress of the reform programme. Moreover, Philip actively defended and promoted the interests of Catholicism beyond Spain's borders. [Historian] Geoffrey Parker has argued that Philip's sense of religious mission crucially shaped foreign and imperial policy. This article explores both the nature of Philip's religious policy and the centrality of religion to his thinking.

The Assault on Heresy

Philip's reign opened with a wave of persecution against 'Lutheran' heretics, discovered by the Inquisition in Valladolid and Seville in 1557. From May 1559, autos-da-fe, huge ritualised 'trials' and demonstrations of penance, were held, attended by huge crowds and the King himself. At these, some of the prisoners prepared to confess and do penance were publicly shamed and released, but many others, despite confessing, were committed for execution. The stubborn were burned alive. Although he professed himself to be uplifted by the ceremony and public exhibition of piety of the autos-da-fe, Philip did not personally attend the subsequent burnings of 77 heretics.

Although the campaign quickly subsided, it signalled a change of direction for Spanish religious policy, after a period of relative quiet. The 1560s saw the revival of limpieza (purity of blood) statutes, excluding from the Church and certain monastic orders anyone of converso (converted Jewish) or Morisco (converted Moslem) origins. Doctrinal uniformity was also enforced more rigorously. Even Catholic mystics and humanists came under close scrutiny by the Inquisition and became much more guarded in their activities. Even such a prominent figure as St Teresa of Avila, Spain's most famous religious reformer, escaped arrest only through the patronage of the King himself. Alongside these measures, the Inquisition created an index of 'heretical' books, forbidden to be printed in Spain or imported:

> No bookseller, book merchant or any other person . . .
> may bring, smuggle, have or sell any book, printed or
> unpublished work which has been prohibited by . . . the
> Inquisition . . . under penalty of death. (Extract from
> Decree establishing the Index, issued, Sept. 1558)

The Index was periodically updated and expanded, eventually including more than 2,000 works by many prominent Spanish religious thinkers and European literary heavyweights such as Dante and Erasmus. Additionally, the vernacular Bible was banned and all Spanish students studying abroad were recalled.

However, these measures proved impossible to enforce. It was the 1590s before the Inquisition managed to extend its control over printed materials beyond Castile to the rest of Spain, and any resourceful person with a taste for suspect literature could obtain prohibited texts from Italy, France, and the Low Countries. Moreover, the Inquisition's duties extended far beyond the simple eradication of heresy. It fulfilled an educative role and was instrumental in driving forward Church reform. After 1570 it was mainly employed in monitoring the orthodoxy of the 'Old Christians' (non-Jewish or Morisco Spaniards) in rural Spain, where the majority of the people had little understanding of either doctrine or the liturgy.

Its limited budget and resources (a mere 45 inquisitors were responsible for 8 million Spaniards) meant that it could not possibly carry out this broad range of duties. Instead inquisitors relied heavily upon familiars (locally-appointed, often unpaid officers) to maintain contact with local communities. [Historian] Sara Nalle has shown that, in the Cuenca district near Madrid, 88 per cent of denunciations during the period 1561–1631 originated from the laity; and this popular involvement suggests that the small village communities of central Castile regarded the Inquisition as a means of enforcing communal moral standards and acceptable religious behaviour. Thus, contrary to its popular image as a sort of secret police of the Church, recent historians have regarded the Inquisition as an accepted feature of religious life.

Reforming the Spanish Church

The Spanish Church at the time of Philip's accession was in dire need of reform. Contemporaries commented scathingly on its weakness amongst poorer folk in the remotest corners of the kingdom. One Jesuit priest complained that, in Huelva, 'many live in caves, without priests or sacraments; so ignorant that some cannot make the sign of the cross'. Religion was a communal affair, serving the villagers' need for sacramental 'magic' to ease their daily struggle, and some historians have argued that Christianity was still only surface-deep in the remotest areas of Spain, despite the missionary efforts of the religious orders, notably the Jesuits and Franciscans, to raise standards of religious observance during the sixteenth century.

As the century advanced, this state of affairs was challenged by the Catholic Reformation. The stimulus for this re-launching of Catholicism was the Council of Trent, a council of the whole Roman Catholic Church that sat, on and off, from 1546 to 1564.

Spain's finest theologians participated, and Philip threw Spain's diplomatic and moral weight behind the Council, which concluded in 1563 with a series of decrees dealing systematically with Catholic doctrine, the reform of abuses and the nature and structure of ecclesiastical authority. Philip promulgated the entire body of decrees in Spain in July 1564.

The King's personal religious commitment was evident in his energetic efforts to promote the reform of the Spanish Church. The Latin Vulgate Bible, and later the Roman Missal and Breviary (published in 1568 and 1570), were introduced. In the years that followed, the Spanish Church attempted to raise standards of discipline and education among the clergy, who were often impoverished, poorly educated and morally compromised around 1556. Only 10 per cent of Barcelonan priests were resident, for instance, and one in five possessed a mistress. Seminaries were established, and a new archdiocese at Burgos and several new bishoprics were created. Philip promoted a generation of educated, energetic bishops, men like Juan de Ribera, Archbishop of Valencia from 1568, and Gaspar de Quiroga, Archbishop of Toledo from 1576.

However, the Spanish Church as a whole was unenthusiastic about the monarchy's reforming efforts, only gradually and reluctantly adopting Tridentine standards of education, behaviour and dress. Whilst in some dioceses surplus feast days and irreverent rituals were suppressed and religious instruction and the wearing of vestments improved, elsewhere the campaign barely got off the ground. Only 20 seminaries had been established by 1598, and even Toledo, the richest diocese in Europe, resisted the establishment of a seminary—claiming, implausibly, poverty! Attempts to expel non-Christian practices from everyday religious life made similarly disappointing progress. Many festivals were banned, and plays, public meetings, business and games were prohibited inside churches, but the attempt to ban bullfighting on holy days was a miserable failure, despite the personal support of the King.

As part of the reform programme the Inquisition increasingly devoted its attention to the encouragement of religious orthodoxy amongst 'Old Christians'. [Noted expert on Spain] Henry Kamen has argued that, after the Protestant scare of 1557–60, the Inquisition mainly concerned itself with 'Old Christian' morality and religious practices, whilst both the clergy and the Inquisition sought to eradicate sexual offences, which were regarded as blaspheming the sacrament of marriage.

[Historian] J.-P. Dedieu describes the Holy Office as 'a gigantic teaching machine', and Nalle has shown that, in Cuenca between 1550 and 1600, 'thousands of ordinary Spaniards appeared before the inquisitors to account for their lax speech, and loose morals'. These local studies reinforce Kamen's argument that the Holy Office gradually became a means of social control and education.

The Impact of Reform

Despite voluminous recent research, it is difficult to assess whether Philip II's reforming efforts bore fruit. There were achievements. El Greco and Titian decorated churches and cathedrals with spectacular devotional art, and the special place of the priesthood in the daily life of the church was restated. Remote regions were brought fully into step with the Mother Church, local saints were replaced with officially approved ones, and a generation of highly educated and energetic bishops led a spiritual revival. But were Spanish people fully 'christianised' by 1600? It is hard to be certain. Recent studies of inquisitorial records in Toledo and Cuenca suggest that basic religious knowledge improved, for example the ability to recite the Lord's Prayer rose from around 40 per cent of parishioners before 1555 to around 82 by 1600. But other evidence suggests that, especially in rural areas, many barely Christian practices endured well into the seventeenth century. An inquisitorial report of 1588 into the Catalonian chapter of the Augustinian order illustrates the limitations of the reforms:

> They have women in their houses. . . . In some monasteries, they have stopped performing the masses and the ceremonies to which they are obliged by the terms of their foundation. They carry offensive weapons. . . . Most of them are totally ignorant and cannot even read. They used to dance publicly with women. Some have been found guilty of very serious crimes, adultery, fornication, theft, homicide, simony, enmity and . . . of being friendly with bandits.

Overall, historians paint a rather disappointing picture of the progress made by the Catholic Reformation by the end of Philip's reign.

The Moriscos' Revolt

The most spectacular episode in Philip's efforts to purify Spanish religious life was the rebellion of the Moriscos of Granada in 1568. The fifteenth-century reconquest of Spain from the moors (North African Moslems) had left a substantial population of converted Moslems (Moriscos) in Spain, especially in Valencia and Granada, where they comprised around half the population. Despite the efforts of successive monarchs and the Inquisition, the Moriscos remained only nominally Christian, continuing secretly to practise their former faith, wearing their traditional clothes and, in more remote areas, retaining their language and customs. Consequently, 'Old Christians' suspected them of collusion with the Islamic pirates who raided the Spanish coast so freely.

During the 1560s, Philip's government stepped up attempts to eradicate Morisco customs and culture. The use of convivencias (arrangements whereby, in return for a fine paid to the Inquisition, Morisco communities were left alone) was abruptly ended and the taxes on leather and silk, the Moriscos' principal industries, were increased. Consequently, following the failure of the 1567 harvest, the Moriscos of Granada, 30,000 mostly unemployed silk-weavers, rose in revolt on Christmas Eve 1568.

The uprising centred on the Alpujarras hills above Granada. The government, fearing that the revolt might spread or that it might attract Turkish support, dispatched 20,000 Spanish troops, commanded by Philip's half-brother Don Juan, to restore order. Two years of savage civil war followed, with massacres on both sides; at Galera, 2,500 men, women and children were slaughtered by Spanish troops. By 1570, however, the rebels had been forced into the most inaccessible and inhospitable corners of the mountains and, when the authorities offered a free pardon to all those willing to surrender, including the rebel leader Aben Humeya, the final resistance crumbled.

The government then decided to scatter the Granadan Moriscos across Spain, with tragic human consequences. In fact 120,000 died during their forced resettlement, from disease, famine and maltreatment, and thousands more fell victim to the Inquisition in the years that followed. The Granadan economy suffered, the population falling by 28 per cent, and industrial and agrarian activity declined too; but the Moriscan problem remained unresolved until the reign of Philip III.

Foreign Policy

How significant Philip II's religious principles were in his conduct of foreign affairs remains a hotly contested debate. The nineteenth-century German historian [Leopold] von Ranke argued that religion was the driving force of his foreign policy, and more recently [Historian] R.A. Stradling has concurred: Philip's 'unquestioning task was to defend in arms the interests of God and His Church'.

However, whilst there is no doubt that, at times, religion motivated his foreign policy, it is not possible to elevate religion to a pre-eminent position amongst his objectives. His long conflict against the Turks was motivated as much by a sense of Spain's strategic needs in the Mediterranean as by any desire to join the Pope on a religious crusade against the 'Infidel', although he was alive to the propaganda value of victories over the Turks. After the victory at Lepanto in October 1571, at which 117 Ottoman ships were captured and dozens more sunk for the loss of only 20 Christian ships, Philip's propagandists trumpeted both Philip's faith and the blessings of God upon Spain and the court artist, Titian, was commissioned to paint a valedictory canvas.

But when Pius V sought to follow up the victory at Lepanto with a crusade against the Turks in the Eastern Mediterranean, Philip demurred, preferring 'to gain some benefit for my own subjects and states from this league and all its expenses rather than employ them in so risky an undertaking as a distant expedition in the Levant'. His fleet was ordered not to co-operate in any such crusade. This demonstrates the extent to which his primary concern was the security of the Spanish empire.

Yet while religion may not have been dominant in Philip's considerations during the 1570s, it appears to have become more influential towards the end of his reign. Certainly one motivation for sending the Armada against England in 1588 was religious. The Armada's commander, Medina Sidonia, told the fleet before they set sail for England: 'The principal reason which has moved his Majesty to undertake this enterprise is his desire to serve God, and to convert to His Church many peoples and souls who are now oppressed by the heretical enemies of our holy Catholic faith.'

Nor was Philip's conviction that he was engaged in God's work shaken by defeat. He told his Council of State in November 1588 that 'I was moved to undertake the Armada campaign for the service of Our Lord, the defence of His Cause, and the advantage of these realms', and he ordered the construction of a new fleet for a second expedition.

In the 1580s and 1590s Philip allowed himself to be drawn into the French Civil Wars, intervening militarily between 1590 and 1598. In doing so, he seems to have been motivated by a combination of fear for Spanish security and religious zeal. Writing to the Duke of Parma in the Netherlands, he argued: 'My principal aim is to secure the well-being of the Faith, and to see that in France Catholicism survives and heresy is excluded'. He did, however, admit to a secondary aim, for: 'If the heretics were to prevail (which I hope that God will not allow) it might open the door to worse damage and dangers and to war at home'.

Overall, it seems that, as the reign progressed, Philip allowed religious considerations to loom ever larger in his shaping of foreign policy. Did this reflect an old man's growing awareness of his mortality and the need for his soul's salvation?

Papal Relations

Given Spain's importance in the defence of Catholicism against its enemies, Philip's relations with the Pope ought to have been close. However, the Pope, as ruler of the Papal States, felt threatened by the power of Spain, which controlled the Italian states of Naples, Sicily, Sardinia and Milan. The Papacy traditionally sought room for diplomatic manoeuvre by playing Spain off against the other great Catholic power, France, but the weakness of late sixteenth-century France made this impossible, and the Pope's consequent reliance upon Spanish arms against Ottoman and Protestant threats only made him more resentful. Philip was aware of this and his ambassador in Rome showered the Papacy with bribes in an effort to form a pro-Spanish party in the Vatican. Yet Spanish interference in papal elections ultimately backfired when, in 1592, the pro-French Clement VIII was elevated to the Holy See.

Philip's determination to control the Spanish Church, from episcopal appointments to the implementation of the Tridentine reforms, complicated matters further. [Historian] John Lynch has famously observed that the Crown's control over the Church was 'probably more complete in Spain than in any other part of Europe'. Philip was entitled to present benefices to clergymen, bishops and archbishops, and this gave him control over an enormous fund of patronage. Moreover, he stoutly defended the Inquisi-

tion's jurisdiction over heresy and prosecutions involving church-
men, most famously during the protracted and bitter battle over
the trial of Archbishop Carranza of Toledo, arrested by the Inquisition in 1557. Carranza was detained by the Inquisition until 1566, when the Pope finally persuaded Philip to transfer the
case to Rome.

Philip and the Pope quarrelled over foreign policy too. The
Pope constantly hectored Philip to embark upon crusades against
the Turks, against Elizabeth of England, against heresy in the
Netherlands, but Philip, knowing full well the costs of such an
aggressive policy, resisted until the 1580s. Thereafter Philip, at war
with England, France and the Netherlands complained that, since
he was engaged upon God's work, he deserved more substantial
support from the Pope. After intervening in France in the 1590s,
he was outraged to discover that the Pope recognised Henry IV
as the rightful ruler of France and was working to obtain his
conversion to Catholicism. The reality was that the Papacy, fearing that Spain might become dominant in Europe, trod a deli-
cate line between supporting Europe's most ardent defender of
Catholicism and avoiding becoming a Spanish puppet.

Was Philip a "Champion of Catholicism"?

Philip is often portrayed as a 'champion of Catholicism' and the
evidence of his religious policy at home and abroad largely bears
out this judgement, despite his tetchy relations with the Papacy.
It is arguable, however, whether his efforts to champion the cause
of religion were successful. The achievements of the Catholic
Reformation in Spain have been questioned in recent years, some
historians concluding that Spain was barely more 'christianised'
by 1600 than in 1500. Others point to real progress in raising
clerical standards and in resisting Protestantism. However, the intolerant and brutal treatment of perceived heretics, all too often
merely humanists or harmless mystics, drew condemnation from
all sides, including Spaniards like Juan de Mariana. Proponents of
the 'Black Legend' have echoed such denunciations, portraying
Philip II as a fanatic, bent on exterminating those who did not
share his faith. A nineteenth-century historian, [John] Motley,
wrote of the Inquisition that: 'The fear of its introduction froze
the ... heretics of Italy, France and Germany into orthodoxy. ...
It condemned not deeds but thoughts ... it arrested on suspicion,
tortured till confession, and then punished by fire'. Indeed, the

persecution endured by conversos and Moriscos and the en-
forcement of codes of limpieza look to modern eyes like an attempt to 'ethnically purify' Spanish Catholicism. Recently [Ben-
zion] Netanyahu has taken up this theme, asserting controversially
that sixteenth-century Spain's treatment of minorities foreshad-
owed later Nazi racial-religious persecution.

However, revisionist historians have challenged this critical assessment, stressing the reforming efforts of both the State and the
Inquisition and pointing out that, of the 40,000 or more 'heretics'
investigated under Philip II, only around 250 were executed. They
paint a more positive picture of a regime striving, certainly, to purify the nation, but also to educate and reform its morals and worship; and they cite as evidence Spain's relatively enlightened attitude to 'witchcraft', the Inquisition concluding as early as 1526
that there was little evidence for the existence of witches.

The contents of inquisitorial archives and church records have
revealed a complex picture. On the one hand, the power of the
State and the Inquisition appears less all-pervasive than we once
believed; and on the other, the Spanish people themselves appear
as both the agents of the Inquisition and its principal 'victims'. If
Philip did indeed seek to champion the cause of Catholicism,
both his success in doing so and his very ability to do so, need to
be reevaluated in the light of this.

The Defeat of the Spanish Armada

By Garrett Mattingly

*Although relations between England and Spain were good during the
early part of the sixteenth century, as the century drew to a close the two
nations inched toward war. Spain's king Philip II allied himself with
Mary, Queen of Scots, who was the cousin and enemy of England's
queen Elizabeth. In 1588 Philip sent an armada to England in an attempt to destroy his enemy. A series of battles ensued throughout the
summer. Despite the superiority of the Spanish fleet, England emerged
from the confrontation victorious.*

*In the following selection historian Garrett Mattingly describes one
day in the naval battle between Spain and England in the summer of
1588. Mattingly is the author of the book* The Armada.

Appropriately enough, the first modern naval battle in history began with gestures out of the middle ages, out of
romances of chivalry. The [Spanish] Captain General of
the Ocean Sea [Alonso Perez de Guzman el Bueno, Duke of
Medina Sidonia] hoisted to his maintop his sacred banner as a signal to engage, as Castilian commanders at sea had always done
since first they sighted the Moorish galleys. And the Lord Admiral of England [Charles Howard] sent his personal pinnace
[small ship], the *Disdain*, to bear his challenge to the Spanish admiral. . . . Then, his defiance delivered, at about nine in the morning, Howard led the English fleet in line ahead, *en ala* the Spanish called it, single file, one ship behind another, against the
northern, shoreward tip of the Spanish crescent.

The wing attacked was [Spanish Commander Don Alonso]
de Leiva's, mainly the Levant squadron [made up mainly of Italian ships], which had been the vanguard as long as the Armada
had been reaching north towards the shore in an effort to cut off

the leeward detachment of English ships. In most accounts of the battle de Leiva's squadron is still called "the vanguard," although in taking its new formation the Armada had changed front to flank, each ship turning east ninety degrees or more, so that de Leiva was on the left wing, and his Levanters formed the horn of the crescent projecting towards the rear on that side.

The rearmost ship, in the post of honor and of danger, was de Leiva's own *Rata Coronada*, and as Howard's *Ark Royal* began to cross his stern Don Alonso put down his helm, meeting the English flagship broadside to broadside and steering a course parallel with it across the chord of the arc formed by the Spanish crescent as he tried to edge to windward to close the range. Behind him swung into action [Spanish Commander Martin de] Bertendona's great carrack, *Regazona*, the biggest ship in the Armada, almost as big as the queen's *Triumph*, and following Bertendona, the rest of the Levant squadron. Howard, under the impression that the *Rata* was "the admiral," that is, the flagship of the Spaniards, "wherein the duke was supposed to be," exchanged broadsides with her for some time, "until she was rescued by divers[e] ships of the Spanish army." Or that is how Howard tells it. In fact, the Levanters, not the most weatherly ships in the Armada, were quite unable to close the range, and Howard had no intention of doing so, so the two lines kept well asunder. As far as we know, nobody got hurt in that part of the action, or was in the least in need of rescue.

Meanwhile, a group of English ships, led by [Sir Francis] Drake in the *Revenge*, and including [John] Hawkins in the *Victory* and [Martin] Frobisher in the *Triumph*, assailed the other wing of the Armada, the "rear guard," commanded by the vice-admiral, Juan Martínez de Recalde. They met a rather different reception. Recalde in the *San Juan de Portugal*, the largest of the galleons and a powerful ship, swung round to meet the attack, but the rest of the galleons sailed on. Later, when he discovered what was happening, Medina Sidonia seems to have been under the impression that Recalde either got separated from the rest of his squadron by accident or was deliberately deserted by them. His report to the king leaves both alternatives open. Neither seems at all probable. The galleons of Portugal were manned and commanded by veterans who would scarcely have panicked at the mere noise of a cannonade. Throughout all the rest of the fighting no squadron in either fleet behaved with greater gallantry.

Nor can one easily imagine Recalde's own Biscayans [northern
Spaniards] deserting him. On the other hand, of all the squadron
commanders Recalde was the least likely to get into trouble by
accident. He was famous for the way he handled his ships and almost equally famous for the way he handled his men. If he left
the duke with a choice between two improbabilities, it must have
been because he did not want to confirm the only likely con-
jecture, that he had disobeyed orders, parted from his squadron,
ordering them not to follow him, and deliberately thrust himself
into the midst of the enemy.

Recalde knew better than anyone that, now the fleet had lost
the weather gauge [a positional advantage], its only chance of
victory was to precipitate a general melee. He had seen enough
of the action already to be sure that he had read the English admiral's intentions correctly, and that Howard meant to stand aloof
and knock the Spanish ships to pieces with his culverins [long
cannons] at a range at which his ships could not get hurt. But it
was unheard of in the previous annals of war at sea for a single
ship surrounded by enemies not to be boarded. Boarding was the
only way a superior force could make sure of taking a valuable
prize intact, and among the group bearing down on him Recalde
saw one ship, surely larger than his, and with bow and stern castles at least as high. It would be strange if her captain could not
be tempted to close. Recalde knew that if he could once get his
grappling irons on one English galleon or, better still, on two, he
could hold on until help came. Then, if the English in their turn
should attempt a rescue, perhaps the general melee, on which
everything depended, could begin. Even if he could lure the English close enough for him to use with full effect his big short-
range ship-smashers, cannon and demi-cannon and perriers, he
might accomplish something. It was worth risking a single ship
for, even worth disobeying a formal order.

The Rest of the Battle

Drake must have read Recalde's mind as clearly as Recalde had
read Howard's. *Revenge, Victory, Triumph* and their companions
closed the range, but only to a cautious three hundred yards or
so, and proceeded to pound Recalde with the long guns which
were their principal armament. He could not get at them and
they would not come to him, though Martin Frobisher in the *Triumph* must have been, as Recalde hoped, sorely tempted. So, for

over an hour the *San Juan* alone withstood the battering of the English squadron, until the great [Spanish ship] *Grangrin* came up, followed by the rest of the Biscayans, drove the English away, and guarded *San Juan* back into the midst of the fleet where she could patch her wounds.

The rescue of Recalde's ship seems to have been begun by the movement of the *San Martín* which also led to the breaking off of the action. Recalde may have been willing to be bait in the trap a little longer, but whatever he had told his captains, he could, of course, have told the Captain General nothing. As soon as Medina Sidonia saw his vice-admiral in danger, he spilled the wind from his sails and put his helm hard over. Immediately all the fighting ships in the main body, the Andalusians, the Guipúz-coans [both from regions of southern Spain], and the rest of the galleons, imitated his action, waiting, with their sails flapping, un-til the slow drift of the rearguard fighting should come abreast of them or, if the English were completely preoccupied, perhaps even pass them, giving them the advantage of the weather gauge. Instead, at the critical moment, the English sheered off, out of range. That was the end of the first day's fight.

When the English broke off the action, about one in the af-ternoon, Medina Sidonia immediately went over to the offen-sive, and tried to get to windward of them. Since the crescent was strictly a defensive formation which could only be maintained with a following wind, the duke formed his fighting ships for at-tack in squadron columns, each squadron in line ahead, leaving the sluggish hulks to pursue their course to leeward. No doubt the galleons made a pretty sight, heeling over, close-hauled in the fresh breeze, but the English easily kept whatever distance they pleased, now and then tossing in a derisive salvo of round shot, and the abrupt rushes of the Spanish fleet, first to port and then to starboard, had less chance than the brave, blind rushes of the bull against his agile persecutors. For three hours the duke kept up his futile attempts; then he put up his helm and turned away, back towards the laboring hulks. "The enemy having opened the range," reads the official log, "the duke collected the fleet, but found he could do nothing more, for they still kept the weather gauge, and their ships are so fast and so nimble they can do any-thing they like with them."

For both sides the first day's fighting had been a somewhat frustrating experience. The Spanish were exasperated rather than hurt. No ship in the fleet had taken as much mauling as Recalde's, and its injuries amounted to no more than two cannon balls in its foremast, some stays and rigging shot away, and a handful of killed and wounded. But if the English long-range bombardment had inflicted, so far, only annoying jabs, they were jabs

KING PHILIP'S LETTER TO THE DUKE OF MEDINA SIDONIA

In this letter, King Philip II gives instructions to the duke of Medina Sidonia concerning the Spanish armada and its upcoming clash with the British fleet. The duke was the admiral in command of the Spanish armada, but he was inexperienced and somewhat incompetent.

The undertaking being so important in the service of our Lord which has moved me to collect these forces, and my own affairs depending so greatly upon its success, I have not wished to place so weighty a business in any other hands than yours. Such is my confidence in you personally, and in your experience and desire to serve me, that, with God's help, I look for the success we aim at. In order that you may thoroughly understand my wishes, and be able duly to carry them out, I send you the following instructions:

In the first place, as all victories are the gifts of God Almighty, and the cause we champion is so exclusively His, we may fairly look for His aid and favour, unless by our sins we render ourselves unworthy thereof. You will therefore have to exercise special care that such cause of offence shall be avoided on the Armada, and especially that there shall be no sort of blasphemy. . . .

When you receive a separate order from me, you will sail with the whole of the Armada, and go straight to the English Channel, which you will ascend as far as Cape Margate, where you will join hands with the Duke of Parma, my nephew, and hold the passage for his crossing, in accordance with the plan which has already been communicated to both of you.

that had to be suffered, apparently, whenever the English chose, and with little prospect of effective retaliation.

As for the English, if they were not hurt, they were beginning to be alarmed. This was a bigger, tougher enemy than they had bargained for. Spanish seamanship and discipline all day had been

---

It is important that you and the Duke should be mutually informed of each other's movements, and it will therefore be advisable that before you arrive thither you should continue to communicate with him as best you can, either by secretly landing a trustworthy person at night on the coast of Normandy or Bologne, or else by sending intelligence by sea to Gravelines, Dunkirk, or Nieuport. . . .

Although it may be hoped that God will send fair weather for your voyage, it will be well, when you sail, to appoint a rendezvous for the whole fleet in case a storm may scatter it. . . .

It must be borne in mind that the enemy's object will be to fight at long distance, in consequence of his advantage in artillery, and the large number of artificial fires with which he will be furnished. The aim of our men on the contrary, must be to bring him to close quarters and grapple with him, and you will have to be very careful to have this carried out. . . .

You will be wise enough, in case you gain the victory, not to allow the squadrons of our Armada to get out of hand in their eagerness to chase the enemy. Keep them well together, at least the great mass of them, and give them full instructions beforehand. . . .

Whenever in the course of expeditions dissensions have occurred between the commanders they have caused victory to be turned into defeat; and although your zeal for my service leads me to expect from you the loyal co-operation with my nephew the Duke, upon which success depends, I nevertheless enjoin you to keep this point well before you, carrying it out straightforwardly, without varying the design or seeking to interpret it otherwise.

"From Philip II, to the Duke of Medina Sidonia, 22 March/1 April 1588."

impeccable, and the Spaniards had been as full of fight at the end as at the beginning. The Armada was more heavily gunned than they had looked for, with enough long guns to return their fire and, on its best ships, more short-range ship-smashers, cannon and perriers than the queen's galleons. If they could close the range sufficiently, the Spaniards could do serious damage, even without boarding. And if the Spanish guns had done no damage that day, why neither, so far as anyone could see, had the English. The Armada looked even more formidable at a nearer view than it had at a distance. At the end, as it stood away into the darkening afternoon, it was more than ever like an impregnable wooden wall, like a grim fortress bristling with towers.

The English were not proud of their performance. They had hunted the Spanish past Plymouth, and if the Armada had had any intention of looking in there (it had shown none), that, at least, was foiled. But now the Armada was proceeding with majestic deliberation, in unbroken order, up the Channel, towards its rendezvous with [the Duke of] Parma [Spanish captain and nobleman]. If that rendezvous were to be prevented, they would have to do better. Howard, who had been willing to encounter the whole Spanish fleet with some sixty-five sail, now hesitated to join battle again until the rest of the ships in Plymouth had come up, and was writing everywhere for reinforcements, men and ships. His council of war concurred. To [Secretary of State Francis] Walsingham he wrote, "We gave them fight from nine o'clock until one and made some of them to bear room to stop their leaks [this was rather what he hoped than what he knew]; notwithstanding we durst not adventure to put in among them, their fleet being so strong." Drake, warning [English captain Lord Henry] Seymour of the approach of the enemy, was even more laconic. "The 21st we had them in chase, and so, coming up to them, there hath passed some cannon shot between some of our fleet and some of them, and as far as we perceive, they are determined to sell their lives with blows."

Spanish Disaster

The first serious Spanish losses came after the battle, two accidents, unrelated to enemy action, but destined to cost the Armada two capital ships. The first seemed minor. Some time after four in the afternoon as the Spanish were re-forming their defensive crescent and the Andalusian squadron was closing up on the duke's right, its *capitana* [flagship], Pedro de Valdés's flagship, *Nuestra Señora del Rosario*, collided with another Andalusian and lost its bowsprit. Then, only a few minutes later, on the duke's left, there was a tremendous explosion. [Commander Miguel de] Oquendo's *almiranta*, the *San Salvador*, was seen to be ablaze; her poop and two decks of her stern castle had disappeared. Obviously, the gunpowder stored astern had blown up.

The farther we get from this event, the more detailed and dramatic does its story become. In the diary or smooth log of his voyage sent to Philip on August 21st, Medina Sidonia says simply that aboard the *San Salvador* some barrels of gunpowder blew up.

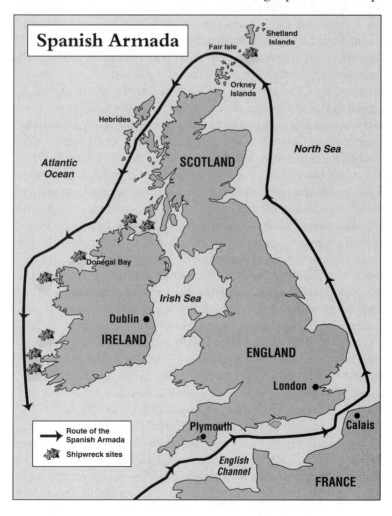

Presumably the duke had made some sort of inquiry, and he had some of the survivors from the *San Salvador* aboard the *San Martín*, but if he found out no more than he reported, it would scarcely be surprising. Everyone anywhere in the vicinity of the explosion seems to have been killed. Naturally, various conjectures were soon bruited in the fleet. Fray Bernardo de Gongora, who ended his voyage aboard the *San Martín*, heard that the explosion was due to some gunner's carelessness, a plausible guess. On another ship it was said that a gunner had set fire to a powder barrel, nobody knew why. Probably he was an Englishman. Some deserters, not from the *San Salvador*, picked up after Gravelines [a later battle], had a much more definite tale. A Dutch master gunner, rebuked for carelessness, laid a train to the magazine, lit it and jumped overboard; his subsequent whereabouts not stated. In Amsterdam an enterprising newsmonger had a better idea. The master gunner (a Hollander, of course, and pressed for the service), reproved by Oquendo for smoking on the quarter-deck, calmly knocked out the dottle of his pipe into a powder barrel and so blew up the ship. . . . In Hamburg, some weeks later, the master gunner was a German whom a Spanish officer struck with a stick.

By the time [Italian journalist and chronicler] Petruccio Ubaldini took hold of it, the story was ready for the full treatment. The master gunner, a Fleming this time, was injured not only in his professional but his personal honor, the Spanish officer who reprimanded him had already cuckolded him, and was now threatening the happiness and safety of his daughter, both wife and daughter being, by some poetic license, aboard the *San Salvador*. The Fleming fired a powder train and sprang into the sea, destroying them all, and Ubaldini has a moving peroration on the folly of arousing in the human breast the savage passion of revenge. The baroque luxuriance of Ubaldini's version should have swept all before it, but it already had too many competitors, and northerners may have found it, as they found some Italian baroque churches, a trifle too exuberant. In one form or another, however, the story of the liberty-loving, or patriotic, or revengeful, Dutchman, or German, or Englishman, or Fleming has become . . . firmly imbedded in the Armada legend. . . .

The catastrophe it was invented to explain was real enough. Medina Sidonia acted promptly, fired a gun to call the attention of the fleet, and steered back towards the *San Salvador*, meanwhile sending off pinnaces and ship's boats with messages. Small craft converged on the burning ship to tow her stern around away from the wind so that the fire would not blow forward, to reinforce the depleted crew now desperately fighting the fire amidships (there was another great store of powder under the forecastle), to take off the maimed and burned and transfer them to one of the two hospital ships among the hulks. The *San Martín* stood by with the duke on the poop deck, within easy hail, supervising and encouraging the operation, until two galleasses appeared to tow the *San Salvador*, her fires now under control, in among the hulks.

By this time it began to look like a squally evening, the sky lowering, the wind blowing in unpredictable gusts, and a heavy, choppy sea making up. Just as the ranks of the fleet opened to admit the two galleasses and their helpless charge, Pedro de Valdés's ship [that is, *Nuestra Señora del Rosario*], which was steering badly without the balance of her head sails, was taken aback, and lost her foremast, weakened, perhaps, by the collision and the breaking of the bowsprit. Again the duke acted promptly. Again he fired a gun to stop the fleet, and stood across to the *Rosario* where she wallowed in the rear. This time the *San Martín* was first at hand. There were few better seamen in the Armada than the flagship's sailing master, Captain Marolín de Juan, and rough as the sea now was, and wildly as the *Rosario* was behaving, Captain Marolín succeeded in passing her a cable. The *San Martín* herself would take the crippled *Rosario* in tow. Scarcely had the cable been secured, however, when *Rosario* bucked like a bronco, and it parted. The wind was increasing, the sea was getting rough, and it proved unexpectedly difficult to pass another line. The duke, on the poop deck, stood watching the work with painful attention.

It had begun to grow dark, and a couple of pinnaces were standing by, when Diego Flores de Valdés came charging up to the poop deck to protest. An experienced officer, commander of the galleons of Castile, he was serving on the flagship at the king's suggestion, as the Captain General's chief-of-staff and principal adviser on naval and military matters. The duke, he declared, absolutely must resume his station, and the fleet must resume its course eastward. Standing by like this in this increasing sea, the ships might do each other mischief, and would certainly scatter so during the night that by morning the duke would not see half of them. It was impossible to continue this disorder in the face

of the enemy, and to go on imperiling the success and safety of
the whole fleet for the sake of a single ship.

There seems to have been a bitter, excited argument. Diego
Flores was, apparently, supported by another officer, perhaps
Bobadilla, *maestre de campo general*. Finally the duke gave way,
though he insisted on standing by until he saw [Captain Augustin
de] Ojeda, in the small galleon that was the flagship of the screen,
coming up with four pinnaces to take over, and received word
that his orders to one of the galleasses and to the *almiranta* of the
Andalusians to assist in the rescue had been received. Then, at last,
he turned away, took up his station in the main body, and the
fleet, in close formation, resumed its march. It was disturbing to
hear, some time later, out of the darkness astern where the *Rosario*
was drifting, the thud of heavy guns.

The duke had been on deck all day and had eaten nothing
since breakfast. He did not go below now. He had a boy bring
him a crust and some cheese to the poop deck, and stood a long
time, leaning on the taffrail, watching the wake and the blackness
beyond. Abandoning the *Rosario* was his first real failure, and he
knew that whoever advised it and however wise had been the advice, his would be the blame. Perhaps it was only then he re-
membered that Diego Flores de Valdés and Pedro de Valdés were
not only cousins, but inveterate and implacable enemies.

The Eighteenth and Nineteenth Centuries

Spain Under the Bourbons

By Henry Kamen

*Henry Kamen is a noted scholar of the history of Spain who has pub-
lished numerous books and articles on the subject. He received his doctor-
ate from Oxford University and currently lives and does research in
Barcelona. He describes Spain during the Enlightenment under the ascendancy of a new dynasty, the Bourbons. Under the "enlightened despotism" of Charles III, Spain was exposed to the ideas of French thinkers
and experienced a number of social, economic, and cultural advances, including a rise in population, the growth of commercial capitalism, and the
creation of the royal academies and libraries. Simultaneously, Spain clung
to old traditions, particularly those of Catholicism. Moreover, not all benefited from these advances; most notably, the condition of the poor generally deteriorated. When France, under Napoléon, took control of Spain in
1808, the Spanish people rose up against this foreign rule, launching the
War of Independence. By 1813 the French were driven out and Spanish
rule was reestablished under Ferdinand VII.*

The eighteenth century, during which western Europe experienced the Enlightenment, was in Spain a century of
extremely slow rebirth. The accession of a new dynasty
made no immediate impact on the nation. Charles II died child-
less and willed the throne to Philip, Duke of Anjou, grandson of
Louis XIV of France. The testament was immediately disputed
by powers—mainly England, Holland and the Empire—hostile
to a further extension of French might, and Europe was plunged
into the War of the Spanish Succession (1702–13).

Castilians were on the whole overjoyed by the succession of
the young seventeen-year-old King, which promised them a part
in the achievements of Europe's greatest ruler. The provinces of
the Crown of Aragon were more apathetic. This made it easier

for the invading armies (principally English and German) to overrun half the peninsula. But the Franco-Spanish forces eventually won the day. On the specious pretext that the population of the Crown of Aragon had rebelled, Philip V abolished the constitutions or *fueros* of Aragon and established in their place the laws of Castile. With this measure (1707), claimed one contemporary Aragonese noble, 'arrived the time so desired by the Count-Duke of Olivares, for the kings of Spain to be independent of all laws save that of their own conscience'. For the first time in history, Castile and Aragon became one political unit, sharing the same administration, laws and taxes. The creation of one Spain was carried through, however, more in form than in spirit. Essentially an act of military violence, union was always resented by the eastern realms. The Catalans in particular resented the loss of their ancient constitution. Their defeat, with the fall of Barcelona in 1714, symbolized the defeat of regional separatism by centralist Castilian power.

Despite the radical turn of events during the War of Succession, the reign of Philip V was essentially one of quiet continuity. In Catalonia and Valencia, where Catalan was the main language, all public business was henceforward transacted in Castilian. Discontent was surprisingly muted, and all Spaniards grew to accept the Bourbons as their own. 'What was the whole of Spain before the august House of Bourbon came to the throne?' asked the eighteenth-century Catalan historian Capmany. 'A corpse, without spirit or strength to feel its own debility.' Peaceful internally, the reign was quite the reverse externally. An aggressive foreign policy meant that the forty-five years of Philip's reign (this includes the interlude of a year when he abdicated in favour of his son Luis) witnessed only ten years of peace. This warlike activity was a result of the Treaty of Utrecht (1713) which ended the War of Succession. By it, Spain gave up Italy and the Netherlands, and the English were ceded Gibraltar and Minorca. Deprived at one blow of control of the western Mediterranean, Spain devoted its energies to making good the loss and to rejuvenating its own internal administration. England, the rising power in the Mediterranean, now became for a century Spain's chief enemy. The rapid growth of the Spanish navy under Philip's greatest minister, José Patiño, was testimony to the nation's new energies under Bourbon rule.

The steady rise in population was a sign of better times. Imprecise figures suggest a growth from over six to eleven millions between 1700 and 1800. The increased labour force was recruited for the new factories set up during the war (textiles, munitions), for the army and for the expanding mercantile marine. Agricultural production increased considerably in the course of the century. An era of commercial capitalism dawned, as moneyed men explored new ways of putting their capital at the service of the state. Catalans and Basques attempted to set up trading companies, directed in part to the American trade. . . .

The early eighteenth century, a period long neglected by historians, was not merely a prelude to the Enlightenment. It exists in its own right as an epoch when significant steps were taken to end the cultural isolation in which the Habsburgs had kept Spain. The great official academies founded by Philip V (Spanish Royal Academy in 1713, Royal Academy of History in 1738) were based on French models. The National Library of today (housed in a nineteenth-century building) was founded in 1711 as the Royal Library, incorporating books brought by the King from France and others confiscated from the libraries of rebellious nobles. The great new palaces built by Philip, such as La Granja (his 'Little Versailles'), or the Royal Palace in Madrid, were executed by Italian architects. Aranjuez, the other great palace of this period, had been started by [architect Juan de] Herrera in the sixteenth century, and was completed in the course of the eighteenth by French and native engineers. Italian styles proliferated under the early Bourbons, thanks to the connection established by Philip's marriage to the Italian Princess Elizabeth Farnese. Italian architects, sculptors, printers and musicians came to the court at Madrid. [Guiseppe] Scarlatti and [Luigi] Boccherini were among the eminent composers who visited Spain. Under their new dynasty, Spaniards—while not ceasing to develop their own skills—began to appreciate the achievements of other nations. This bred new standards of culture and erudition. One of the most outstanding products of the new outlook was the late eighteenth-century Valencian scholar Gregorio Mayans y Siscar. In the north of Spain, in Asturias, the writings of a Benedictine monk, Feijóo (d. 1764), were to be taken by the subsequent generation as a harbinger of Enlightenment philosophy. 'While abroad there is progress in physics, anatomy, botany, geography and natural history,' Feijóo complained, in Spain there was a 'preoccupation against all novelty'. Through his works, Feijóo prepared the élite to accept foreign novelties, particularly the think-ing of English and French writers.

The loss of the European empire made it possible for the gov-ernment to turn its mind to internal reconstruction. A new bu-reaucracy was introduced into united Spain in the form of in-tendants; military academies were established, uniforms adopted; the navy was expanded into one of the most powerful in Europe; reforms in taxation were projected. Many of these ventures were the work of the remarkable chief minister of Ferdinand VI (1746–59), the Marquis of Ensenada.

Spain Under Charles III

Charles III (1759–88), Ferdinand's half-brother, had already been King of Naples for twenty-four years when he succeeded his brother on the Spanish throne. His mature age and long experi-ence were to help make his reign in many ways the most brilliant in all Spanish history. Charles kept control of the Spanish state within his firm and capable hands; his ministers were servants, who could be dispensed with when necessary. He was the one king in eighteenth-century Spain who can be called an 'enlight-ened despot'. He was admittedly despotic in that his policies and reforms were often adopted without reference to public opinion ('My subjects', he said on one occasion, 'are like children: they cry when they are washed'); but he never went to extremes, and compromised readily. Strongly anti-English in his foreign policy, he continued the previous attempts to expel the English from Gibraltar and to restrict their presence in the Mediterranean.

The social advances under Charles III were achieved by a lib-eral, free-thinking élite. Well-educated nobles and ministers like [Gaspar Melchor de] Jovellanos and the Count of Campomanes [Pedro Rodríguez Campomanes y Perez] were the spearhead of both political and economic reform. Other nobles maintained private cultural and scientific links with England, France, Swe-den and other countries. Among them were the Count of Aranda, friend of [French writer] Voltaire and Spanish ambas-sador to France; the Duke of Alba, friend of [French philosopher and writer Jean-Jacques] Rousseau and likewise ambassador to France; and the Count of Peñaflorida, who studied in France and later in 1765 joined a group of other Basque nobles to found the Basque Society of Friends of the Country (Amigos del País). Foreign books, such as the works of [English philosopher John]

Locke, Rousseau, [Sir Isaac] Newton and many others, were ea-
gerly imbibed by Spaniards. It was impossible to check the
growth of new ideas. On the notable occasion in 1778 when the
Inquisition succeeded in imprisoning a leading government official, Pablo de Olavide, the confession of a friend of his impli-
cated so many of the Crown's ministers that the Holy Office was
obliged to let the matter drop. The Enlightenment in Spain drew
heavily on French and foreign influences: a writer of the stature
of [José de] Cadalso [y Vázquez] openly modelled his *Moroccan
Letters* on [French political philosopher] Montesquieu's *Persian
Letters*. But the Spaniards adapted foreign influences to their own
tastes. All the great progressives remained firm Catholics, and officials of the Inquisition could be found among members of the
economic societies of Amigos del País. As long as traditionalist
forces coexisted, albeit uneasily, with the new trends, the government remained unworried. This explains why Charles III,
when asked why he did not abolish the Inquisition, replied, 'the
Spaniards want it, and it does not bother me'.

There were several clashes between the old and new. Church-
state relations were made difficult by the active alliance of Jesuits
and Inquisition against French influences and certain aspects of
state policy. In these circumstances it was not surprising that
when the government sought out those responsible for the popular riots in Madrid in 1766 against the widely hated Italian minister Squillace, it was the Jesuits who were chosen as the scapegoat. The extent of their alienation from the great forces in
Church and state is shown by the fact that forty-six out of the
sixty bishops voted for the decree, issued in 1767, to suppress the
Society of Jesus and expel its members from Spain. The expulsion, and the evacuation of the great Jesuit colleges, enabled the
government to proceed with another controversial measure, the
reform of the universities. Olavide (who later fell foul of the Inquisition) in 1769 presented a plan for educational reform, which
was adopted as the basis of the decree of 1770 reforming the syl-
labuses of all Spanish universities.

The economic progress of the late eighteenth century was notable. A new attitude to economic growth was stimulated by the
diffusion of the economic societies of Amigos del País. Between
1765 and 1789 fifty-six societies were founded throughout Spain.
Sponsored by provincial nobility, their task was to promote technical knowledge and encourage investment. The favourable eco-

nomic climate of the period had a beneficial effect on production, but little would have been achieved without the crucial help given by state legislation. Ministers pioneered the way with incisive studies of what was required, works such as Campomanes's two *Discourses on Industry* (1774–75), and the famous analysis of Spanish agriculture (*Informe de ley agraria*, 1795) written by Jovellanos. Government policy directed the building of canals and roads, the equitable distribution of land, the free internal trade of agricultural produce, the opening of rural banking facilities, a ban on the acquisition of land by the Church.... Belief in freer trade led to a relaxation of the traditional monopoly system by which only Cadiz and Seville had been allowed to trade to America. In 1765 and 1778 the American trade was progressively opened to all Spain's major ports.

These steps gave a positive stimulus in particular to the periphery. In Valencia the silk industry expanded rapidly, from eight hundred looms in 1718 to five thousand in 1787, making it a major European producer. The iron and shipbuilding industries of the Basque provinces experienced boom conditions. But it was Catalonia that benefited principally: it forged ahead to the industrial leadership it was to attain in the following century. By the end of the eighteenth century it had a cotton industry second in size only to that of England. Much of this progress was related to the opening of the American trade, on which Catalonia was heavily dependent for raw cotton.... The centre of the peninsula, which had exercised leadership throughout the Habsburg centuries, now lost its primacy as the expansion in population and production shifted (as in ancient Hispania) to the periphery.

Agriculture, in which the overwhelming majority of the working population was engaged, remained stunted. The area of greatest agrarian distress, Andalucia, was the subject of reform projects that failed largely because no steps were taken to alter the system of land ownership. A rise in rents and prices in the late eighteenth century increased the misery of the landless rural labourers in the arid south.... Side by side with intellectual progress there was an alarmingly rapid deterioration in the condition of the lower classes both in the countryside and in the towns. This poverty contrasted starkly with the wealth of the upper orders in Church and state. The Church had too many clergy and too much money. As the owner of vast estates (in Galicia it owned half the territory) it was often directly responsible for the poverty of labourers. There was good ground for the anti-clericalism that has become a common feature of Spain's modern history.

Despite progress in many fields, the social problem remained unsolved. Castile was slow to provide leadership. The great reforming ministers were non-Castilians: [Zenón de Somodevilla y Bengoechea, Marquis of] Ensenada came from Logroño, Campomanes and Jovellanos from Asturias, the Count of Floridablanca [José Moñino y Redondo] from Murcia. Castilian literature blossomed with writers like Leandro Moratín (d. 1828), a distinguished playwright well acquainted with foreign culture. But the cultural rebirth of non-Castilian Spain was perhaps even more notable: in medicine the outstanding names included the Catalans [Antonio Gimbernat y Arbos] Gimbernat and Casal, in natural history the Valencian, [Antonio Jose Cavanilles] Cavanilles, in economics the Catalan Capmany. The foreign artists [Anton] Mengs and [Giovanni] Tiepolo were the most influential at court, and when the native genius of Spain broke through it was in the stupendous canvases of the Aragonese painter Francisco Goya (1746–1828). Goya's vast output and his wide range of themes mercilessly caricatured every aspect of Spanish character; at the same time he managed to convey the underlying strength and vision of Spain in all its moods, from the bright sunshine of the bullfight to the savage heroism of the War of Independence. . . .

Charles III had given Spain a new spirit internally and a new strength abroad. His vigorous anti-English maritime policy was most successful in North America, where he actively supported the colonists in their struggle for independence. His son and successor, Charles IV (1788–1808), had little opportunity to display his rather limited talents, for the year after his accession coincided with the outbreak of the French Revolution. All the efforts of his prime minister, Floridablanca (a former progressive who had also been a chief minister of Charles III), were devoted to sealing off the peninsula against Jacobin influence. Floridablanca's successor, [Pedro Abarca de Bolea] the Count of Aranda (who had been chiefly responsible for the expulsion of the Jesuits in the previous reign), held on to power very briefly. At the Queen's instance, his place was soon taken by her handsome favourite, a young man of doubtful ability named Manuel Godoy.

The Spanish government did what it could to shield Spaniards from the world-shaking impact of the French Revolution, but though a heavy curtain of censorship was drawn it was never as effective as in the sixteenth century. The presence of a large French colony in the trading centres of Spain, and the volume of commerce with France, meant that information was bound to filter through. To combat this, Frenchmen were compelled to become Spanish citizens or leave the country. Their departure was countered by the arrival in Spain of thousands of French refugees (by 1793 over six thousand French clergy alone had reached Spain). Floridablanca went to extreme lengths to stop any news of events in France reaching Spain. In 1791 he annihilated the intellectual movement by a decree which suspended all private periodicals. Aranda's rather milder ministry could not afford to relax the restrictions because of the active republican propaganda coming from France. In the peninsula political excitement had been stirred up to a high pitch. One contemporary reported that in Madrid, 'in the inns and over the tables you hear of nothing but battles, revolution, convention, national representation, liberty and equality'. However, the growth of pro-French sentiment was rapidly dampened by the news first of the execution of Louis XVI (1793) and then of the beginning of the Jacobin Terror.

French Intervention and the War of Independence

After the King's execution, the Revolutionary Convention in Paris declared war against Spain. It was one of the most popular wars in Spanish history: all classes and the whole nation were united in their detestation of the republicans. Regional patriotism, particularly that of the Basques and Catalans, was aroused for Spain against the foreigner. Though French forces managed to penetrate Spain, their progress was halted by the Treaty of Basel (1795), by which Spain gave up Santo Domingo to France. The next year Godoy was obliged to sign a treaty of alliance with France against England. This disastrous agreement, which drew down on Spain England's far superior naval power, began the break-up and loss of Spain's overseas territories. Trinidad was annexed by Britain at this period. In 1797 the impossibility of protecting America against British aggression forced Spain to cut the colonies free and allow them to trade with neutral powers. South America was now for all practical purposes lost to Spain, which never regained control.

Internally the government faced a critical situation. Military burdens crippled the treasury, and while government credit crumbled the cost of living soared. Between 1780 and 1800 a labourer's wages rose by only 12.5 per cent while the price level rose by 50 per cent. When Napoleon became First Consul of France in 1799, he increased his demands on Spain. A treaty in 1800 forced the government to cede Louisiana (in effect, most of Spain's territory in North America) to France. Bullied by France and harassed by the English, Spain was also suffering internally from economic difficulties and epidemics. In 1804 the government declared war on Britain. The next year brought the great Franco-Spanish naval disaster at Trafalgar.

It was clear that subservience to France was ruining Spain. In Madrid Charles IV found that the French alliance had in reality become a French occupation. The annexation of Portugal by French troops in 1807 was followed by the imposition of French garrisons on Spanish cities in 1808, when General [Joachim] Murat took over control of Spain. Differences over policy at court led to disagreements between Charles and his son Ferdinand, who mounted the throne as Ferdinand VII in March 1808 after Godoy had been displaced and Charles forced to abdicate. The French command refused to recognize the change of monarch, and the royal family was induced to go to Bayonne, just inside the French frontier, to lay their differences before Napoleon. Once at Bayonne, Charles and Ferdinand were in Napoleon's power. The latter persuaded Ferdinand to renounce the Crown but immediately made Charles surrender it to France. Napoleon then chose his brother Joseph as the new King of Spain.

The economic distress of these years made popular unrest inevitable. When in addition the people of Madrid found that Murat had seized control from the royal family, they registered their protest on 2 May 1808—the *Dos de Mayo*, immortalized in Goya's canvases—by rising against the French army of occupation and so setting ablaze the War of Independence. Most historians adopt the year 1808 as the beginning of Spain's modern history, and with good reason. The popular uprising at Aranjuez on 17 March, when Godoy's palace was sacked (the favourite was found hiding in a rolled-up carpet) and Charles forced to abdicate after dismissing Godoy, signalled the first violent irruption of the masses on to the field of Spanish politics. The revolt of 2 May, tragic in its consequences, confirmed the leadership of the common people in the forthcoming struggle.

Almost without a signal from their leaders, the Spanish people rose against the intruders. 'My position is unique in history,' Joseph wrote to Napoleon, 'I have not a single supporter here.' Asturias was the first province to rise, to be followed by the whole nation. A delegation to London brought the British in on the side of Spain. It was both a heroic and a brutal war. Goya's etchings *The Disasters of War* capture vividly the extreme cruelty and savagery which were never to be absent from subsequent conflicts in the nineteenth and twentieth centuries. Because of the bravery of Spaniards in the War of Independence, there has been a tendency among older historians to idealize their position. The reality was a little more complex. Most placed their hopes in the absent Ferdinand, their 'Desired One' (*el Deseado*). But beyond that there was a division into roughly two attitudes. For the mass of the people and for the upper levels of society, the war was a conservative one in defence of tradition, religion and local rights. France for them represented impious republicanism and wicked atheism. Despite being firmly wedded to such traditional values, the common people were frequently also capable of spontaneous acts of ferocity against the upper classes. The other principal attitude, held by a small minority, resented French aggression but was sympathetic to many French ideas. People in this group looked forward to the day after liberation when the reforms and enlightenment of the eighteenth century could be extended. Here essentially was the split into 'two Spains'—traditionalist on one side, reformist on the other—that set the pattern for all subsequent Spanish history.

Spain was split even further by the breakdown in public authority. Because Spaniards refused to recognize the French government in Madrid, control reverted to the local level. Regionalism received a massive stimulus. Each area set up a provincial junta with sovereign powers, and the country broke into federal units, the only centre being a weak supreme Central Junta at Aranjuez. The French found themselves fighting not one concerted war but a series of fragmentary actions against Catalans, Valencians, Asturians and so on. Their operations were bogged down by having to fight off sporadic guerrilla attacks, and to conduct sieges of individual towns and cities. The difficult Spanish campaign (Napoleon was later to attribute the beginning of all his ills to intervention in the peninsula) forced the Emperor himself to march into the country. Spaniards were less effective in pitched battles, at which they were poor, than in guerrilla warfare. For the former they relied on the all-important aid of British troops under the Duke of Wellington. Together both British and Spaniards drove out most of the French by the end of 1813. . . .

The end of the War of Independence in 1814 brought the return of the 'Desired One', but raised problems as well. The French occupation had brought about major changes in the state, and had opened up an irreconcilable gulf between the liberals and the conservatives. Ferdinand VII chose to follow the old absolutist path, and began his new reign by abolishing the Constitution and imprisoning members of the liberal opposition. The Crown commanded great prestige thanks to its attitude in the war, and Ferdinand managed with some success for a few years, during which all the apparatus of the old régime was brought back. Below this repressive surface the differing political aspirations of Spaniards continued to seethe. The liberals strengthened their links with the army; secret societies such as the Freemasons became the resort of underground parties. This was a situation that was bound to produce extremes both of repression and of revolutionary violence, so setting the tone for nineteenth-century politics.

In 1820 a Colonel Riego raised the flag of military rebellion in Andalucia. . . . Riego's stand was for the Constitution. When risings for the same cause occurred elsewhere, Ferdinand gave in and accepted the men of 1812. But the liberal success led immediately to a split in their ranks between the moderates and the radicals. This weakened their cause within Spain. Abroad the proclamation of the 1812 Constitution by Italian liberals aroused the anxiety of those European powers opposed to constitutional government. When the administration at Madrid fell into the hands of the radical liberals, there was widespread hostility to their harsh policies. This supplied the pretext for the French to send armed help to the royalists. The 'Hundred Thousand Sons of St Louis' (a phrase of Louis XVIII) entered the country in 1823 and helped Ferdinand to resume full absolute power and to abolish all liberal legislation. Counter-revolutionary terror claimed its toll of lives as the liberals went into exile. Once again the pattern of modern Spanish politics was being set. The victorious conservatives, however, found that matters were still not wholly to their liking. Ferdinand relied to some extent on moderate counsels, so that the extreme rightists began to place their hopes rather on his younger brother Carlos. The birth of a daughter and heir to Ferdinand in 1830 dashed royalist hopes that Carlos might succeed to the throne, but since Philip V had in 1713 introduced a law excluding females from the succession it was held by many that Carlos was still the legitimate heir. This created a succession dispute, and also a Carlist party (modern Carlists still claim that their branch of the Bourbon family should succeed to the Spanish throne).

Ferdinand's reign left major problems for Spain. Both economically and politically the country was in a precarious state. Political labels meant little: 'moderates' were no less extreme in their resort to brutal repression than their enemies. Absorbed in domestic affairs, the King was powerless to stop the loss of the American colonies.

The occupation of Spain by French armies after 1808 had given the Americans a pretext for declaring their independence from the Francophile government in Madrid. But loyalty to Ferdinand soon changed into separatism. First Venezuela in 1811, then other states later, declared their independence. Upon the restoration of Ferdinand the American rebels were faced with the return of Spanish control. At this point the Venezuelan General Simón Bolívar, named 'the Liberator' by his country in 1814, undertook leadership of the struggle for independence. Helped by Britain and the United States, and by commanders such as [José Francisco de] San Martín, the Americans began a systematic overthrow of Spanish power. At Ayacucho in 1824, Bolívar's lieutenant [Antonio José de] Sucre crushed the last Spanish resistance. Save for Cuba and Puerto Rico, all southern Spanish America was free.

The American Colonies Revolt

PART I: THE CONGRESS OF VENEZUELA; PART II: *GACETA EXTRAORDINARIA*; PART III: BERNARDO O'HIGGINS; PART IV: DON JAVIER DE BURGOS

These documents represent the end of Spain's control of its remaining colonial possessions in the Americas. One by one each colony sought and achieved its independence from Spain. The first document, Part I, is the declaration of independence by Venezuela, wherein its citizens declare their rights to self-determination without interference from Spain. Part II is a report in the Spanish newspaper Gaceta Extraordinaria *on the expulsion of representatives of the Spanish crown in Argentina, signaling the start of the Argentinian rebellion seeking independence from Spain. In Part III, Bernardo O'Higgins, leader of the Chilean revolt against Spain, declares that Chile would no longer "remain dependent on a speck of the old world." In Part IV, Don Javier de Burgos, Spanish representative in the New World, reports that the last Spanish holdings in the Americas, Mexico and Peru, would soon fall into the hands of the revolutionaries, ending Spanish control in the New World.*

I

In the name of Almighty God. We the representatives of the provinces ... which make up the American Confederation of Venezuela on the Southern Continent, meeting in session to consider the complete and absolute possession of our rights which has been justly and legitimately ours once again since the 19th April, 1810, as a result of the journey to Bayonne and the occupation of the Spanish throne by conquest and the succession of another dynasty arrived at without our consent, wish, before making use of these rights of which we have been forcibly deprived for over three hundred years and which have now been restored to us by the political order of human events, to make

W.N. Hargreaves-Mawdsley, *Spain Under the Bourbons, 1700–1833: A Collection of Documents*, edited and translated by W.N. Hargreaves-Mawdsley. Columbia: University of South Carolina Press, 1973. Copyright © 1973 by W.N. Hargreaves-Mawdsley. All rights reserved. Reproduced by permission.

plain to the whole world the rationale which has emerged from these very events and which empowers us to make full use, as we intend, of our own sovereignty.

We do not want, nevertheless, to start by alleging the right which every conquered nation has to recover its own country and its independence . . . we shall only present the true facts which are well known and which were bound to split the old world from the new, as indeed they have done, through the up-heaval, disorders and conquest which now have the Spanish nation in a state of disunity.

It is against natural order, is impossible for the Spanish Government and has dreadful effects for America, that a country so much more vast and with an incomparably greater population should be dependent on and subject to a peninsula at the corner of the Continent of Europe. The surrenders and abdications of Bayonne, the journeys from El Escorial and Aranjuez and the orders of Lieutenant the Duke of Berg to America, must induce Americans to make use of those rights which they have until now forsworn in the interests of the unity and integrity of the Spanish nation.

We have for three years lived in a state of indecision and political uncertainty of so dire and dangerous a nature that this alone would be sufficient justification for our taking this resolve which our promises and our family ties led us to postpone until necessity forced us to go further than we had intended, driven by the hostile and unnatural conduct of the Spanish authorities, which conduct has released us from the limited oath with which we were called to the awesome office of representatives, which office we are now filling. . . .

We, therefore, the representatives of the United Provinces of Venezuela, with the Supreme Being as a witness of the justice of our proceeding . . . in the name and with the support of the virtuous people of Venezuela, solemnly declare to the world that our provinces are and shall be from this day forward de facto and de jure free, sovereign and independent nations, owing allegiance to no one and independent of the Spanish crown and from all who claim either now or at any time in the future to be her proxy or her representative. . . .

Given in the Federal Palace at Caracas, signed by our hands and sealed by the great provisional seal of the Federation and countersigned by the Secretary to Congress, the fifth day of the month of July, 1811, the first year of Independence. Juan A. Rodríguez Domínguez, President, etc.

II

When the Royal High Court in Buenos Aires demanded that the Council which had been set up there should recognise the authority of the Supreme Council of the Regency about June of last year, 1810, the Council replied that it would do so as soon as official advice of the constitution of that body reached it, since it only knew of the existence of that body through the accounts of individuals, and none of the formalities usually observed in such cases had been observed in this instance. This reply did for a little while allay the fears of those well intentioned persons who looked for the restoration of the monarchy and who hoped for the unity of all Spaniards to safeguard untarnished the rights of the King during the bitter days of his captivity.... But they soon had cause to view the Council of Buenos Aires with suspicion when they saw how intent it was on distorting events in Europe, painting an absolutely desperate picture of the situation and heaping incrimination on the conduct of those who were for the union of the Provinces on both sides of the Atlantic, and who, it claimed, could be suspected of wanting to hand over these enormous and wealthy lands to the thief of Europe. Finally unmasked, the dissidents kidnapped the Viceroy, D. Baltasar Hidalgo de Cisneros, and the Ministers of the Realm and expelled them from the country. They deposed the Ministers that made up the cabinet of the city and sent them into exile because they had, in secret session, given recognition to the Council of the Regency, and they appointed another cabinet from among their own supporters, without any reference to the people, not even for the election of the attorney general. They exiled the most respectable citizens, confiscated all their property and ordered the execution of many who were not happy with the changes, under the pretext that they were plotting a revolution.

III

The Regency had informed us that we would for ever associate that name with the period of regeneration of monarchy and restitution of happiness both in the old world and the new....

The peoples of the Peninsula have not built their revolution save on the demands of necessity—why cannot the peoples of America just as equally be judges of whether they are or are not faced with the same demands? Since the Regency and Parliament have proclaimed that the only basis for their authority is the sovereignty of the people, they have lost all pretext for giving orders to any people who wish to exercise their sovereignty for themselves. If their authority emanates from the Spanish people and they have no power over the peoples of America who, like them, are an integral and chief part of the nation, why cannot we ourselves represent the King and act in his name as they do themselves when they declare us rebels? . . .

Let us look at the map. . . . Twenty two thousand square leagues and one million people . . . are these to remain dependent on a speck of the old world which begs all its resources from them? . . . In a Parliament with equal representation we find one member for every thirty thousand people in the Peninsula while we have to have nearly a million for ours. . . .

Free peoples of the world . . . convince her (Spain) of her powerlessness and the mutual advantages which would accrue from our independence . . . and persuade her to make close appraisal of the outcome which threatens her and to lay down her arms and make a sacrifice, in the interests of justice and freedom, of those trappings which hasten her down the road to obliteration. Cry out to her on our word of honour that Chile The Magnanimous will open her heart to the friendship of her brothers and will share with them, in due observance of the law, the benefits of her undying independence.

Presidential Palace of Chile, 15th February, 1808—Bernardo O'Higgins.

IV

From your crown, my lord, two great and triumphal laurels with which [Hernán] Cortés and [Francisco] Pizarro wreathed the crown of Carlos I have been untimely plucked. The Spanish Monarchy has today fifteen million fewer subjects than it had in 1808. The flag of the Mexican Revolution now flutters over the battlements of San Juan de Ulúa and it is to be feared that that of the rebels in Perú shall soon be flown over the battlements of Callao. In place of the unbounded trade of such vast possessions which fed both the city and the enormous stretches of countryside, there has sprung up paltry coastal trafficking daily molested by pirates from those very countries which learned from Spain the arts of peace and the benefits of civilisation.

The Church in Spanish Society

By Adrian Shubert

Adrian Shubert is an assistant professor of history at York University, Ontario, Canada. He is the author of numerous articles on the social and labor history of modern Spain. In this article he describes the role of the Catholic Church in nineteenth-century Spanish society. Despite its ever-important place in a traditionally religious culture, Shubert demonstrates the decline of the church's influence in the wake of the growth of liberalism in modern Spain.

F ew countries have been more closely identified with Catholicism than Spain. For some, Spaniards and outsiders alike, the Church has been an integral part of the nation's identity, if not the very basis of that identity. Yet, in the nineteenth and twentieth centuries, the Church has been the most controversial institution in the country, struggling to determine how to relate to an emerging liberal society while that society, and the governments to which it gave rise, sought to delimit an acceptable sphere for the Church and religion.

But, as severe as were the difficulties in defining the institutional role and nature of the Church within the new society, even graver was the alienation of an increasing segment of the population from the Church and its ministers, and from religion itself. By the early part of the twentieth century religious belief had ceased to be the common heritage of all Spaniards and turned into yet another point of conflict. In large part this growing 'dechristianization' was a product of the Church's inability to formulate an effective response to the challenges of urbanization and industrialization. But not entirely; its roots lay in certain features of that impressive structure that was the Church of the Old

Regime, the consequences of which became evident only when the protective political environment of the absolute monarchy disappeared.

If the identification of Spain with Catholicism was debatable, the identification of Spaniards with their new, liberal state was no less in question. Spanish liberals were not very successful in creating a secular, national identity to supplant the country's long-held religious identity. In fact, one can question the extent to which any nationwide form of identity, sacred or profane, has ever managed to impose itself on top of deeply ingrained local identities of small communities.

The Church, Religion and Belief

In the eighteenth century, the Catholic Church was an institution of great political, economic and social power. There were about 200,000 clergy at mid-century but they were very unequally distributed geographically, with many more in the north than the south. There were also many more clergy in the cities than in the countryside. Old Regime Spain had an urban church in a rural society. The clergy who had direct contact with the faithful, the parish priests, were the smallest part of the ecclesiastical population, greatly outnumbered by the members of the orders and benefice holders who were concentrated in the cities and were most common in the wealthier parts of the country.

The vast wealth of the Church came from a variety of sources. The Church received a quarter of the agricultural income of the Castiles, 45 per cent of the tithes and urban property rents, 70 per cent of the interest on loans and 10 per cent of the livestock. In total, it received 'just over one fifth of all the income produced by the leading sectors of the economy'.

Where did the money go? Certainly not on the salaries of the parish priests, who were miserably paid and frequently had to take on other jobs, such as tutors or administrators for noblemen. The greatest expenditure went on buildings, decoration and 'the splendour of the cult'. This included large numbers of cathedral staff. In 1805 the cathedral of Toledo had 143 ecclesiastical positions, plus a choir of 175, Seville had 137 and Santiago 166. Charity was another major expense, reaching what [historian William] Callahan calls 'unprecedented levels' in the latter part of the eighteenth century.

During the reign of Charles III (1759–88) there was a

government-supported movement for Church reform. However the failure of this program left the Church poorly equipped to deal with the decades of turmoil touched off by the intrusion of the French Revolution into Spain and the radically new political environment which was produced. The institution which emerged from the crisis in the 1840s would be very different from the one that had entered it in 1789.

The Place of the Church

The resistance to the French occupation was fully supported by the Church—which treated it as a crusade—and seemed to reaffirm its role as a leading national institution. The hierarchy supported the election of a parliament in non-occupied territory which, when it met in Cádiz in 1810, had a strong ecclesiastical contingent, 97 of 308 members. Yet when the Cortes passed legislation such as the abolition of the Inquisition, freedom of expression, freedom of the press and reform of the regular clergy, the Church was in opposition. When Ferdinand VII (1808–33) returned to the throne in 1814, the hierarchy hoped to restore the position of privilege that the Church had enjoyed under the Old Regime.

The rift between reformers and traditionalists which had been present in the eighteenth century remained and was even wider than before. Reform came to be identified with liberalism and the reformers within the Church were isolated. In the archdiocese of Toledo, ecclesiastical authorities became concerned with the political behavior of their subordinates and there were a large number of trials of priests who had collaborated with the French or supported the liberals. After 1814 political ideas became an important consideration in the recruitment of priests. The persecution of the liberal clergy increased following the liberal interlude of 1820–3. There was an avalanche of denunciations, and supporters of the Constitution were brought to trial. The best positions were given to older, strongly anti-liberal priests while the liberals were exiled to the least attractive villages.

The experience of 1820–3 drove the Church definitively into the arms of reaction. Initially there was little opposition to the Constitution and most bishops took the oath of loyalty, as did the clergy, although the members of the orders were substantially less co-operative. However, proposals for reform, including the closure of purely monastic orders, drove large parts of the clergy into opposition. Local political authorities began to act against those priests who did not support the Constitution: in Toledo eighty-two were removed from their posts and twenty more listed as disaffected.

Following his second restoration in 1823, Ferdinand annulled liberal legislation and appointed a clerical ultra as his chief minister. He did resist ecclesiastical demands for a restoration of the Inquisition but allowed unofficial Juntas de la Fe to function until 1827. In the last decade of Ferdinand's reign, the majority of the Church supported the government but there was an activist minority, especially strong in Catalonia, which participated in royalist secret societies and turned to the king's brother, Carlos. When the Carlist War broke out in 1833 most of the hierarchy recognized Ferdinand's daughter, Isabel. Support for the rebels came mostly from monasteries and convents in the north and in Andalucia.

Between 1835 and 1843 progressive governments legislated a new, reduced place for the Church and in the process destroyed the institutional base of the Old Regime Church. In October 1835 the monasteries were suppressed and in February 1836 their properties sold. Finally, in July 1837, the male orders were abolished. During the regency of [Baldomero] Espartero (1840–3) the government attempted to create a streamlined Church, subservient to the state. The property of the secular clergy was put up for sale and in 1841 a major reorganization of parishes and dioceses was proposed, along with limitations on contacts between the Spanish Church and Rome. Attempts were made to purge politically disaffected clergy by requiring a loyalty certificate to be issued by the civil governor.

Neither the progressives nor the moderates considered the question of the Church as a choice between religion and atheism. Both groups saw religion as important to social order and both sought to find a role for a Church molded by reason. The question at hand was the type of Church, and religion, the country was to have. The progressives attacked what they saw as the excessive size and wealth of the Church, but they never questioned its spiritual hegemony. The Constitution of 1837 made Catholicism the state religion and declared that the clergy were to be publicly supported. Catholicism had an important role to play as a unifying force in a society already divided in a number of ways, a point made by [Spanish politician] Salustiano

Olózaga when he urged parliament to 'do nothing that may lead Spain to lose its religious unity'. The moderates, who came to power following the overthrow of Espartero in 1843 and remained there until 1854, had their own ideas about the relation of the Church to the state and society. For them, the Church had an indispensable role in the maintenance of public order. The clergy had a duty to preach obedience to the laws and resignation to the lower classes.

The moderates emphasized the utility of the clergy, but demanded that the clergy abjure fanaticism, the Inquisition and any political role. It must also meet certain personal and intellectual standards: 'a virtuous, national, Catholic clergy, capable of putting itself at the head of society to uproot through Christian charity the discord among us'. This charity had to be one which respected the established authorities and 'the legitimate inequality of wealth', that is, the existing social order. It was a role that the Church proved willing to take on.

The moderates began to work on improving relations with the Church early in 1844. Exiled bishops were allowed to return and the loyalty certificates were abolished. The next year properties of the secular clergy, which had not been sold were returned. The Constitution of 1845 confirmed Catholicism as the 'religion of the Spanish nation' and bound the state 'to maintain the cult and its ministers'. Negotiations towards a definitive reconciliation began in 1848 and culminated with the Concordat of 1851.

The Concordat affirmed that the 'Apostolic Roman Catholic religion remains the only religion of the Spanish nation to the exclusion of any other religion'. The secular clergy were to be supported by the state and the religious budget was set at one-seventh of total government expenditures. The state also agreed to support the seminaries, permit the Church to hold property and allow a limited number of male orders to function; it also promised that all education would conform to Catholic doctrine. In return, the Pope recognized the land sales which had already taken place, agreed to limited parish and diocese reorganization and affirmed the Crown's right of episcopal appointment. The Concordat resolved the contentious question of Church–State relations but did not settle the question of the place of the Church and its influence in society.

This settlement remained intact until the Second Republic except for the revolutionary interlude of 1868 to 1874. The government suppressed religious communities, prohibited the orders from owning property, abolished the special ecclesiastical jurisdiction and introduced civil marriage and the civil registry. It also proposed to allow freedom of religion. On August 1, 1873, the government of the First Republic announced a plan for the separation of Church and state, in which the state renounced its powers of appointment and let the Church run itself. The law was criticized by clerical opinion and died with the Republic.

The Constitution of 1876 reaffirmed the 1851 settlement but with one significant alteration. Article 11, which dealt with religious matters, was by far the most controversial aspect of the attempt by [Spanish premier Antonio] Cánovas [del Castillo] to reconcile all liberal opinion and create a stable political system. Cánovas' solution retained Catholicism as the state religion, and even gave nineteen bishops seats in the Senate, but allowed other faiths to be practised in private. This generated vocal opposition from the hierarchy and even Pope Leo XIII's attempts to rally Spanish Catholics behind the monarchy met with 'rather indifferent results'. By the end of the 1880s the bulk of the Spanish Church was willing to accept the Constitution, albeit without enthusiasm, and the Church continued to push its claims for a larger role in education, censorship and public morality.

There were some elements within the Church which continued to reject the liberal state. In the Rioja, the lower clergy and the religious orders continued to support Carlism. When in 1889 a canon of Santo Domingo de Calzado who had preached against freedom of the press and the 'damned error of liberalism' and called it a sin for Catholics to vote for Liberals, was brought to trial for 'having condemned political liberalism from the pulpit' he was supported by many of the region's clergy. The bishops of the diocese frequently condemned press freedom and in 1883 banned some radical papers. In the Basque Provinces, the clergy preached more frequently just before elections and they preached in Basque in order to attack the government. Funerals were also a common occasion for treating political themes. In 1890 Minister of the Interior Romero Robledo issued a Royal Order on the subject which criticized Basque priests for using Basque to attack the Constitution.

The Effects of Spain's Defeat in the Spanish-American War

By Laura Rodriguez

Laura Rodriguez is a historian and journalist who lives in Spain. She has recently cowritten a documentary on the Spanish-American War produced in London for the Discovery Channel and Canal Plus, Spain. The Spanish-American War arose as a conflict between the United States and Spain over the sovereignty of Cuba and the Philippines, with the United States intervening under the pretext of protecting Cuban and Filipino self-determination. The war was precipitated by the explosion of the U.S. battleship Maine *in April 1898, which the Americans used as an excuse to declare war on Spain. Rodriguez details the aftermath of the Spanish defeat in war, examining the repercussions within Spanish society. She finds that although the defeat was considered disastrous and affected Spain in a highly negative manner, it forced many to reevaluate the ailing aspects of the nation, such as the inefficacy and corruption of the government and the need for modernization of the economy, and to seek new solutions to such problems.*

Around 600,000 Spanish, Cuban, Filipino and American lives were lost before Spain and the United States signed the peace treaty in Paris on December 10th, 1898, that formally put an end to the war between the two countries over Cuba and the Philippines.

The consequences of the 'splendid little war', as the US ambassador to London, John Hay, called it, were enormous. The United States won its first overseas possessions, and in less than

Laura Rodriguez, "'El Desastre': Spain in Defeat, 1898," *History Today*, December 1998, pp. 33–39. Copyright © 1998 by History Today, Ltd. Reproduced by permission.

three months had acquired Cuba, Puerto Rico, Guam and the Philippines, driving Spain out of the Western Hemisphere. American public opinion was divided over what to do with its new empire, but the expansionists defeated the anti-imperialists and the country shed its isolationist skin establishing a new identity as a world superpower—an awkward position for a nation founded on rebellion against the colonial tyranny of the Old World.

For the Cuban, Filipino and Puerto Rican patriots who had been fighting against colonial Spain for decades, and who had welcomed the Americans as their allies, the outcome of the war of 1898 meant a *'pérfida traición'*: the betrayal of their aspirations for independence. Their fight for national liberation had ended simply with the exchange of one colonial power for another. As José Martí, leader of the *Cuba Libre* movement, put it, 'to change masters is not to be free'. For Spain, the war meant the final loss of her New World and Pacific empire after four centuries. It became known nationally as *El Desastre*. 'It was a time of lies and infamy', said Antonio Machado, the most distinguished poet of the group of artists and intellectuals who became known as the Generation of '98. Spain had to confront the implications of her military defeat as soon as her troops arrived home, ill and ragged in the summer of 1898. 'The soldiers bring us something more terrible than the plague, anaemia, dysentery or tuberculosis. They bring with them the truth', wrote the weekly *Blanco y Negro* on September 3rd.

Some 10,000 Spanish men died in combat during the war in Cuba and the Philippines; a further 50,000 died of disease. Around 125,000 were shipped home, but over 4,000 died on the voyage back, 'During the two-week sea journey back home, five or six *repatriados* died daily . . . most soldiers were sick. We arrived at Santander looking like ghosts,' wrote soldier Alvarez Angulo. The food on board consisted of onions, dried sardines and more onions. The writer Vicente Blasco Ibáñez complained:

> The ships that brought our men back to our shores have not been like boats from the Motherland, but something closer to Charon's boat, taking them to a hell of misery and sufferings. It's clear to all that the blood of the poor is cheap and their death matters very little.

Once back in Spain, the soldiers were put in improvised hospitals by the Red Cross, but with poor sanitary conditions the hospitals quickly became incubators of fresh disease. On arrival, veterans were supposed to receive a new suit and a third of their pay, the rest to be paid once they reached their final destination. In fact, all they got was a glass of brandy, a packet of cigarettes, and a few pesetas. They were forced to take private charity or to beg wandering around towns and villages.

The Socialist Party (Partido Obrero Socialista Español), which had consistently opposed the war, launched a campaign demanding pay for the veterans. There were demonstrations in many towns, but it wasn't until the following year that a Royal Decree was finally issued designating a meagre five pesetas to each of them. That or nothing. (The daily wage of an unskilled worker was 2.50 pesetas and it cost some 3.50 pesetas to feed a family of four.)

The press and public opinion, so pro-war until then, were shocked. Writers wrote about the importance of family, home and village, and complained about the lack of interest of most of the population in the plight of the veterans. During the Cuban War, prominent Spanish writers like Leopolde Alas 'Clarín' and Emilia Pardo Bazán had denounced the histrionic patriotism and the horrors of the war, demanding a peaceful end to what they saw as a fight between brothers. They condemned the injustice against the poor who were doing all the fighting, but none of them questioned the political attitudes that had led Spain into such a catastrophe.

Following the restoration of the Bourbon dynasty in 1874, Spain became a constitutional monarchy under Alfonso XII, with the Liberal and the Conservative parties taking turns to hold office. The political system was based on the manipulation of the electoral machine as agreed by both parties. The Republicans rejected the monarchy as an illegitimate and obsolete form of government, while the right-wing Carlists rejected the branch of the Bourbon line that had brought Alfonso, and then his widow, Queen Regent María Cristina to power, and the liberal institutions that they had established. The Socialists, then a minority of little importance, denounced the monarchy as a reactionary institution, and the Anarchists, a very active minority, rejected any state *in toto*.

When the Cuban insurrection began in February, 1895, the press and the whole political spectrum—with the exception of a number of Republicans, the Socialists and the Anarchists—supported the decision of Prime Minister Marco Práxedes Sagasta, leader of the Liberal Party, to fight 'to the last man, to the last peseta' to keep Cuba under Spain's control. The Conservative Party, led by Antonio Cánovas del Castillo, replaced the Liberals in March and maintained the same policy. The 'Cuban question' for Spain was not merely a colonial issue. The ties between 'the Pearl of the Antilles' and the metropolis were very special. Cuba had then a population of around 1.5 million of which 200,000 were born in Spain and 800,000 were creoles of Spanish descent. Spain considered Cuba as part of herself, because Spanish people, culture and language dominated the island. The Cuban insurrection was presented by the Spanish government and the press as led by bandits and supported by mulattos and the discontented. To win against it became a question of 'national honour', particularly when the United States threatened to intervene. This was a domestic conflict that Spain was quite capable of resolving, she maintained.

El Desastre represented not only the humiliating defeat by the US, a nation presented by the Spanish press as a bunch of greedy pigs without honour, but also the destruction of Spain's image as a great power. Francisco Silvela, leader of the Conservative Party after Cánovas's assassination, described the national feeling in a

Spain suffered a disastrous defeat during the Spanish-American War.

famous article, '*Sin Pulso*', '... a cloud of quiet sadness hangs over the country ... a peculiar state in which the pulse of Spain cannot be felt.' Miguel Santos Oliver, editor of Barcelona's leading newspaper, *La Vanguardia*, diagnosed the disease that had eaten away at the country:

> It was never so evident the split between shallow opinion (written in newspapers or expressed at the Cortes) and the truth. Almost everyone felt a prisoner of the opinions held by the others. The core of our pedagogy in relation to patriotism rested on the continuous cajolery of national vanity. We were the bravest, the most intelligent, our land the most blessed, our women the most beautiful, our poets the best. All the country's attention was focused on appearances.

Santiago Ramón y Cajal, a scientist who had served in Cuba as a doctor in the Ten-Year War (1868–78) and later won the Nobel Prize for Medicine, wrote in his memoirs:

> In the war against the United States it was neither the soldiers nor the people who were defeated, but a government who lacked foresight. The only solution to the brutal ultimatum from the United States should have been the immediate recognition of Cuban independence. How difficult it is to adopt sensible measures in an ignorant and dazzled country! Such a solution, the only rational one, intimidated our government, fuelled by the popular press and the threat of an Army uprising. The majority of the country, the sensible majority, never wanted war. We were led into it by the ignorant and the crazy.

Overawed by the disaster, the nation sought a scapegoat. The first shot was fired against the armed forces. The press and some members of the opposition in the Cortes (the Spanish parliament) demanded that certain army and navy officers who had been in command, accepted responsibility, among them Captain General Primo de Rivera and Admiral Montojo in the Philippines, Admiral Cervera and Captain Generals Weyler and Blanco in Cuba. The army and navy counter-attacked; if the officers were not defended with justice, the generals would take justice into their own hands. Cervera was acquitted, and other officers were sent to join the reserves. Prime Minister Sagasta advised prudence and tried to draw a discreet veil over the matter: 'What is important now is to return peace and tranquility to Spain, filling factories and workshops with the hands that the war took away from industry and agriculture.'

Both Republicans and Carlists withdrew from the Cortes after the government refused to discuss the terms of the peace protocol signed with the United States in August. Washington had demanded the relinquishment of all Spanish sovereignty over, and title to, Cuba and the immediate evacuation of the island; the cession by Spain to the US of Puerto Rico and Guam as war indemnity, and the right to hold Manila 'pending the conclusion of a peace treaty which shall determine the control, disposition and government of the Philippines'. José Canalejas, a prominent Republican politician, denounced both the Conservative and the Liberal parties for lying to distract and mislead public opinion, concealing the seriousness of the military and diplomatic situation that led to defeat.

General Camilo Polavieja, former Captain General of the Philippines, issued a manifesto blaming the politicians and demanding a radical transformation of the political system based on popular participation. His programme included administrative decentralisation, something that pleased Catalan nationalists, but made little impression on the rest of the country.

It was unfair to blame the political system entirely for *El Desastre* since the problem was that Spain, a second-rate nation, was incapable of saving what remained of her empire in a confrontation with the United States, the emerging power of the twentieth century. Prime Minister Sagasta explained the dilemma that had confronted his government:

> We went to war because we had no choice. We were faced with a terrible dilemma: war with all its consequences or dishonour, and dishonour would have meant the end of everything and of all of us.

In fact, the Spanish government's decision to go to war was a carefully calculated strategy seen as the lesser of two evils. At home, the political system of the Restoration and the monarchy were both at stake. The government and most politicians preferred to risk a confrontation with the American forces rather than a popular uprising or a military coup in Spain. For this reason the government acted on reasons that were beyond traditional military considerations: fear of public opinion and of its own army. Both politicians and naval officers were well aware that a war against the United States was a foolishness that would end in disaster and that the sensible thing would be to negotiate peace. However, to surrender Cuba to the Americans without a fight would unleash popular rage and could provoke a military uprising. The arm-wrestling between politicians and the military was resolved by sacrificing Spain's naval fleet because the navy, unlike the army, was unable to stage a successful *coup d'état*. So Spain went to war and her fleets in Manila and Santiago de Cuba were destroyed by the US navy in a matter of hours. Spanish honour was saved and the government was ready to sign for peace under the terms imposed by the United States.

Without a scapegoat for *El Desastre*, everyone and no one was responsible, but all paid the bill. The war had been financed by an inflationary policy that put the burden on consumers. However, the main means had come from war loans guaranteed by the Cuban and Filipino revenues and the debt was paid off gradually without financial trauma. The capital sent home from Cuba, some 1,600 million pesetas, was a healthy injection for the country.

Criticism of the Restoration political system intensified following the defeat and *El Desastre* began to be seen as a national problem. Castelar summed it up: 'In the Cuban question we might quote the poet who wrote about Jesus's crucifixion: you all stained your hands with His blood.' The voices of Castilian wheat producers and of Catalan industrialists, the most severely affected by the loss of the colonies, joined the chorus for 'regeneration':

> From Cádiz to Gijón,
> from Lugo to Castellón
> all Spain, or almost all,
> after the last pruning
> cries out: Regeneration!

The *'regeneracionistas'* wanted to solve the 'national problem', as it became termed. The problem hinged on the apparent incapacity of Spain to jump on the wagon of progress and modernity. This had been confronted before, but the crisis of 1898 revived the discussion and broadened its audience. Spain at this juncture needs to be understood in the context of the times, when Social Darwinism and the supposed superiority of Anglo-Saxon people touched a chord among what Lord Salisbury referred to in a speech of 1898 as 'the dying nations'. The mood across Europe had a lot to do with a sense of *'fin de siècle'* [the end of the nineteenth century]. France went through a period of introspection after her defeat by Prussia in 1870; so did Italy after Adowa in 1896. Austria was consumed with uncertainties about the future of her decrepit empire, and Spain had now lost hers.

'Regenerationism' was like a fever that swept the country, infecting the whole ideological spectrum. Some reiterated old conservative themes: decadence was the result of the erosion of traditional values of national unity, Catholicism, the family, social hierarchy, the rise of materialism and so on. Others blamed racial characteristics and portrayed Spaniards as an apathetic, lazy and arrogant bunch whose individualism undermined civic spirit, wrapped up in quixotic delusions.

The most influential and tenacious regenerationist was Joaquín Costa, a lawyer with a noble, but naive, programme of reforms that was heading for failure. Costa put his faith in the mobilisation of what he called 'the neutral masses', which was a myth; the 'neutral' ones were only willing to support the status quo. Miguel de Unamuno, a philosopher and writer, discarded 'the horrid regenerationist literature' as pseudo-scientific, grandiloquent, provincial, morbid and masochistic and allowed his pessimism to flow:

> It's useless to silence the truth. We are all lying when we talk about regeneration, because nobody believes in his own regeneration. Only the intellectuals and some public men talk constantly about regeneration, but the people contemplate the loss of the colonies with supreme indifference because those possessions had no influence at all on their happiness or misfortunes, nor on the hopes that sustained them. What do they care about national glory? Let them sleep and dream their slow dreaming! For God's sake! Do not sacrifice them to progress.

Ramón y Cajal also cautioned against the futility of regenerationism:

> The regenerationists of '98 were read only by themselves; like a sermon, the austere preachers preached to the converted. The masses remained passive.

Despite these criticisms, and regenerationism's failure to topple the political regime, the reforms proposed by the *regeneracionistas* offered concrete solutions to real problems: an efficient administration, education, modernisation of the economy and an end to political corruption. Its proposals for industrialisation and educational reform formed the framework for Spain's modernisation. Its most coherent principles have remained on the agenda: the relationship with Europe, democratisation, modernisation, and the recognition of a plurality of peoples and cultures within Spain.

Other positive solutions to 'the problem of Spain' came from the artists and writers who responded to the challenges of the twentieth century in what became the most impressive cultural movement to have emerged since the Golden Age. These artists and intellectuals were the first as a group to take a leading role in the vanguard of everything. They were the modernists, who resisted anything that was old, any continuity in doing and feeling things. They established the roots of a modernity becoming role models for generations to come. 'Spain should create, not simply absorb from abroad,' the philosopher José Ortega y Gasset declared some years later. Ortega coined the name *'Generación del 98'* as an example to push intellectual and moral reform in 1914 Spain.

The artists, writers and intellectuals who rose from the ashes of *El Desastre* were all very different, but they had in common a dislike for conformism, the rhetoric and ignorance of their country, and the organised corruption of the political system. They were full of contradictions and pessimism. Miguel de Unamuno critisised both Spanish obscurantism and European progressivism but was incapable of resolving the dilemma. Angel Ganivet, who had committed suicide the previous year, shared with Unamuno the idea that 'the problem of Spain' was essentially psychological and philosophical, a sort of spiritual crisis. He felt a nostalgic yearning for an idealised preindustrial society that in itself was a myth. Another writer, Azorín left behind his anarchism to take refuge in the contemplation of landscape.

For Ramiro de Maeztu, Spain's problem was that the country had never previously considered the question. Maeztu, who understood and accepted the burdens of modernisation, preached redemption through imitation of the Anglo-Saxon work ethic:

> *El Desastre* revealed to us that our bloodless body was nothing more than skin and bones. The United States

have battleships, machines, money. That's what Spain needs.

Many of these people felt an intense repulsion against their own society, but deep down they believed that there was still a 'real' Spain—a peculiar genius capable of enormous achievements. They set themselves the task of creating a new national culture based on history and imbued with a national character that accentuated Spain's emotional features. They believed that the spirit of the people could be expressed through language, literature and art. It was their intention to put that culture at the service of a progressive and democratic political system.

The influence of German philosophers such as J.G. Herder and K.C.F. Krause, with their emphasis on a common culture as the basis for national identity, was enormous. The educational efforts of the Institución Libre de Enseñanza; regenerationism; Unamunos's ideas about *'intrahistoria'*—the inner history—the quixotic and tragic sentiment of life; Azorín's reappraisal of literature, geography and society; the poetry of Antonio Machado; the revival of artists like Velázquez, El Greco and Zurbarán, and the reinterpretation of landscape with an emphasis on local customs and manners by painters such as Zuloaga, Regoyos, Sorolla, Solana and Romero de Torres, were all signs of a desire to transform Spain through an understanding of her historical past, through education and political reform, creating a shared culture within a democratic framework. For many, then and now, *El Desastre* was a blessing in disguise. In an article written in 1898, Unamuno predicted:

> With the empire lost and confined within our own home, we will soon have to confront two social problems that would absorb all the rest: that posed by the working-class movement and that posed by the regionalist movement.

The loss of Cuba meant the loss of a secure and profitable market for Catalan industrial products, and was seen as a failure of the Madrid government. The growing Catalanist movement offered a new perspective to the middle class. The region responded to the 1898 crisis with outward-looking optimism: it embraced Art Nouveau, applauded [composer Richard] Wagner and read [philosopher Friedrich] Nietzsche. The Catalans concentrated their efforts on industrialisation and commercial expansion and encouraged the rest of the country to follow suit. Barcelona wanted to be more than a provincial capital; it demanded a place against Madrid, the capital dominated by bureaucrats and rentiers. Castile had to learn the lessons of the disaster and move forward. Times were changing. Catalonia began considering itself as a 'nation' regarding Spain as 'the State'. The Catalan nationalists demanded home rule, a protectionist industrial policy and official recognition of Catalan as their language. Many years later, their aspirations would be fulfilled.

The Crown managed to survive intact after the disaster, but the ruling elite did not learn its lesson and in 1904 joined France in a colonial campaign in Morocco that proved a long-lasting military disaster over the next century. The war and its sequels left an exacerbated anti-militarism among the working classes, its most dramatic repercussion was the Tragic Week in Barcelona in 1909, an uprising led by anarchists against the military draft and the colonial policies in Morocco that was bloodily crushed. Alfonso XIII came of age in 1902. He had written in his diary a year earlier:

> I can be a king whose name will remain in history because of his achievement regenerating our Motherland, but I can also be a king that will be governed by his ministers and eventually will be put over the border. It's up to me whether Spain remains a monarchy or a republic.

The outcome was decided thirty years later, when Alfonso went into exile and the Second Republic was proclaimed. As for Cuba, the ties with Spain were not broken; in fact, the links between the two countries became stronger with new waves of Spanish immigrants arriving at the Pearl of the Antilles (800,000 between 1902 and 1931). A hundred years after the Cuban War, Spain, the defeated colonial oppressor, remains the motherland for Cuba, while its former ally against colonialism, the United States, is enemy number one.

Twentieth-Century Spain

Spain Enters the Twentieth Century

BY JAIME VICENS VIVES

Jaime Vicens Vives, the distinguished Catalan historian, was a professor of modern history and the founder and director of the Center of International Historical Studies at the University of Barcelona. Vicens Vives examines the multiple crises faced by Spain during the early years of the twentieth century, encompassing political, religious, social, and international dilemmas, as well as a serious crisis of identity. In so doing, he establishes the framework for the impending civil war and triumph of fascism.

During the first half of the twentieth century Spain was convulsed by a profound crisis. That it can be considered a regional version of the general European crisis in this century does not diminish its importance. Granting that many problems were identical and developed along parallel lines, some facets affected Spanish life exclusively.

The very first of these was that malaise had been manifest in Spain far earlier than elsewhere in Europe, at the height of the gilded and prosaic *fin de siècle* [end of the century]. Although there had been many indications of a profound spiritual change, it crystallized under the impact of Spain's defeat by the United States in 1898. The frivolous official optimism and the facile patriotism of the man in the street gave way to universal consternation, which some felt as simply a level stretch before Spain moved on to another inconsequential era; others felt it as humiliation and shame, as an avowed determination to change, either along the paths of exalted nationalism, or along those of revolutionary internationalism. Both groups agreed that if the situation—the government, the society, the vulgar and silly way of life,

Jamie Vicens Vives, *Approaches to the History of Spain*, translated and edited by Joan Connelly Ullman. Berkeley: University of California Press, 1970. Reproduced by permission.

the deceit, the routine, the lethargy—continued, it would lead to the extinction of Spain.

But what was Spain? The question was answered in a great variety of ways: Spain was Castile, Spain was Africa, Spain was an entelechy, Spain was the sum total of the autonomous regions in the era of the Catholic monarchs, and so on. That generation did, however, set forth two unanimous and incisive affirmations: they did not like Spain as she was at that moment, and they believed it necessary to Europeanize her at any cost.

On the form to be given to the future Spain that those men so ardently desired, there was a divergence of opinion. This was the second specifically Spanish facet of the European crisis. Those on the periphery, especially the Catalans, predicated an optimistic solution—one that was constructive, bourgeois, and historically oriented. Castilians, in contrast, were characterized by pessimism, by a break with the past, by an aristocratic tenor, by a tendency toward abstractions. Both groups found their *razón de ser* [reason for being] in an ardent nationalism that longed to burn intervening stages and to restore the grandeur of Spain. If that were not possible—if Spain were dead—then the Catalans, the Basques, and the Galicians would have to refuse to continue shouldering the added burden of Castile. Therein lay the entire problem. The effect of this restless regional mentality on the Spanish structure as a whole was to stimulate an intellectual and literary revival of the first order, one that maintained its momentum throughout the following two decades. But the ideas that it contained—explosive ideas, capable of shattering the country—did not reach the political scene until 1917, by which time the revival had undergone a philosophical process of defining its ideology and a historic process of gaining public support.

The fact that there were two different generations—which we express in a double code, 1898 for Castile, 1901 for Catalonia—stimulated dissension between Castile and Catalonia on the question of how the Spanish state should be organized. Fundamentally the dispute involved not only the possibility of accepting the indigenous and authentic culture of Catalonia as representative of one mode of the Hispanic essence, but also the possibility of providing the state with an efficient and modern structure whose leaders, instead of playing politics, would seek solutions for the country's most urgent and dramatic problems. In order to present both tendencies in the best possible light, Catalan nationalists asked for an autonomous regime. Their proposal was encumbered by its own antiquated concepts and by the fear that it would lead either to the breakup of the Spanish state that had emerged at the Renaissance, or else to the decline of Castile's historic mission as the national entity that had founded that state.

At the height of the intellectual controversy and of the political game, theoretical positions were established that verged, ideologically, on mutual separatism; such positions were used to advantage by those who captivated facile enthusiasms. But the strict reality of the events reveals that, as part of the nationalist tendency mentioned previously, Catalans participated in the scientific, social, and economic life of Spain far more than they ever had in the past.

The third facet of the Spanish crisis concerned religion. The attacks upon Catholicism and the alienation of the masses from the Church were of course general throughout Europe. But the manner in which the problem was presented—entwined with politics and even with war—was specifically Spanish.

The aristocratic and bourgeois Liberalism of the nineteenth century had been moderately secular and had favored a Church subject to state controls. Its great objective was to eliminate the religious orders and acquire their property; but the secular Church was to be defended and protected by the state itself (the Constitution of 1845 and the Concordat of 1851). Meanwhile Democratic, Republican, and Federalist movements were preaching not only anticlericalism in general but also—and for the first time in Spain—an atheistic point of view. Beginning in 1868, anti-religious propaganda opened wide cracks in the old-time bloc of Spanish Catholicism, especially in the proletarianized industrial zones. The schism created within the country in 1869, at the time of the arguments over the Catholic unity of Spain, had of necessity profound repercussions in the succeeding era.

If we except the group of apologists led by Jaime Balmes, the reaction of the Church was quite weak throughout the nineteenth century. At its close only one individual, Marcelino Menéndez y Pelayo, was able to rise above the vulgarity and defend the Catholic roots of Hispanic life. However, during those same years the generous policies of the Restoration governments benefited the Church by allowing new and old religious congregations to expand their educational activities. A new factor that should be pointed out is that regionalist movements were supported by a large sector of the clergy on the periphery, and this in turn stimulated a powerful current of religious revival. Thus the Spanish Church also had its "Generation of 1898." From those focal points (particularly Catalonia, Valencia, Asturias, and the Basque provinces) came a surge of liturgical revival that secured new and fervent public support for the Church, especially among the nobility, the bourgeoisie, and the middle classes. Because Catholicism was thus revitalized, its clash with the first anticlerical wave of the century—unleashed in 1901 in the wake of the French and Portuguese campaigns—was more violent.

This wave of demagogy inundated the proletarianized masses and prepared a break between them and the Church, which it accused of being an instrument used by the bourgeoisie and the landowners to oppose the demands of labor. This psychology of having been defrauded might explain the assaults upon the church buildings that have been so rife in recent Spanish history, beginning with the Tragic Week of Barcelona in 1909. The Church, however, did not abandon the course that she had set for herself: the reconquest of society by means of education.

Although many and varied, the Church's efforts in the social field were very timid, in both the industrial and the agrarian zone. Unfortunately, those who directed these activities, even high-ranking members of the hierarchy, did not find the support that they deserved. In 1917—in the general crisis of labor relations—the Catholic labor movement was sacrificed and left to its fate. "Yellow syndicalism" gained support within this group and diverted it into combat positions that promoted neither social peace nor religious tolerance.

Far more than in other Western European countries, the conservative classes of Spain were intransigent in their attitude toward labor demands, because of the presence of a violent and destructive anarchist movement. It still remains to be clarified whether anarchism developed as a consequence of the lack of vision and the harshness of Spanish employers, or whether employers adopted a position of strong resistance when confronted with anarchist syndicalism's tendency toward lawlessness or avowedly revolutionary action. In either case, whereas the bourgeoisie and even the government reached a stage where they were able to negotiate with the UGT (Unión General de Trabajadores, the Socialist labor organization), and while the Socialist party participated in Spain's national and municipal politics, anarchistic syndicalism remained intractable.

As a matter of record, one must distinguish between the two components of this movement: pure syndicalism and militant anarchism. Syndicalism—an imitation of the French movement, apolitical and advocating direct action—began to organize in Barcelona in 1902. It gave rise to Solidaridad Obrera (first a federation of labor societies of Barcelona, and then a regional confederation of Catalan labor), the National Confederation of Labor (CNT—Confederación Nacional del Trabajo), and the Single Syndicates (Sindicatos Únicos, 1918). The second component was militant anarchism. Weakened by the failure of individual terrorism at the end of the nineteenth century, anarchism slowly gained control of organized labor and finally, after 1909, imposed upon it the ideals of a cataclysmic and definitive social revolution. This is the way that anarchism and syndicalism consolidated; the street fighting in Barcelona from 1919 to 1923 made their symbiosis indissoluble.

During these years syndicalists, theoretical anarchists, professional terrorists, and hired gunmen mingled in one of the most explosive, destructive movements—and until now the least studied—of that general European social complex which emerged from World War I. They were people disposed to wrest power from the hands of the bourgeoisie and their coercive forces, to annihilate the state in one great revolutionary blow, and to initiate a life of collectivized property organized into free municipalities and based on an agrarian and patriarchal economy. An enervated utopia, with no possible counterpart in the world, it was purely the reaction of an illiterate peasant transformed into the mechanized worker of an urban enterprise.

Finally, the last of the Hispanic features of the twentieth-century crisis concerned the agrarian problem. Although not exclusive to Spain, for she shared it with other nations in Eastern Europe and the Balkans, it was a differential factor inasmuch as it did not occur in other Western European nations. This difficult problem (simultaneously a moral, economic, technical, and social problem) was circumvented by the parties who alternated in office (*los partidos turnantes*) and who were selected from the great landowners. The First World War had momentarily provided a solution because of the demands of belligerent nations for rural products and for raw materials, but the subsequent decline in prices and the resulting unemployment darkened the already stormy horizon of the Spanish countryside.

The remaining facets of the Hispanic crisis were identical with those of Europe in general: diversity of opinion as between directed and free economies; between authoritarianism and democracy; between private property and collectivization of the means of production; between a humanistic and a materialistic concept of life. But given the Hispanic temperament and the magnitude of these problems, the differences of opinion developed on Peninsular soil into an extremely violent conflict.

Prior to 1936, there were three attempts to overcome the difficulties that obstructed the organization of Spanish society. The first solution, attempted during the actual reign of Alfonso XIII (1902–1931), consisted of implementing the parliamentary system correctly, exactly as it had been set forth in the Constitution of 1876, but as [Premier Antonio] Cánovas [del Castillo], its author, had not wanted it to develop. Antonio Maura was the architect of this policy. His grand idea was to reform local government, in the belief that this would have a twofold result: it would uproot bossism (caciquismo) and it would provide an outlet for Catalonia's desire for autonomy. But Maura's policy was doomed to failure by the workers' explosion in Barcelona in 1909—an explosion that had been foreseen since 1901 but that nothing had been done to avoid, because the labor problem was considered only in terms of public order. A shift to the left, proclaimed publicly by José Canalejas, made some further progress for a little while, but his assassination in 1912 and the declaration of World War I canceled this promising experiment in reforming the parliamentary system.

Although Spain remained neutral, the war began to undermine her nineteenth-century society. The process of transformation was stimulated by the two torrents from the battlefields of Europe—money for supplies, and ideas to maintain faith in the struggle. Even the army felt the impact of subversion from within; officers organized *Juntas de Defensa*. Their activities and proclamations helped demolish the principles that were the basis for the parliamentary governments—purely caretaker governments harassed by demands for redress of political and social grievances, and for regional autonomy. In 1917 this situation turned into a crisis. The labor strike of that year was quelled by the army and by the Catalan bourgeoisie, who, although themselves leaders of a movement for political renovation, allowed themselves to be detoured into the attractive, sheltered harbor of positions in the government.

The crisis of 1917 led to years in which grievances were exacerbated. Disjointed and invertebrate was the way that [philosopher] José Ortega y Gasset defined this juncture. Each sector of society sought a drastic solution: labor syndicalism blindly devoted itself to fighting in the streets, precisely the site preferred by the most reactionary bourgeoisie, who specialized in summoning the army to their aid; Catalan regionalism, which had achieved its first administrative structure (*la Mancomunitat*, 1913), demanded a definitive legal document as part of its campaign for self-determination, which was derived from President [Woodrow] Wilson's principles; Castilian radicalism spied out the slightest occasion for an attack on any government whatsoever. And in chorus, all of these groups exclaimed that a new political solution must be sought.

Contrary to the forecasts of many persons, the solution—the second one attempted—was the establishment in 1923 of a dictatorship under General Miguel Primo de Rivera. The Constitution of 1876 was suspended and the very principle of the Crown's legitimacy was transgressed. But given the circumstances—terrorism, ill-starred colonial campaigns, the disintegration of the state—the monarch and the army believed that they should intervene and reorganize the life of the country. It was a propitious moment to attempt such a project, for Western Europe was reorganizing in a conservative fashion and [Italian dictator Benito] Mussolini had already carried out his march on Rome. Primo de Rivera set up a system of purely defensive, paternalistic government that lasted as long as the wave of general prosperity that followed the end of the First World War. The economic crisis of 1929 removed him from power. His fall revealed the immensity of his failure: aside from the pacification of Morocco and the construction of some public works, everything still remained to be done. What was even worse was that the problems had become inflammatory because they had been going on for so long and because of the wave of radicalism that the Great Depression had prompted throughout Europe.

The mystique of revolutionary reform, the general feeling of a large majority of the Spanish population in 1931, gave rise to a third solution—the Second Republic. Swept into power by an initial movement of popular enthusiasm, the Republic proclaimed a state that was democratic, regionalist, secular, and receptive to broad social reforms. Such a program would benefit leftist businessmen, a professional middle class, and skilled workers—precisely the classes which (except in such peripheral territories as Catalonia) were the least vital ones in the Spanish panorama. For this reason the progress of the Republic was totally obstructed by the demands of labor (the syndicalists of the CNT inspired by the mystique of the Third Revolution, and the socialists of the UGT inspired by revolutionary Marxism) and the opposition of great landowners (the revolt of General José Sanjurjo, 1932). Catholics also harassed the government because their consciences were threatened; instead of democratically and sincerely attempting to take over the places of command, they helped to undermine the Republic.

To these deep gashes in the hide of the Hispanic bull, no other balm was applied than the apologia of violence—learned in the Germany of [Adolf] Hitler, the Italy of Mussolini, the Austria of [Engelbert] Dollfus, the Russia of [Joseph] Stalin, and even the France of February 1934. Europe fell upon Spain, obscured her vision, and plunged her into the tremendous crisis that occurred in Catalonia and Asturias in October 1934. From this she emerged with a revolutionary mentality, both on the right and on the left. And thus it was that, just as many drops of water form a torrent, the Hispanic peoples allowed themselves to be propelled toward the dramatic vortex of July 1936 [the start of the Spanish civil war].

The Spanish Civil War

By Robert Wernick

Robert Wernick is a freelance writer and a contributor to Smithsonian *magazine. In this article Wernick describes the events of the brutal civil war in Spain from 1936 to 1939. Nearly half a million people were killed during the conflict between left-wing Communist, anarchist, and socialist forces and right-wing conservative and Nationalist forces. The turning point of the war, he contends, was the massive battle at Brunete on July 6, 1937, when the Nationalists routed the Republican forces. The Nationalists, commanded by Generalissimo Francisco Franco, ultimately won the war because, as Wernick asserts, they were better organized and more professional as an army, under the decisive leadership of Franco. The Republicans, on the other hand, quarreled among themselves and never achieved the level of discipline required for a victorious army.*

The roads are empty leading to Brunete in summertime: no one wants to drive 15 miles from Madrid to visit a sleepy little town baking among brown fields under the merciless sun of the Castilian plateau. There are no tour guides, no flags, no souvenir shops, no postcards, no monuments, nothing but a few stone bunkers, a couple of tarnished bronze plaques and a street named after Generalissimo Francisco Franco to remind the visitor that in July of 1937 . . . more than a hundred thousand men were fighting here in a battle that passionate bystanders all over the world believed might decide the future of Europe. Though no one realized it at the time, Brunete was the Gettysburg, the climax and turning point, of the Spanish Civil War, which had begun a year earlier with a rising by army generals to overthrow the government of the Second Spanish Republic and would last almost two more years after Brunete. When it was over, an estimated half-million Spaniards had been killed.

Robert Wernick, "For Whom the Bell Tolled," *Smithsonian*, vol. 28, April 1998, pp. 110–22. Copyright © 1998 by Robert Wernick. Reproduced by permission.

Spaniard vs. Spaniard

It was the first war in history that could be followed almost minute by minute by a horrified world—in beleaguered Madrid, reporters could take a taxi or the subway to the front lines at the edge of the city, and their stories would be in the papers everywhere the next day. What they saw was a particularly brutal war that cut to the heart of almost every city and village in Spain. Each day brought its share of atrocities. Some of them were new to warfare, like the mass bombing of helpless civilians in cities, but to the watching world they all served as a reminder that what it feared most, the outbreak of another and much greater war, might not be avoidable. That war began in September 1939, only months after the Spanish conflict ended. After presiding over a victory parade among cheering crowds in Madrid, General Franco ruled as dictator of Spain for the next 36 years.

The people of Spain were divided almost exactly in half with regard to broad political loyalties. But in most every other way—religion, region, ideology, standard of living—they were hopelessly fragmented. In the election of February 1936, the last free vote Spain was to know for nearly half a century, a Popular Front of liberal and extreme left-wing parties, some dedicated to revolution now, nudged out the conservatives of the Right by less than two percentage points. The electoral laws allowed this uneasy coalition to form a sizable majority in parliament, but the new government it formed was too splintered to rule effectively, and could only watch helplessly while the country—which had already seen five years of riots, general strikes, church burnings, a failed putsch by army officers and an armed rebellion by miners—slipped further toward chaos. There would soon be a new common word in the vocabulary of everyday life, *paseo*, meaning "ride," as in the phrase "take him for a ride" made popular by Hollywood gangster movies. It was just such a ride—one on which the monarchist party leader Calvo Sotelo was taken to be murdered in the early hours of July 13, 1936—that set off the armed uprising hardly a week later.

Both the Left and the Right in Spain had moderates and centrists who hoped for compromise. But by the time the guns began to play on July 18, extremists ran the show. For the defenders of the government, who called themselves Republicans or Loyalists, all their enemies were Fascists. For the supporters of the insurgent generals, who called themselves Nationalists, all their enemies were Reds. Men who were ready to die to protect Catholic Spain now assumed a license to kill anyone, school-teacher or government official or working man in blue overalls, whom they suspected of having voted for the Popular Front. Men who were ready to die for an imagined future Spain in which—as the two-million-member anarchist workers' union demanded—the state, the army, the church and private property would be abolished all at once, were now ready to kill any oppressor of humanity, landlord or employer or priest or anyone who owned a car or an expensive-looking house. Armed gangs on both sides roamed the country, shooting, stabbing, strangling, while firing squads worked overtime in prison courtyards. The bodies would be left for days in the streets as a warning. . . .

The original rising was badly executed. Three of the top Nationalist generals who had planned the coup died or were taken prisoner within 48 hours. When officers of the Mediterranean fleet joined the rebellion, their crews mutinied and, in some cases, shot the officers and dumped their bodies into the sea.

Military Insurgents

At the beginning a part of the army and the air force stayed loyal to the government, which still loosely controlled more than half the national territory, the principal ports, and most of the country's industry and mineral resources—not to mention its gold reserves. The military insurgents had only two major advantages, but they turned out to be decisive. One was political: the fact that the elected government so clearly could not keep its revolutionary left wing under control. One was military: in Spain's strip of the North African coast, General Francisco Franco had taken command of the local garrison of Moroccan troops and the Spanish Foreign Legion. As armies go, it was small—no more than 25,000 men at the start—but it was the only efficient fighting force in the country. In a few weeks, in the first major troop airlift ever, Franco began to bring his forces over the sea to the Spanish mainland, many in German planes.

Troops and officers in a number of cities rallied to the rebellion. In the north an insurgent army, led by Gen. Emilio Mola, drove to the coast, cutting off the Basque provinces from the French border. In the south, starting from Seville, Franco's army pushed north to Madrid, outmaneuvering and slaughtering undisciplined and poorly armed worker and peasant militias that tried to stop them. In November, when Franco's troops approached Madrid, the Republican government commandeered all available trucks and fled in panic to set up shop in Valencia on the Mediterranean coast. But the people of the city rallied to build barricades, and the advance bogged down in costly fighting in the southwestern suburbs.

In the following months, the scattered, uncoordinated forces of the early days grew into more or less well disciplined, more or less well equipped armies, eventually approaching half a million men each, and things settled down into the pattern of conventional war. As the Battle of Brunete was about to begin, these armies were stalemated along a front that snaked its way 1,000 miles across the country from just north of Gibraltar to the Pyrenees.

An impoverished, predominantly agrarian society like the Spain of the 1930s could not possibly have maintained a war on this scale. But the war—though the armies that fought it were made up overwhelmingly of illiterate boys from the desolate countryside and villages of Spain—soon became international.

The totalitarian powers were delighted to be able to push their political and strategic agendas. [Nazi leader Adolf] Hitler thought the conflict a "convenient side-show" that would distract the attention of the Western democracies from the much bigger war he was preparing. [Soviet premier Joseph] Stalin hoped that Hitler would get bogged down in Spain and have to postpone any adventures to the east. Hitler sent 600 planes, aviators, 200 tanks, military experts and 17,000 men. [Italian dictator Benito] Mussolini sent planes, tanks and at least 75,000 so-called volunteers. Stalin sent planes, guns, tanks and military "advisers," no fewer than four of whom went on to become marshals in the Red Army, which would crush the German Army only a few years later.

On both sides aid was doled out carefully, and never as a gift. Stalin got much of the gold reserves of the Bank of Spain, 158 truckloads of it, some in direct payment for matériel, some for "safekeeping" in Moscow. Hitler got much of the output of the Spanish copper, iron and tungsten mines to provide steel for the Wehrmacht. Mussolini got a naval base on Majorca and a chance to demonstrate Italy's "iron military strength."

Foreign Involvement

For the Western democracies, the choice was more difficult. While public opinion, partly driven by intense and skillful Communist propaganda, might favor the Republican government of Spain, public and governments alike were haunted by memories of the Great War, which only two decades before had killed or maimed millions of their young men. To a considerable extent pacifist, and militarily unprepared, they were desperately anxious to avoid another one. The United States had just passed a neutrality act. The British got all the great powers of Europe to sign a nonintervention pact, which Germany and Italy promptly broke.

In all the democracies, however, there was a large minority, passionately concerned and loudly vocal, who would have nothing to do with neutrality or nonintervention, and who insisted the overriding question for the world was the sudden and terrifying rise of Nazi barbarism. Nobody had dared to stand up to Hitler so far, and now behind their improvised barricades the people of Spain, bombed by Nazi planes and assaulted by Nazi tanks, were stoically accepting shells and bombs, and hunger, shouting, *No pasarán*! They shall not pass! . . .

To writers, artists, students, intellectuals, as well as to unemployed workers living out the Great Depression, Spain became a rallying cry. [Artist Pablo] Picasso made a world-famous painting deploring war and the Nationalist bombing of Guernica. [Writer Ernest] Hemingway wrote a world-famous novel, expressing support of the Spanish people. Huge meetings from London to Los Angeles thundered with demands for lifting the embargo and shipping arms to Republican Spain.

Others felt that only direct physical action, here and now, could stop the terrifying onrush of the brown tide of Fascism. André Malraux, the French novelist, recruited a squadron of airplanes. English idealists like George Orwell joined workers' militias that believed revolutionary actions like redistributing land and setting fire to churches were more important than learning how to fire a gun. On the more realistic premise that the first order of business was not revolution but winning the war, some 35,000 volunteers from almost every country in the world, including 2,800 Americans, joined the International Brigades.

The Brigades were formed and directed by Communists, many of whom were old party stalwarts—like Josip Broz, later to be Marshal Tito, ruler of Yugoslavia. But others were idealistic young people to whom Soviet Russia, which claimed to have solved all social and economic problems, was a beacon of light pointing to a utopian future. Most joined the Brigades for the same reason that ordinary Spaniards began joining the Spanish Communist Party, which grew from 130,000 to nearly 400,000 members in one year: the Comintern (Communist International) had prudently abandoned its call for world revolution in favor of a united front against Fascism, and even those who distrusted it figured it was the only group disciplined and ruthless enough to run a war against Franco.

The Battle of Brunete: Turning Point

In July 1937 a large number of the Brigades—including some 900 Americans—were picked to be in the front line for the Battle of Brunete, the first major offensive to be mounted by the Republican Army. They had been trucked by night into the woods of a former royal hunting lodge west of Madrid. After a Fourth of July celebration that brought the Americans double rations of Hershey bars and Lucky Strikes, they were on the march, picking their way through the pinewoods, elated to be in the forefront of an 80,000-man force, the most powerful army that had ever gone into battle in the whole history of Spain, with some 130 tanks, 40 other armored vehicles, 300 planes, and 220 heavy guns. They were singing the "Internationale": "Arise ye prisoners of starvation. . . . A new world's in birth. . . ."

As dawn came up on July 6, and all the guns, planes and tanks went into action, the Americans could see the whole battlefield spread out before them: gently rolling countryside with a few villages and clumps of trees, a few narrow streams, no serious physical obstacle between them and Brunete, 15 miles to the south.

Their battle plan described by Colonel Rojo, who drew it up, as possessing a "rigorous technical beauty, almost perfect." A giant pincer was to close on the insurgent army dug in at the doorstep of Madrid.

Franco had sent his best troops and many of his German planes 200 miles to the north to capture the major port of Bilbao, near the Bay of Biscay. The army he left behind at Madrid was badly outnumbered, Russian planes controlled the air, and the ten-ton Russian tanks could brush off their three-ton Italian counterparts like so many flies.

Franco's spies must have picked up mountains of talk about the coming offensive in the noisy sidewalk cafés of Madrid, but when the blow struck on July 6, the Nationalists were not ready for it. The left pincer stroke ran into heavily fortified positions and could make no headway at all. But the right-hand stroke succeeded beyond its leaders' wildest hopes. Ahead they saw the enemy in disorderly retreat. The Nationalist front disintegrated within hours, and Republican troops sped forward under a bright cloudless sky, their only worry the 100-degree heat, which emptied all their canteens by 10 in the morning.

The enemy was so disorganized and demoralized that an en-

GEORGE ORWELL'S IMPRESSIONS OF CIVIL-WAR SPAIN

George Orwell was a British journalist and the author of Animal Farm *and* 1984. *He went to Spain in 1936 with the intention of writing newspaper articles about the civil war, but upon arriving in Barcelona, he was moved by the cause of the Socialists and joined the militia to help them fight the Nationalists. He describes the atmosphere he encountered there, one of seeming classlessness and social equality.*

I had come to Spain with some notion of writing newspaper articles, but I had joined the militia almost immediately, because at that time and in that atmosphere it seemed the only conceivable thing to do. The Anarchists were still in virtual control of Catalonia and the revolution was still in full swing. To anyone who had been there since the beginning it probably seemed even in December or January that the revolutionary period was ending; but when one came straight from England the aspect of Barcelona was something startling and overwhelming. It was the first time that I had ever been in a town where the working class was in the saddle. Practically every building of any size had been seized by the workers and was draped with red flags or with the red and black flag of the Anarchists; every wall was scrawled with the hammer and sickle and with the initials of the revolutionary parties; almost every church had been gutted and its images burnt. Churches here and there were being systematically detire division—commanded by Enrique Lister, the Communist quarrier who had risen from the ranks to become one of the Republicans' most successful and most charismatic generals—was able to slip unobserved all the way to Brunete and beyond, leaving one battalion to capture the town far ahead of schedule. They had punched a wide-open hole in the enemy line through which tanks and cavalry and foot soldiers could have poured to spread

molished by gangs of workmen. Every shop and café had an inscription saying that it had been collectivised; even the bootblacks had been collectivised and their boxes painted red and black. Waiters and shop-walkers looked you in the face and treated you as an equal. Servile and even ceremonial forms of speech had temporarily disappeared. Nobody said '*Señor*' or '*Don*' or even '*Usted*'; everyone called everyone else '*Comrade*' and '*Thou*', and said '*Salud!*' instead of '*Buenos días*'. Almost my first experience was receiving a lecture from an hotel manager for trying to tip a lift-boy. There were no private motor cars, they had all been commandeered, and all the trams and taxis and much of the other transport were painted red and black. The revolutionary posters were everywhere, flaming from the walls in clean reds and blues that made the few remaining advertisements look like daubs of mud. Down the Ramblas, the wide central artery of the town where crowds of people streamed constantly to and fro, the loudspeakers were bellowing revolutionary songs all day and far into the night. And it was the aspect of the crowds that was the queerest thing of all. In outward appearance it was a town in which the wealthy classes had practically ceased to exist. Except for a small number of women and foreigners there were no 'well-dressed' people at all. Practically everyone wore rough working-class clothes, or blue overalls or some variant of the militia uniform. . . . I did not realise that great numbers of well-to-do bourgeois were simply lying low and disguising themselves as proletarians for the time being.

George Orwell, "Homage to Catalonia," *The Complete Works of George Orwell*, vol. 6. London: Secker & Warburg, 1986.

havoc in the enemy rear and deliver a decisive blow, as the Germans would do to the French Army at Sedan just three years later.

Then almost everything went wrong. On top of the usual muddle of battle, many of the officers who ran the Republican forces were not up to their job. They may have been able to inspire men to hold a position to the death, but they had no experience of a war of maneuver. According to one Republican colonel, most militia leaders did not even know how to read a military map. They had no way of handling the immense traffic jams of troops, trucks and ambulances that turned their breakthrough into a bottleneck.

A combination of tradition and inexperience in the Soviet and Republican armies dictated that all decisions be referred to headquarters, and by the time approval came it was too late. They were cautious when they should have been bold, reckless when they should have been cautious. The American troops, who might have been pouring through the hole in the enemy lines on the first day of the battle, were ordered instead to make a frontal attack on the village of Villanueva de la Cañada, where a small force of Nationalists had dug in for a last-ditch stand. They took the village but suffered crippling casualties, and wasted 15 hours that could never be made up.

On the other side, in the crucial hours following the fall of Brunete, three Nationalist lieutenant colonels, cut off from communication with their superiors, handled their few troops with such skill and made such an artful commotion that they bluffed overwhelmingly superior attacking troops to stop and wait for reinforcements. At least one managed on his own initiative to scrape together some 300 men—clerks, drivers, men who had barely handled a rifle before—and set them to work digging trenches.

Then, in a remarkable display of speed and efficiency, reinforcements were hurried to Brunete from all over Nationalist Spain, traveling great distances over the same kind of rickety railways and wretched roads as those of the other side, but these arrived in time. By the third day the Republican advance had ground to a halt, and men who had left shovels and other equipment behind so that they could advance faster were forced to dig trenches with bayonets and helmets in the stony Castilian soil.

The mastery of the air provided at first by Russian planes frittered away with the arrival of new German equipment, like the Messerschmitt 109 fighter plane and the 88-millimeter antiaircraft gun, which would later do such deadly work in World War II. What was to have been a battle of maneuver turned into a small-scale replica of World War I battlefields like Ypres and Verdun. Masses of troops surged back and forth over a devastated countryside of burning fields and trees, burning tanks and screaming men, and the rattle of machine guns, trying to chase each other out of holes in the ground. It went on for 21 days. The scorching sun turned dead bodies to mummies and dried up all the watercourses on the battlefield. Men actually went mad from thirst. Six decades later the surviving veterans of the battle are obsessed with memories of the experience.

Harry Fisher, a veteran of the Abraham Lincoln Brigade, who was in action all 21 days, can never forget the frantic hour-long minutes he spent digging with a soupspoon down into the hard-baked bed of the Guadarrama River, down to where there were little pockets of mud, out of which he could squeeze a few drops of water.

When it was all over, and more than 40,000 casualties had been added up, each side claimed victory—the Nationalists because they had retaken Brunete in the last days of the battle, the Republicans because they had conquered and held on to about 20 square miles of devastated Spanish soil. In the long run, it was a disaster for the Republican Army, which lost 100 airplanes and 80 percent of its tanks and more than 20,000 soldiers. (Of the 900 Americans who started the battle, only 280 were fit for action at the end.)

The war would go on for almost two years, but it was largely a replay of Brunete. At Belchite, at Teruel, even on the Ebro, the Republicans made a surprise attack and advanced for a few heady days to occupy pockets of often strategically unimportant terrain, only to be ground down yard by yard in long bloody counterattacks till at last their armies collapsed, and eventually Francisco Franco became dictator of Spain.

The German generals who were advising Franco were critical of his strategy. They said that if he had just let the Republican attacks peter out, and not insisted on costly counterattacks, he could have won the war much more quickly and with fewer losses. They were probably right, but they were shortly to end up in the dustbin of history, while General Franco made the remarkable and almost unbelievable achievement of not only winning his war but managing to remain the master of Spain for 36 years.

Franco's Leadership

No one at the start of the war, least of all his fellow generals, could have suspected that such a role could be played by Francisco Franco y Bahamonde. Though he had proved himself a genuine war hero of the Moroccan campaigns and a capable military administrator, he was a colorless little man with a piping voice, no oratorical skills, no political sex appeal.

Franco won the war not because his army was stronger or braver than that of his enemies, but because it was better organized, more professional, more at home in the complexities of modern warfare. He turned out to be the very man to create and lead such an army. He was a fierce disciplinarian with an obsessive concern for detail. He once had a soldier shot for refusing to eat his rations. He was responsible for building the network of training schools for young Nationalist soldiers who became the *alféreces provisionales*, or temporary officers, whose willingness to take individual initiatives without waiting for orders from headquarters helped determine the outcome of the war. With immense skill he wrangled, cajoled and bullied all the antagonistic groups in his camp to form a single movement with himself as its unchallenged political and military boss.

No Unity of Command

The Republicans, on the other hand, never achieved real unity of command. They were torn by conflicts between different parties, different regions. There was civil war in the streets among Communists, Socialists and anarchists. Anti-Stalinist and anarchist worker militias believed they should be fighting not just for a republic but for a revolution as well—particularly in Catalonia. In *Homage to Catalonia*, George Orwell, who sympathized with these policies at the time, described how they "collectivized" factories and farms, theaters, even restaurants, often at gunpoint; established local police forces; and replaced the local government. In militia companies everyone wore the same uniform—overalls. It was considered demeaning to waiters to offer them a tip.

There as elsewhere, the church was a target, which troubled moderate loyalists. Some 7,000 priests, monks, nuns and bishops were put to death during the war. Throughout Republican

Spain, churches were regularly burned, sacked or pressed into revolutionary service.

All through the fighting, Spanish officers in the Republican Army continually bickered among themselves and grumbled about the high-handed ways of their Soviet advisers. Franco, meanwhile, kept all the reins firmly in his hands. He would take advice but never orders from his German and Italian advisers.

The Franco Regime

BY SEBASTIAN BALFOUR

Sebastian Balfour is a reader and the assistant director of the Canada Blanch Centre for Contemporary Spanish Studies at the London School of Economics and Political Science. He describes the regime headed by Generalissimo Francisco Franco, which came to power as a result of the victory of the Nationalists during the Spanish civil war in 1939. Franco's rule was characterized by repression and economic stagnation. Although Franco held tight to the reins of power for more than thirty-five years, he could not restrain the cultural transformation brought about by economic growth and modernization, which ultimately clashed with the archaic values of the dictatorship and led to its demise.

The new Nationalist state that replaced the Republic at the end of the Civil War was forged during the conflict itself. In April 1937 all the political parties supporting the rebellion had been united into a single state party, the National Movement. Franco became the personification of the new regime, enjoying absolute authority both as chief of state and head of government granted by his fellow generals in September 1936. His power rested on three institutions, the church, the army, and the Falange [the Fascist party that ruled Spain after the war], but within the regime there existed an unofficial pluralism of 'families' representing the different political tendencies that had joined the uprising—the original Falangists, Carlists, Catholic conservatives, and monarchists. Beyond them lay the diverse social forces that had backed the uprising. In addition to a common religious, nationalist, and antidemocratic ideology, what welded these contradictory interests together was the so-called 'pact of blood', a bond forged during the violence of the Civil War and the bloody repression practised or sanctioned by all in its aftermath.

Sebastian Balfour, *Spain: A History*, edited by Raymond Carr. Oxford, UK: Oxford University Press, 2000. Copyright © 2000 by Oxford University Press. All rights reserved. Reproduced by permission.

The Francoist state was essentially a conservative and authoritarian regime. Its totalitarian tendencies, represented by the Falange, were displayed in the pageantry of the state in the early years, when it appeared the Axis would win the world war. They were kept on a leash, however, by the church, the generals, and the monarchists. Towards the end of the war the Falange's power as a mass party was effectively emasculated. They felt compensated to some extent by their continued control over the compulsory social organizations of the regime, the state syndical system modelled on Italian corporatism, and the youth and women's organizations. Franco's own ideology was deeply conservative but it was subordinate to the perpetuation of his own power. He maintained control by repeatedly shifting the balance of influence within the regime according to internal and external pressures, and he continued to command loyalty by allowing the self-enrichment of his elites through the institutions of the state.

The victorious regime was consolidated by a prolongation of the civil war by other means. Despite its espousal of Christian values, the new state showed no forgiveness for the defeated. 'Spaniards, alert', the state radio announced on the day of victory: 'Peace is not a comfortable and cowardly repose in the face of History. The blood of those who fell for the Fatherland does not allow for forgetfulness, sterility, or treachery. Spaniards, alert, Spain is still at war against all internal and external enemies.' The repression carried out in the Nationalist rearguard was institutionalized in a series of laws aimed not just at the political supporters of the Republic but also at class and regional identities. The Law of Political Responsibilities, issued in February 1939 shortly after the Nationalist troops marched into Barcelona, declared 'serious passivity' towards the Republic to be a crime, and it was made retroactive to 1934. The definition of crime itself was broadened so as to enable the prosecution of trade-union activities carried out during the Republic.

The overt objective of the repression was to rid Spain of the systems and ideologies that had 'corrupted' her 'true identity'. Among these were democracy, atheism, and, at least in the early years of the regime, capitalism as a liberal market system. The beginning of the process of Spain's corruption was located in the eighteenth-century Enlightenment. The most immediate enemies were the communists, Jews, and freemasons who had been feeding off the decaying body of Spain. The true Spain was to be sought in the imperial and hierarchical traditions of the Catholic Kings. Her health lay in a mythologized Castilian countryside, while the city was seen as the source of her sickness. Combining the language of religion and medicine, the new regime sought the spiritual disinfection of Spain. The means to achieve this end were mass executions, imprisonment, redemption through penal labour, and the inculcation of the regime's values through education, psychological programming, and media propaganda.

It would be hard to exaggerate the consequent suffering of millions of Spaniards. Apart from the immediate effects for Republican supporters of defeat and repression—exile, imprisonment, execution (according to cautious Foreign Office estimates, some 10,000 people were executed in the first five months after the Civil War), most families in the early years of the Francoist regime suffered semi-starvation, disease, and exploitation. For all those who did not share the aims of the new regime, life was claustrophobic; without freedom of expression, their beliefs, and—in Galicia, the Basque Country, and Catalonia—their own language, were confined to private spaces. In public, they had to give the fascist salute and make sense of the official slogan 'For the Empire towards God'. Language became a tool of the victors. Even footballing terms were renamed to eliminate words with foreign derivations.

Autarky

The Francoist cure for a 'sick' economy was withdrawal from the world market, the creation of import substitution industries, and state intervention to supplement the weakness of private capital. The motor of the economy was to be the brutal exploitation of a tamed labour force. The autarky thus adopted was modelled on that of European fascism and reflected the admiration felt by Franco and his Falangist supporters for Nazi Germany and Fascist Italy. Although Spain remained officially neutral during the Second World War, close links were maintained between the Francoist regime and the fascist dictatorships from the beginning of the conflict. Franco and his advisors, led by his brother-in-law Ramón Serrano Suñer, first as minister of the interior and then as foreign secretary, attempted to negotiate Spain's entry into the war on the Axis side. For [Nazi leader Adolf] Hitler, however, Spain was of peripheral interest to the German war effort; moreover, the price Franco was demanding for her participation, the award of French Morocco, was, Hitler believed, more than Spain's contribution was worth. An awkward meeting between the two on the French-Spanish border at Hendaye on 23 October 1940 resulted in a formal undertaking by Spain to join the war, but no date was specified when she would do so. Hitler later complained to [Italian dictator Benito] Mussolini about his meeting with Franco (whom he subsequently called 'that fat little sergeant'): 'Rather than go through that again, I would prefer to have three or four teeth taken out.' Franco, for his part, was not impressed by Hitler, whom he found 'a stage actor'. In the meantime, flouting its official policy of non-belligerence, the Francoist regime recruited a volunteer force, the Blue Division, to fight for Germany on the Russian front.

In the wake of the Allied invasion of North Africa in November 1942, Franco began to hedge his bets, assuring the Allies of Spain's friendship while continuing to provide material support to Germany. On the eve of peace in April 1945 Franco announced a series of cosmetic reforms, including a Charter of Rights for Spaniards, aimed at persuading the Allies of his democratic credentials. Spain was henceforth described as a Catholic and organic democracy. A corporative parliament, the Cortes, was set up, based not on universal suffrage, but on the 'natural organs of society', and later a Law of Succession was promulgated defining the regime as a monarchy without a monarch, with Franco as regent. The survival of his regime in the post-war world order, however, derived above all from the growing tensions of the incipient Cold War, encouraging the West to tolerate Spain under Franco. Despite the efforts of the exiled monarchist and Republican opposition, international disapproval of the Franco regime was reduced to a token gesture, the diplomatic boycott of Spain agreed by the United Nations in December 1945.

Spain's self-imposed economic isolation was abandoned when it became clear by the late 1940s that autarky had failed. In comparison to countries experiencing rapid industrial growth thanks in part to the Marshall Aid denied to the Spanish, Spain's economic situation had not improved significantly. Inflation was rising steeply and the balance of payments had plunged into a chronic deficit. The crisis of the late 1940s obliged the regime to modify its policy of autarky. Franco reshuffled his cabinet to permit a timid liberalization of the economy. Diplomatic isolation also came to an end in 1953. In that year the Vatican signed a concordat with Spain, and the United States, keen to extend its Cold War defences, signed a pact with the regime allowing for the creation of US military bases in Spain in exchange for financial aid amounting over six years to some $625 million. Two years later, the UN voted to readmit Spain.

Economic Liberalization

Despite its semi-liberalization, the Spanish economy was still in trouble in the mid-1950s. The balance-of-payments deficit had doubled and record inflation was eating into the value of wages, which were as little as 35 per cent of their pre–Civil War level. The first wave of illegal strikes swept across Spain. A new generation of university students was also beginning to mobilize against the state from within the official student association previously dominated by the Falange. Within the regime itself, the first stirrings of opposition took place. Cracks appeared in the

WOMEN UNDER THE FRANCO DICTATORSHIP

Mary Nash is a professor of contemporary history at the University of Barcelona. She describes the status of women during Franco's rule of Spain, finding that they suffered a number of setbacks on the road to liberation and equal opportunity. During this period, women's roles were relegated to motherhood and domestic responsibilities and their public participation was severely limited.

Under Franco, women's primary social function was motherhood. Hence, women's aspirations related to work, education and self-betterment, social activity, and emancipation were perceived as a threat to their biological destiny as breeders of the nation's future generations. Women could be politicized only through the notion of fulfilling a common female destiny based on their reproductive function. Female sexuality, work, and education were regulated in accordance

church's formerly ardent support, and tensions were growing between the Falange and the military, many of whom were monarchists disappointed by Franco's refusal to install a monarch in the person of Don Juan, son of Alfonso XIII. Against his will, Franco was persuaded in 1957 to sack his ministers and appoint a new cabinet with more pliant Falangists and an economic team made up of neo-liberal technocrats linked to the Catholic lay organization, the Opus Dei.

The technocrats' objective was to dismantle the 'orthopedic apparatus' of autarky and open up the economy to the boom of the West without political, cultural, or social liberalization. It was driven by the belief that economic growth and an accompanying rise in living standards would be sufficient to sustain the regime. In doing so, the regime's 'legitimacy of origin' based on victory in the Civil War would be replaced by the 'legitimacy of exercise', the provision of prosperity. A reluctant Franco was forced to accept the technocrats' Stabilization Plan of 1959,

---

with this gender designation, while motherhood was idealized and considered a duty to the fatherland, Francoist ideology marked women off as a separate natural species, identifying them exclusively as mothers whose offspring would check the tendency toward declining birthrates and thus prevent the decadence of Spain.

Women's path to emancipation was brutally closed by the repressive Franco dictatorship. Women's voices were lost, their organizations disbanded, and their newly gained presence in the public arena disallowed. The new regime espoused a gender role of submission, docility, and unquestioning obedience to the traditional tenets of domesticity. As stressed by Pilar Primo de Rivera, the leader of the Sección Femenina, the only official Francoist women's organization, women's inevitable and absolute destiny was maternity. She qualified this role as "a biological, Christian and Spanish function."

Mary Nash, *Defying Male Civilization: Women in the Spanish Civil War.* Denver: Arden, 1995.

which turned the peseta into a convertible currency, thereby cutting its value by half. It also reduced public expenditure, and opened the gates to foreign investment. The Plan had a radical effect on a hitherto protected economy. After a brief recession, it began to enjoy higher rates of growth than any other country in the West, for a while more than twice that of the European Community. Once a mainly agrarian economy only partially integrated into Europe, Spain became part of the industrialized, urban, and consumer society of the West by the early 1970s.

The engine of this growth was the economic boom of the western economy. Foreign investment was attracted to Spain by her potential for expansion, by government subsidies, and by low labour costs. The rise in living standards in Europe and a cheap peseta in Spain drew increasing numbers of tourists. Four years after the Plan was put into effect, their number had increased from 4 million to 14 million, and earnings from tourism had risen from $129 million to $919 million. The restructuring of the economy also led to the emigration of one-and-a-quarter million Spaniards to Europe between 1960 and 1973. The money they sent to their families in Spain in the same period amounted to some $5,000 million. Foreign investment, tourism, and emigrant remittances helped to balance the deficit in Spain's balance of payments resulting from economic growth.

Apologists for the regime attributed the boom of the Spanish economy to the *dirigisme* [planning and control] of the technocrats. In reality, much of the economic growth in Spain was unplanned. Despite attempts to reduce regional disparities, economic growth was concentrated in areas where industry had traditionally been located, the Madrid region, Catalonia, Valencia, and the Basque Country. While foreign firms came to play an increasing role in capital formation, the Spanish tradition of state patronage and protection through nepotism and shared ideology became an instinctive practice in the Franco regime, favouring the development of inefficient domestic monopolies.

Economic growth transformed Spanish society. Contrary to the regime's exaltation of rural life, the countryside was emptied of its inhabitants. Rural exodus was accompanied by a massive and largely unplanned growth of cities characterized by speculation, overcrowding, and a lack of urban infrastructure. Yet there were considerable improvements in health, nutrition, and education. Modernization also changed Spain's occupational structure.

From a largely agrarian society, Spain became dominated by the industry and service sectors. The size of the professional middle class burgeoned. The speed of Spain's insertion into the consumer market can be illustrated by the rise in the number of television sets. In 1960 only 1 per cent of households had a television; nine years later 62 per cent owned a set.

The ensuing transformation of culture clashed with the archaic values of the regime. Franco had feared the effect of 'breezes from foreign shores corrupting the purity of our environment'. However, the cultural contradictions that accompanied modernization were largely domestic in origin. A remarkable example of these was the metamorphosis of the church. From the most ardent defender of the regime, the church became an outspoken critic from within, spurred on not just by the change in world Catholicism after the Second Vatican Council but also by the radicalization of its lay organizations and urban priests. In 1971 the church voted to ask forgiveness from the Spanish people for its role in the Civil War, and in 1973 the bishops asked for the separation of the church and the state. To Franco, this was a 'stab in the back'.

Protest and Opposition

Modernization also bred protest. The vertical, authoritarian syndicates of the regime were increasingly out of tune with the needs of a mobile, educated, and pluralist society. As a result, social and cultural protests adopted a more political character. Of these, the greatest challenge came from the labour movement that had never ceased, even in the 1940s, to stage strikes in protest against the desperate conditions of workers. The wave of stoppages that swept through Spain from 1962 was in part the result of the transformation of production. The reluctant introduction by the regime of collective bargaining in 1958 undermined the legitimacy of its vertical industrial relations model, because it led to the growth of democratic structures on the shop-floor and in offices. The clandestine organization that emerged in workplaces throughout Spain was the Workers' Commissions, dominated by militants of the Communist party. Labour protest overflowed into the surrounding neighbourhoods and workplaces in the form of solidarity movements. It also influenced other agitations such as the neighbourhood associations. In the process the ideals of citizenship and democracy were fostered.

After the 1950s the regime faced a new challenge from students and intellectuals. Spanish universities changed from elite to mass institutions in which violent protests were staged against the lack of democracy in the official union and the poor conditions of university life. These culminated in the declaration in 1969 of a state of emergency throughout the country. The repression launched by the regime against the protesting students evoked widespread solidarity, since the students came overwhelmingly from middle-class families.

The regime soon had to face a resurgent regional nationalism. By the 1960s regional rights in Catalonia and the Basque Country had become the focus of the widespread demand for democracy. Catalanism in particular was seen as a modernizing and democratic project linked to European models, as opposed to the archaic and repressive nationalism of the Franco regime. On the fringes of Basque nationalism, on the other hand, there was a more xenophobic ideology. Heavy migration into the region had intensified the insecurity and exclusivism that lay at the origin of the movement. Regional protest in the Basque Country took violent shape with the creation of the terrorist organization ETA [Euskadi Ta Askatasun (Basque Fatherland and Liberty)] in 1959. Between 1968 and 1975, when ETA was at its most active, forty-seven people associated with the regime and its repressive apparatus were assassinated. ETA became a symbol of resistance against the Franco regime. The Burgos trial of ETA members and sympathizers in 1970 generated a widespread movement of solidarity in Spain, and throughout Europe.

Out of the agitation of the 1960s a new political opposition emerged. In contrast to the socialists and anarchists, whose clandestine organization had been largely destroyed by repression (though the socialists, in particular, retained much residual support in a number of regions, such as Asturias), the communists succeeded in engaging with the new grievances generated by modernization. Having renounced the guerrilla struggle of the 1940s, the party adopted the policy of National Reconciliation; a broad political alliance led by the Communist party would direct Spain on to the path of democracy. Alongside them, new and more radical organizations emerged, closely linked to the revolutionary left in Europe. Despite its considerable growth and influence, however, the political opposition in the 1960s and early 1970s failed to unite around a common programme which could embody a viable alternative to the regime, because it was split by the Cold War divisions and by different agendas for political change in Spain.

The Decline of the Regime

For the regime, modernization without democracy turned out to be an insuperable contradiction. Though it hoped the Spanish economic 'miracle' would bolster its legitimacy, the demands thrown up by socio-economic and cultural change could not easily be reconciled with the structures of the dictatorship. The attempt to win the acquiescence of the population through bread and circuses was only partially successful. Real Madrid became the football team most closely associated with the regime, and the success of the bullfighter El Cordobés led the state to transmit one of his bullfights on 1 May, in the hope that demonstrators could be enticed to stay at home. There were few apologists for the dictatorship amongst artists, writers, and film directors. Creative artists sought oblique, metaphorical means of expressing their dissatisfaction with social and political life in Spain in order to escape censorship. The film *Spirit of the Beehive*, by Victor Érice, portrayed a depressed, listless village, under the surface of which, as beneath the lid of a beehive, a dynamic and restless society was growing.

As part of an effort to renew its image, the regime carried out a superficial refurbishment of its institutions. A Law of Associations was passed in 1964 allowing regime families to set up opinion groups; these were restricted since Franco believed they would degenerate into political parties. A press law was issued in 1966 removing prior censorship. Yet any further liberalization was blocked by the regime's fundamentalists, the so-called 'immobilists'. The essentially reactionary nature of the state was confirmed by the Organic Law of the following year. The nomination in 1969 of Prince Juan Carlos, son of the Pretender to the throne, as heir to Franco and future king of Spain did nothing to resolve these contradictions.

One of Franco's most repetitive self-justifications was that he had brought peace to a society at war with itself. If it still had any purchase, this claim was undermined by the increasing social and political agitation of the early 1970s. The most dramatic expression of that protest was the assassination by ETA at the end of 1973 of Franco's right-hand man and prime minister, Admiral

Carrero Blanco. The explosive charge laid by ETA across the path of Carrero's car in the centre of Madrid was so powerful that the limousine was thrown over the top of a high-rise block, prompting the opposition to nickname him Spain's first astronaut. Unable and largely unwilling to liberalize because of internal splits, the regime turned increasingly to martial law and state brutality, such as the execution in 1975 of five anti-Francoist terrorists. Mounting protest, added to the economic recession induced by the oil crisis in 1973, further weakened the regime's legitimacy in the last two years of Franco's rule. His illness and death in November 1975 dissolved the only glue that had held the regime together in its last years.

The Transition to Democracy

By Fred James Hill

Fred James Hill is a writer and editor who has spent many years living and traveling in Spain. He explains the transition that Spain underwent following the death of Francisco Franco in 1975 and the subsequent dismantling of his regime. The new leadership, under Juan Carlos I, was committed to making Spain into a modern democracy. The democratic government was replaced by the Socialists under Felipe González in 1982, but democratic forms of government were retained under the Socialists' moderate programs. During González's long tenure in power, Spain enjoyed growth, prosperity, and relative peace. There were problems, however, including violence enacted by Basque separatists, high unemployment, and political opposition. In 1996 economic difficulties and corruption scandals cost the Socialists the elections, and José María Aznar, of the Popular Party, became prime minister.

"After Franco what?" was the question that was on everyone's lips before the death of the dictator. Few people knew what was in the mind of the man Franco had chosen as his successor. Juan Carlos I had given very little away, and most had taken this to be a sign that he was little more than Franco's own creation, reared on a diet of the dictator's own values and ready to help keep the regime's torch burning. They were wrong. Privately, Juan Carlos had acknowledged the importance of reestablishing democracy in Spain and peacefully laying to rest the long years of dictatorship; and he was to play a crucial role in bringing this about. What few people knew was that for several years Juan Carlos had secretly met with members of the opposition (in some cases they had to be smuggled into his residence in the trunks of cars), and he was incredibly well-informed of the country's mood.

Yet Juan Carlos had to tread carefully. He had publicly sworn to defend a regime over whose end he was about to preside. In order to dismantle the structures of the dictatorship, the new monarch needed a prime minister who was acceptable to the regime, but who could also initiate a dialogue with the illegal opposition. [Carlos] Arias Navarro [prime minister under Franco] would clearly be an obstacle to the process since he owed not only his job but his ideology to Franco. In July 1976, Juan Carlos substituted him with Adolfo Suárez, a man he felt had the skills to do the job. Suárez did not disappoint. From the beginning, the king and Suárez were clear that it would be impossible to bring about the end of the dictatorship by using the same kind of authoritarian means that had been used by Franco. Neither the regime's supporters nor the opposition would allow such a plan to succeed. Therefore, they worked on the principle that the key to a peaceful transition to democracy was to establish a pact with the opposition in order to negotiate a break with the past. Thankfully the opposition was almost unanimous in its agreement to play by the rules of the pact.

Having managed to get the co-operation of the greater part of the opposition, the government announced the Law of Political Reform, which was designed to legalize political parties and introduce the right to vote. This measure was approved by the Cortes in November, and subsequently endorsed by referendum in December. If democracy was to be successful, all of the opposition parties were going to have to be permitted to participate in the elections. But Suárez had to tread carefully when it came to some of the old enemies of the regime. Free elections would involve the participation of the Communists, and this idea was wholly unacceptable to Franco's diehard supporters (who had already had to swallow the bitter pill of partial amnesties for ETA terrorists). Yet after negotiations with Santiago Solares, leader of the Spanish Communist Party, Suárez went ahead and legalized the party in April 1977. In a clear show of compromise, the Communists put aside their Republican ideals and agreed to work within a constitutional monarchy.

Meanwhile tension was growing in the country as ETA stepped up its violent campaign against the government with a spate of assassinations and kidnappings. Other militant extremists from both sides of the political spectrum became increasingly active too, raising the specter of a bloody showdown. Undeterred, the king and Suárez went ahead with the plan. In March, Juan Carlos decreed that the first free general elections would take place on June 15, 1977—the first in Spain since 1936. It was a momentous occasion. Amidst a wave of national euphoria, the elections were celebrated fairly and freely. The electoral turnout was enormous as the people rushed to the polling stations to play their part in the history that was being made. Two parties took the lion's share of the votes, the Democratic Center Union (UCD) with around 36 percent, led by Suárez himself, and the Spanish Socialist Party (PSOE) with 29 percent. Although many had expected the Communist Party to win the contest, it secured only 9 percent of the votes. UCD and PSOE were both moderate parties that together covered a broad area of the political center ground. The result indicated the understandable caution of the nation and allowed Suárez to continue to oversee the reforms of the country.

On October 31, 1978, a new constitution, drawn up with the participation of the opposition, was approved by the Cortes and then endorsed by referendum. This time the politicians were determined not to repeat the same mistakes made in the past. The Church that was once declared to be "inseparable from the national conscience" and the inspiration of its laws was made to feel a welcome part of the democracy. Although the constitution affirmed that there would no longer be a state religion, it promised a future of co-operation with the Catholic Church in a conciliatory tone. This seemingly minor gesture was of great importance, since it helped to alleviate the tensions created previously by the Republican constitution of 1931. The short-lived republic of the 1930s had attempted to deny the Church any participation in the affairs of the State, going so far as to refuse it the right "to exercise industry, commerce, or teaching." It paid a high price for its bluntness.

An area of utmost sensitivity was that concerning the unity of Spain. The very mention of Basque or Catalan independence was enough to jeopardize the whole transitional process—the army simply would not tolerate such talk. Yet the issue could not be ignored. Accordingly, the new constitution affirmed that the unity of the nation was "indissoluble" but it nevertheless recognized that the regions were entitled to a degree of autonomy. Such a declaration would have amounted to an act of sedition under Franco who, along with his supporters, had elevated the unity of Spain and its people to an almost mystical level. The regions were soon to exploit the concession to great effect.

The democratic elections and the content of the new constitution marked a major turning point in the history of Spain, demonstrating the success of the process of converting Spain into a democracy after many long years of dictatorship. But a weak point was its failure to address the problems of the Armed Forces—victors of the Civil War, and one of the pillars of Franco's regime. With Franco gone, only Juan Carlos I could expect the loyalty of the army. To reduce the possibility of military intervention in the political process, Suárez tactfully appointed a military officer, not a civilian, as Minister of Defense to oversee reforms of the Armed Forces. Lieutenant General Manuel Gutiérrez Mellado, a liberal, began a process of substituting key military officers with others who were more sympathetic to the changes taking place. Gutiérrez was no revolutionary and, in keeping with the spirit of the transition, worked slowly and cautiously. Overall, the process brought beneficial results, helping to neutralize potentially troublesome elements in the army and isolating those that were most reactionary.

However, the intrigues of the ultra-conservative military officers were about to dramatically challenge the fledgling democracy. In August 1978, an ETA faction launched a series of attacks against the armed forces. It was a blatant attempt to sabotage the parliamentary ratification of the constitution and the subsequent referendum. The army was, not surprisingly, incensed by such an act of provocation. In the events that followed, several officers hatched a plan, named Operation Galaxy, to stage a coup. The government was alerted. As a result, two leading conspirators were arrested. One of the officers seized was Antonio Tejero Molina, a lieutenant colonel in the Guardia Civil, the militarized police force. The plan had failed, but the government's timid reaction and the subsequent leniency of the military tribunal was anything but a lesson to deter would-be coup leaders.

Operation Galaxy had never gotten past the planning stage, but the attempted coup of February 23, 1981, did. This time, the very same Tejero and his henchmen stormed into the Cortes, during the investiture of Leopoldo Calvo Sotelo as Spain's new prime minister, and held the assembly at gun-point. The whole democratic process was hanging on a thread. The nation, watching the events as they unfolded live on television, held its breath.

If the goverment lacked influence over the army, could the king persuade it? The authority of Juan Carlos was put to the test. As ministers and parliamentary deputies waited for an end to their ordeal as Tejero's hostages, the king declared that the Crown did not and would not support any attack against democracy. He personally contacted key senior military officials and, by making his position clear, managed to win their loyalty. Deprived of royal support, the coup failed. The fact that the government owed its survival to the king was proof of the fragility of democracy. Although the king met with the political opposition and informed them that he could not repeat what he had just done, the new democracy had passed the biggest test. It had overcome the army.

Spain Under Felipe González and the Socialists

That same year saw serious problems hit the government. Suárez had already been replaced by Calvo Sotelo as prime minister. His UCD party was disintegrating, shaken by internal disputes over the direction it was taking, and Suárez had found his position untenable. The government limped on, but many UCD members defected to other newly created parties. Faced with a crisis of confidence, there was little to do but ask the king to dissolve the Cortes, and announce general elections.

On October 28, 1982, the Socialists, headed by Felipe González, an immensely popular and able Andalucían lawyer who had played a key role in the democratic negotiations after Franco's death, won a sweeping victory in the general elections. UCD gained only 6.5 percent of the votes compared to PSOE's 48 percent. This margin was highly significant. It was now clear that, having elected a Socialist government into power, the Spanish people were determining their own future. The various elements that continued to have an interest in destabilizing democracy, although they did not disappear, were becoming more isolated and discredited. The transition had succeeded. The governing of the country had passed on to the opposition by peaceful and democratic means—a great achievement that owed its success to the moderation and co-operation shown by practically all sides.

From November 1982 to March 1996, Spain was governed by the Socialist government led by Felipe González. It was a period of enormous socio-economic change as the country fully embraced the modern world. Despite its name, the Socialist Party to which González belonged had little to do with Marxist ideology, which it had renounced several years earlier. It was a highly dynamic party that attracted a wide range of supporters from not only the left but also the center. Although moderate in tone, the Socialists demonstrated a tough and active style of government that oversaw major reforms in a variety of areas including education, welfare, industry, and taxation. It also launched into much-needed programs to develop the infrastructure of the country, overseeing the construction of much-needed major roads.

Yet there was one prize the government anxiously pursued—entry into that powerful economic club, the European Community (now the European Union). For a long time, many politicians from both the left and right had dreamed of such a day; and on January 1, 1986, it arrived, bringing to a successful conclusion several years of hard work and negotiations. Also that same year, after putting the issue to the nation in a referendum, Spain's full incorporation into NATO [the North Atlantic Treaty Organization] was approved.

The country enjoyed stability and peace under the Socialists, and the government continued to enjoy huge popular support. Of course, it was not a problem-free ride. The government was unable to bring down the high level of unemployment. By the end of the 1980s, the number of jobless was running at over 20 percent, making it one of the worst hit countries in Europe, and causing a great deal of social hardship. Another seemingly insoluble problem was the terrorist group ETA, a law unto itself, which continued to wage a violent campaign to bring about Basque independence.

Felipe González and PSOE held on to power after a succession of general election victories—four in total. But by the early 1990s, the administration was running into trouble. The economy was seriously affected by a world recession. Furthermore, a series of scandals involving corruption rocked the government. Meanwhile, one of the opposition parties, the conservative People's Party (PP) was growing stronger and stronger. Despite one more final victory in the elections of 1993, PSOE was increasingly beleaguered and on the defensive as yet more scandals emerged. In March 1996, after an extraordinary lengthy tenure in government, Felipe González and his party lost the elections to the Partido Popular. Spain had a new prime minister, José

María Aznar. The pendulum had swung once again, and it had done so once more without blood.

Spain in the Twenty-First Century

The days of Franco are gone and the future for Spain looks secure. After many years of isolation, Spain has embraced democracy and opened its doors wide open to the new political and economic spirit of the European Union. Aznar's government faced many challenges as the 20th century drew to a close, yet Spain enjoyed a period of economic prosperity and mercifully saw some progress in reducing the number of the unemployed. With the inevitable replacement of the peseta by the European single currency, the euro, Spain has shown the world clearly that its future lies in Europe.

One of the greatest challenges facing the Spanish government as the new millennium dawned was the seemingly intractable problem of terrorism in the Basque Country. Sadly, attempts to negotiate an end to the hostilities by ETA continued to end in failure. The organization continued its violent and bloody campaign in the name of Basque independence, despite the clear message from the overwhelming majority of Basques, and the Spanish population at large, that enough was enough.

Nevertheless, Spain enjoys a reputation as a safe and vibrant country to live in and visit, and this ensures that it remains one of the most popular destinations for travelers in Europe. Of course, as we have seen, Spain's history encompasses not only its geographical boundaries, but is inextricably linked to the pasts of Europe, Africa, the Middle East, South America, the USA, and even South-East Asia. As a result, it has proved to be a fascinating example of how different peoples of the world have interacted with each other, shaping each others' identities and destinies. Despite the upheavals of its past and previous attempts to impose regional unity by force, Spain has paraxodically blossomed into a country united by its diversity, which it proudly displays for all to see.

As the world today grows ever smaller, particularly in a Western Europe that has embraced full political and economic unity, it is a cause for celebration to see that differences continue to thrive, making the world all the richer for it.

THE HISTORY OF NATIONS

Chapter 6

Contemporary Spain

The Basque Separatist Movement

By Miren Gutierrez

Miren Gutierrez is a freelance writer who contributes articles to
Gatopardo *in Colombia,* El País *in Spain, and United Press International (UPI) in Washington, D.C. In this article she traces the history of the Basque separatist movement, the ETA, and describes how it attempts to achieve its initially nationalistic goals through violent terrorist acts. ETA attacks, although against military and governmental targets, expanded to include civilians beginning in the 1970s. These tactics, while gaining the ETA support from alienated youth and other disgruntled members of Basque society, have cost the movement wider sympathy for its cause, particularly following the September 11, 2001, terrorist attacks on the United States. Today, the hope is that its goals of self-determination can be achieved without further violence and loss of life.*

With a leg on each side of the Pyrenees, the Basque Country ranges from the gentle mountain slopes of southern France and the rough Bay of Biscay on the Atlantic coast to the sophisticated cities of Bilbao—home to [architect] Frank Gehry's Guggenheim Museum—and San Sebastián. This is also the last terrorist redoubt in Europe.

Fighting for a mixture of old-fashioned Marxism and secular nationalism, the group named Euskadi Ta Askatasuna (Basque Fatherland and Liberty) is still killing after forty years. ETA has murdered almost a thousand people, kidnapped seventy-seven and held the business class hostage by demanding and collecting millions of dollars in "revolutionary taxes." Those who refuse to pay face harassment, abduction or even death. Some 5,000 acts of po-

Miren Gutierrez, "Terror in the Pyrenees: ETA Is Losing Legitimacy, but Many Basques Still Feel Unable to Condemn It," *The Nation,* vol. 274, March 25, 2002, p. 20. Copyright © 2002 by The Nation Magazine/The Nation Company, Inc. Reproduced by permission.

litically motivated vandalism—targeting banks, public property and government offices—were linked to ETA between 1996 and 2000. The organization is on the US State Department's updated list of global terrorist organizations, along with Hamas and Al Qaeda. Last November [2001] London and Washington announced they would freeze ETA's foreign bank accounts, along with those of twenty-four other terrorist organizations, and in February, the Bush Administration blocked the assets of twenty-one people linked to ETA.

ETA's violent struggle for its goal of an independent homeland comprising the seven Basque provinces (four in Spain and three in France) continues even as today the Basque Country enjoys considerable autonomy within the Spanish polity. Spanish policemen have been mostly replaced by Basque officers, who are often welcomed as a buffer between the people and the terrorists. The Basque language is taught in schools and widely spoken. The Basque Country collects its own taxes and pays for central government services; controls the educational, judicial and health systems; and has its own premier and Parliament.

Yet, as Spanish Prime Minister José María Aznar says, the "Basque question" remains the single most important issue in Spanish politics. The two main parties, the conservative ruling Popular Party (PP) and the Spanish Socialist Party (PSOE), refuse to negotiate with ETA unless it renounces violence. In the wake of the September 11 terrorist attacks in the United States, the government has cracked down harder on the group. And with Spain chairing the European Union since January, Madrid has intensified diplomatic pressure on nations that have in the past given ETA members a safe haven.

ETA was founded in 1959, during the fascist dictatorship of Gen. Francisco Franco, by students who were disgruntled at the moderation of the Basque Nationalist Party (PNV) in the struggle for independence. Its first military action was in 1961—an unsuccessful attempt to derail a train carrying war veterans. The police responded with repression. Many Basques went into exile, while others joined ETA's struggle. "Thousands [of Basque nationalists] were tortured under Franco. Once it is in your body, it doesn't go away," says Joseba Zulaika, an expert on terrorism at the University of Nevada. "They are unable to condemn ETA, because it represents the Basque military response to Spanish fascism, even twenty-seven years after Franco died."

Nowadays ETA's funding comes primarily from supporters' donations and from extortion, kidnapping ransoms and armed robberies. The money is used to finance assassinations, bombings and other urban guerrilla attacks. Even though the group's rhetoric is Marxist, it behaves like a fascist organization, and it is often compared to one. It gets its basic support from alienated youth, who in another country would probably become skinheads. Social bile, the exhilarating feeling of power and destruction, and dogma absorbed in many cases at home and at school, are what attract new recruits. The new generations are increasingly in charge of the organization and have gradually distanced themselves from the founding leaders. Authorities estimate that only 200 active members—distributed in commando cells—make up the band, and another 2,500 supporters provide them with shelter and infrastructure. According to Manuel Huertas, secretary general of the PSOE in Guipúzcoa province, "ETA is hiding behind the independence flag" but is devoid of ideology. (Recently seized ETA documents name Huertas as an assassination target.)

ETA has expanded the scope of its victims beyond police and the military to include local civilians. They call this policy the "socialization of suffering." The idea is to exert pressure on different groups so they will demand that the government negotiate. In response, successive governments in Madrid have resorted to state terrorism. During the democratic transition in the 1970s, the infamous Basque-Spanish Battalions killed twenty-nine people supposedly linked to ETA. In the 1980s, under Felipe González's PSOE government, the Antiterrorist Liberation Group killed twenty-eight, some of them innocent bystanders. Disclosures of what became known as the "dirty war" helped defeat the PSOE in the 1996 general elections, paving the way for the ascension of Aznar's PP.

In 1998 ETA unilaterally declared a cease-fire after a police campaign that left it vulnerable. This action brought on the collapse of an anti-ETA alliance among the democratic parties. The PNV took as a partner Our Basque Country (EH), at the time ETA's political arm. This should have paved the way for peace talks, but there was too much lingering distrust. The Interior Minister at the time, Jaime Mayor Oreja, who was in charge of antiterrorism policy, dubbed the cease-fire a "truce trap." It was later discovered that ETA had been rearming in France, but Zulaika of the University of Nevada points out that the truce was also marred by the arrest of one of ETA's two negotiators. "Madrid didn't want [talks] to succeed. And the rearming gave reason to those who were suspicious," he says. "But peace was alarming, because ETA's terrorism is much easier to handle. After all, it is only one killing every two weeks. [Without peace] Madrid keeps the moral legitimacy, goes on being the guarantor of law and order, and maintains international support. In peace, nationalists could do anything!" When the truce collapsed in November 1999, so did the alliance between the EH and the PNV.

Antiterrorism Sentiments

The September 11 [2001] terrorist attacks in the United States, and the revulsion against terrorism kindled by those attacks, had a strong impact on the Spanish government's fight against ETA. The repression-first approach regained some of its luster both at home and abroad, and Madrid has made strong demands for cooperation from European Union members, some of whom have in the past treated ETA as a nationalist organization deserving respect and protection rather than as a terrorist group whose members should be extradited to face criminal justice. Thousands of demonstrators took to the streets on November 8 [2001] to protest the assassination of a Basque judge, José María Lidón the previous day. The murder came just one day after a car bomb in Madrid injured nearly 100 people. An anonymous eyewitness who tailed the terrorists helped to catch them.

Since the end of the cease-fire in 1999, eighteen ETA commando units have been broken up and fifteen members have been arrested, among them the "historic leader" Iñaki de Renteria, considered the head of the organization. After September 11, the rhythm of arrests in Spain and France has accelerated, but there have also been police failures and counterstrikes: On October 31 [2001] twelve members of an organization that provides ETA prisoners with legal assistance were detained, accused of terrorism. In France the police failed to capture the leader of that group, Juan María Olano, when he appeared in a demonstration, even though there was an international warrant for his arrest. He was detained later. Also in October, a pro-ETA, balaclava-helmeted throng attacked San Sebastián City Hall with Molotov cocktails, and a car loaded with eighty-eight pounds of explosives was detonated in the main Court House of Vitoria. Both sites were under police protection. No one was arrested.

Recalling incidents like Olano's initial escape, socialist Huertas says, "If the international community stops providing shelter to the terrorists, and the [nationalist] PNV takes a firm line, we are on the road to peace. But first the PNV must be willing to share the risks of becoming the terrorists' targets" by more vigorously opposing ETA. He believes that a firmer stand by Juan José Ibarretxe's PNV nationalist government in Basque Country can help Spanish endeavors in Europe, where some countries still see the nationalist struggle with sympathy.

Hopes for Peace

In search of a solution for a problem that has cost not only many lives but also 10 percent of the Basque Country's per capita gross domestic product (GDP) politicians of all stripes have tried to crack the same obstinate riddle: Which comes first, peace or self-determination? Basque Premier Ibarretxe has suggested that both aims can be sought simultaneously. He tried to revitalize the coalition of the democratic anti-ETA parties that disintegrated after ETA's cease-fire, initiating a debate on pacification in October. But in Madrid Aznar remains adamant. "I have nothing to state on the question of self-determination," he has said. The understanding among some local constitutionalists, as those nonnationalists who support the 1978 Spanish Constitution are known, is that sovereignty for Basque Country can be a subject of future talks, even if they do not agree with it. But peace must come first. "How can we talk? We cannot articulate with pistols in our mouths," complains Huertas.

Last October ETA issued a communiqué in which it said, "Peace is possible, of course it is, and ETA's hand will always be open," but only if Madrid and Paris allowed a vote on independence for the region. "ETA demands no more than this." Only ETA's followers took the message as a bona fide offer, and a day after the announcement a small bomb exploded close to a car belonging to a member of the Civil Guard, Spain's public security force. Later a bomb exploded in Madrid, and then Judge Lidón was shot at point-blank range. Considering its latest strikes, ETA does not seem to be redefining itself. Most of the people I interviewed place their hopes either on the police campaign against ETA or on the proposed talks on self-determination, which would make the terrorists even more obsolete and out of touch.

There are signs of hope, though. One was the sight, after Judge Lidón's murder, of Basque Premier Ibarretxe marching against ETA alongside his defeated opponents in last May's [May 2000] elections, Jaime Mayor Oreja of Aznar's PP, and PSOE president José Luis Rodríguez Zapatero. Another is meeting people like Cristina Cuesta, who was 20 years old when ETA assassinated her father. She is the spokesperson of a pro-peace NGO [nongovernmental organization]. "Society would be generous with ETA if they gave up arms," she says. "I am a republican, but I don't defend my ideas shooting against monarchists. When terror stops, we can talk about anything."

The Gibraltar Conflict

By JOE GARCIA

Joe Garcia is the editor of the Gibraltar daily Panorama. *He traces the history of Gibraltar from the Muslim occupation in 711 to the present day and describes the conflict over possession of "the Rock." Although the British maintain nominal possession of Gibraltar, the territory has been largely autonomous since the 1980s, when the British delegated powers to the Gibraltarians, making it self-governing in internal affairs. Spain, however, has always asserted a claim to Gibraltar and is still pressing for sovereignty. Currently, the British are negotiating with the Spanish regarding possession of the Rock—despite the wishes of the Gibraltarians themselves, who desire to remain British—in the hopes of strengthening ties with Madrid.*

One foot separates Gibraltar from Spain, that being the distance between the Spanish and the British frontier gates. You show your passport to the Spanish border guard and then, before you pass through, to the British guard as well. You are now leaving the Spanish town of La Linea to step upon the world's biggest pebble, the majestic Rock of Gibraltar, rising almost perpendicularly from sea level to some 1,400 feet at its highest point. This limestone rock of Jurassic age is the lasting symbol of British imperialism, and of injured Spanish pride at having lost it to the British 300 years ago. . . .

Now, as the saying goes, you can feel as safe as the Rock of Gibraltar, but you begin to wonder as the London-like red double-decker bus begins its journey on the only road into downtown Gibraltar—which incredibly cuts across the airfield runway. The barrier is down and the jetliner from London roars as its tires grip onto an airstrip resembling an oversized aircraft carrier. Beyond Winston Churchill Avenue and an old Moorish

Joe Garcia, "The Rock Gets Rolled," *The National Interest*, Fall 2002, pp. 119–26.

castle is the town, which nestles on the western slopes, rising from the one-time busy naval harbor to what is now essentially a commercial and cruise ship terminal. Gibraltar is populated by 30,000 people who call it their homeland, their country.

This tiny outpost of empire is the last remaining colony in Europe, as its claimant, Spain, likes to say. It occupies just under three square miles of the Iberian peninsula, but within its minuscule dimensions it squeezes two cathedrals, four synagogues, two mosques and a Hindu temple. There are 19 banks and nearly as many companies as there are people. About 300 apes roam in the wild, as well. The homegrown Royal Gibraltar Regiment is the Rock's largest military unit; its police force is over 200-strong and is the second oldest in Britain and the Commonwealth. Gibraltar is the leading bunkering port in the Western Mediterranean and, of course, it commands the strategic Strait of Gibraltar, which separates Europe from Africa.

Just what is so important about this shining stone in the British Crown, whose intriguing past gives credence to the notion that fact can be stranger (and also more irritating) than fiction? A case can be made that its importance lies mostly in the realm of military history. But that is not how the people of Gibraltar see things today, as the British government seeks to deal away their sovereign identity and sense of repose to Spain, for equities having to do with the internal diplomacy of the European Union. Gibraltar is not about grand strategy and military history anymore; as its homeborn see it, it is about integrity, about right and wrong. It is less dramatic than sieges, wars and competitive espionage, yes; does that also make it less important?

Strait and Narrow

It all started when a Moorish leader conquered the place in 711 C.E. and gave his name to it: *Gebel Tarik*, the mountain of Tarik. Battles raged, and the land changed hands on numerous occasions between the Moors and the Spanish, until 1704 when an Anglo-Dutch fleet conquered it. Under the Treaty of Utrecht in 1713 the Spanish Crown formally ceded sovereignty "in perpetuity" to the British Crown, but the Spanish were not particularly good to their word. Of the many sieges they staged over the years, pride of place goes to The Great Siege of 1779, which lasted three years, seven months and twelve days. The fortress, outnumbered four-to-one, was attacked with all manner of Spanish contraptions, including floating batteries, which gave the British the idea of setting them ablaze by firing red-hot cannon balls from vantage points along Gibraltar's rocky promontory. After 200,000 shots rained down, the Spanish backed off, and there followed a long period of peace. British Gibraltar became an impregnable fortress.

Through war and peace, the native Gibraltarians emerged. "In this small corner of the world there lives today a people of amazingly mixed stock who represent a fusion of very many races ... basically Genoese, but with much inter-marriage between Spaniards, Portuguese, Minorcans, Italians, persons from the British Isles, Maltese, Jews and many races of Northern Europe," wrote then-British Governor and Commander-in-Chief, General Sir Kenneth Anderson in 1950. Under British protection, this eclectically composed population increased by leaps and bounds. As it did, the British had the penchant of dividing the population into as many classes as they could think of: By 1777, in the 3,000-plus population, residents were known as "British Blood Native Protestant" and "British Blood Non-Native Protestant." There were also "Alien Blood Native Roman Catholics" and a wide range of combinations. By the next century the classifications had been simplified to "British from Britain," "British from Gibraltar" and "Aliens." (Nowadays, we have "Gibraltarians," "Other British" and "Non British.") With no wars to fight, life must have been something of a bore, so the British decided in 1830 that their battle-scarred fortress would henceforth become a Crown Colony (which, unknown at the time, was to provoke a war of words with the Spanish in years to come, for Gibraltar ended up being listed at the United Nations as a colony to be decolonized). So it remained in relative peace for over a century, serving as sentry post for the British Navy over the strait and narrow separating Europe from North Africa.

World War II then brought great change and sacrifice. Military considerations helped make Gibraltar into a city-within-a-city, with tunnels being hewn inside the Rock. A self-contained, underground fortress emerged, with its own power and water supplies, even a hospital. Testimony to the scale of the operation is that there are 35 miles of subterranean roads—more roads inside than outside the Rock. As the weekly dances for military men and women proceeded, the British secret agent Donald Darling recalled that "alarming explosions from within the bowels of the Rock, where Canadian tunnelers worked day and night, interrupted the syncopation of 'The Big Noise from Winetka' or the 'Anniversary Waltz.'" Meanwhile, the lorries, piled high with stones blasted out by the tunnelers, were driven downhill toward the airfield, to be used for its extension into the (still) disputed waters of the bay.

The war effort led to Britain's half of the narrow, low-lying isthmus that links the Rock to mainland Spain being used initially as an emergency landing ground. The then-Governor recalled having received a proposal: "I propose, with Your Excellency's concurrence, to issue an order warning pilots that, should a forced landing be necessary, they are to bear in mind that there may be men working here or in the firing trenches, that cattle may be grazing and people exercising horses." These were the kind of impediments General [Dwight] Eisenhower could do without as his aircraft touched down on Gibraltar in November 1942. He was to command Operation Torch, the invasion of North Africa: the first major Anglo-American amphibious campaign and a turning point in the struggle against Nazi Germany. Eisenhower was installed in what the British called "an office in the maritime headquarters," but which his own aides described as a "cramped, damp, 8-by-8 foot cubbyhole" deep inside the Rock, and accessible only through a tunnel as dark as night.

German agents spied relentlessly on the Allied command in Gibraltar through powerful telescopes from the Spanish port of Algeciras just five miles across the bay. The reason was clear: more than 400 aircraft lay crammed wingtip to wingtip on the airstrip, and warships kept coming in and out. But the Germans were deceived into thinking that the military build-up was intended to relieve besieged Malta, or to prepare a limited landing . . . in Libya. Even before Eisenhower's arrival, however, Gibraltar's importance to the Allied cause had not escaped [Nazi leader Adolf] Hitler's attention. As early as 1940, Hitler had issued Directive No. 18, code-named "Operation Felix"—the German plan to invade the Iberian peninsula, capture Gibraltar and drive the British out of the Western Mediterranean. Hitler was offering the Spanish dictator, General Francisco Franco, the prize of a Spanish Gibraltar, but Spain's demands escalated and the plan was not activated. Speaking in Nuremberg prison, Hermann Goering said that the most damaging mistake to German fortunes was Hitler's failure to march through Spain, with or without Franco's assent, "capture Gibraltar and spill into Africa.... [I]t would have altered the whole course of the war." In February 1945, Hitler admitted: "... we ought to have attacked Gibraltar in the summer of 1940." Indeed, such an attack, as [British prime minister Winston] Churchill himself put it at the time, would have been extremely dangerous.

The exigencies of war led to the entire population, except able-bodied men, being evacuated "for their safety" to places such as bombed-out London. Those who stayed behind initiated vociferous campaigns calling for the repatriation of their loved ones; when they returned after the war they did so all the wiser, having experienced the wider world "out there." As the population bulged after V-E [Victory in Europe] Day, there were more people about to make their weight felt in a new fight for civil and political liberties. Then, suddenly it seemed, the colonial masters allowed the emergence of political parties, workers' unions and the publication of newspapers without a license from the military governor. The Gibraltarians' political emancipation was soon crowned by the visit of the Duke of Edinburgh in 1950 to inaugurate the Gibraltar legislature, the forerunner of today's 17-seat parliament.

Whether this trip irritated General Franco is not a matter of clear public record, but the visit of the recently enthroned Queen Elizabeth II, just four years later, certainly did. By the mid-1960s, Franco had explicitly renewed Spain's quest for Gibraltar. His annexation plan received support at the UN General Assembly from the Soviet bloc, whose leaders in Moscow saw it as an opportunity to weaken the British presence in the Mediterranean and to roil NATO [North Atlantic Treaty Organization] cohesion. In 1968, the Spanish government sealed the land frontier, suspended maritime links and cut telephone communications. Except for a daily air link with London and a ferry service across the Strait to Tangier, Gibraltar was isolated. Thus did a modern siege of Gibraltar incarcerate the Gibraltarians in their small rock of a homeland.

Although Franco insisted that Gibraltar was not worth a war, the British took no chances. The British chiefs of staff believed that Spanish military aims could range from sabotage in the airfield area to the occupation of the whole colony, and they prepared countermeasures in meticulous detail. The level and manner of British response would have depended on the action taken by the Spaniards, but if this was to occupy the whole of Gibraltar, the British planned to attack Spanish forces on Spanish soil, waters and airspace. The situation was so potentially explosive that during a visit to London by President [Richard] Nixon in February 1969, the British appealed to him to dissuade Franco from engaging in military action. The British recognized the reluctance of the U.S. administration to involve itself in Anglo-Spanish problems on account of the American bases agreement with Spain, but they appealed to Nixon to "do what you can to persuade the Spaniards to adopt a policy that can get us out of our present deadlock, which is in the interest of neither country." Whatever messages were passed, Franco decided not to be rash.

Whose Gibraltar?

In February 1895, with Franco gone and democracy restored in Spain, the blockade was lifted. However, much to the chagrin of Madrid, the British had since devolved powers to the Gibraltarians, making the Rock self-governing in internal affairs, with Britain largely responsible only for foreign affairs, defense and internal security. Any transfer of sovereignty to Spain would have to be sanctioned by the Gibraltarians themselves, as stated in the British assurance in the preamble to the 1969 Gibraltar Constitution. That would seem to render moot the fact that the Treaty of Utrecht came with the proviso that Gibraltar would revert to Spain should Britain ever abrogate the treaty. Gibraltarians have held for years that the Rock is not Spain's to claim *or* Britain's to give away—echoing a phrase coined by a former British Governor, General Sir William Jackson. "Utrecht is not worth the paper on which it was written," chorus all five of the political parties here, meaning that such an archaic document cannot deny them the right to self-determination. Anyway, they tell you, a number of sieges by the Spanish broke the treaty, and it is so antiquated that, for example, it prohibits Jews from living here—even though many Jews who do live here can trace their ancestry back several centuries. . . .

The assurance inscribed in the Gibraltar Constitution has now become a matter of urgent practical interest. At London's behest, Britain and Spain initiated serious negotiations in July 2001 seeking to overcome all their centuries-long differences over the Rock. The proposed deal includes the retention by the Gibraltarians of British citizenship, respect for their British way of life and greater self-government, but also some yet-to-be-specified form of joint sovereignty with Spain. Gibraltarians would have the final say, promised Prime Minister Tony Blair. Said Gibraltar's opposition leader, Joe Bossano, British Foreign Minister Jack Straw has told us that "this 'skeleton' will be 'fleshed out' by Gibraltarian participation in subsequent negotiations."

But Bossano demurs. "Our position," he said, "is that Britain has no right to enter into such arrangements to make concessions on sovereignty." In this he is as one with the Gibraltar chief minister, Peter Caruana, who has repeatedly accused the British Foreign Office of betrayal. "It is," he said, "a violation of Gibraltar's political rights for the Foreign Office to do deals above our heads which stay on the table even if we reject them in referendum. The UK parliament is opposed to this, as is British public opinion." This is true. "Sovereignty shared is sovereignty surrendered,"

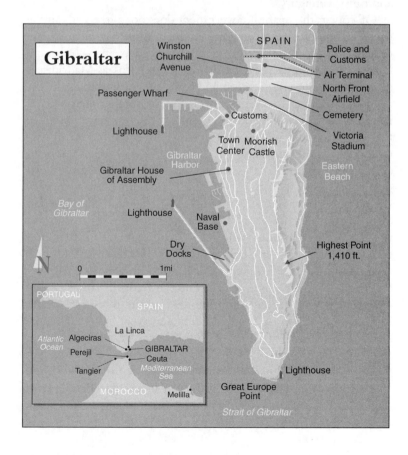

said Michael Ancram, the Conservative Party's foreign affairs spokesman; and a Gibraltar government advertising campaign in the British press elicited nearly 400,000 messages of support. Not surprisingly, then, Gibraltarians gave Mr. Straw a noteworthy reception when he visited Gibraltar on May 3; he was "hailed" as a traitor by rowdy British flag-waving protestors.

To put not too fine a point on it, Gibraltarians are furious that Britain has been negotiating the thorny issue of sovereignty with Spain in the full knowledge that the Gibraltarians are against it. Virtually the whole population have taken part in pro-British demonstrations to make the point as visible as possible, and to support the October 2001 "Declaration of Unity" (by past and present members of the Gibraltar House of Assembly) which stated, *inter alia:* "The people of Gibraltar will never, ever, compromise or give up our inalienable right to self-determination . . . and our sovereignty."

Of course, the Spanish government does not agree with any of this. The question of sovereignty is a matter for Britain and Spain only, said Josep Piqué before being replaced as Spanish foreign minister in a cabinet reshuffle in July [2002]. It is, as Madrid sees it, a matter of de-colonization and Spain's territorial integrity. . . .

Spain's motives for wanting to recover Gibraltar are obvious. But why did Britain's Labor government request negotiations in the first place, and why does it persist with them in face of virtually unanimous opposition in Gibraltar? Everyone in Gibraltar agrees that Britain wants to strike a deal with Spain because London thinks that its interests in the European Union are best served by a closer relationship with Madrid—and the Gibraltar dispute stands in the way. The Spaniards, forever clamoring for the Rock's return but without any real expectation of being taken seriously, could not believe their luck when British officials suggested to them a sovereignty deal over Gibraltar in return for an Anglo-Spanish alliance to counter the dominant Franco-German axis in the European Union. (The plot thickened when, in March [2002], the EU offered Gibraltar what has been generally described as a "bribe" of £35 million as an inducement not to fuss if a deal is struck; "Gibraltar is not for sale," answered Mr. Caruana.) In a UK parliamentary debate in June [2002], the British Labor government's Minister for Europe, Peter Hain, made London's motive plain enough: "Our alliance with Spain in Europe is helping us to deliver a European Union of strong nations . . . however, that relationship remains constrained by the Gibraltar dispute. . . . [W]e must fix the issue."

Given such a rationale, most observers believed that British capitulation to Spain would not take long. Such expectations, however, have not been realized. After Blair and the Spanish Prime Minister José Maria Aznar met in London in May [2002], they let it be known that "difficulties" had arisen. The difficulties center on three points: Spanish insistence that the door of joint sovereignty should be left open, leading possibly to full Spanish sovereignty in the future; the question of Spain's involvement in a British military base; and Spain's concern about a referendum being held in Gibraltar. (Madrid fears that a referendum could be interpreted as an act of self-determination and lead separatists in the Basque region to demand one for themselves.) Seeing the British in such a pliant mood, the Spanish seem to have overreached.

That difficulties have arisen tend to cheer the Gibraltarians, but they remain active in pressing their case. For example, assurances by Foreign Office officials that, in any deal, Britain would retain complete operational control of the base, have not mollified critics. Indeed, a letter sent by the UK defense secretary Geoff Hoon to Mr. Straw, subsequently leaked to the British media, suggested that British strategic interests *were* being put at risk by the planned deal, that there was "growing concern among both British and American Armed Forces that any deal could damage the operational capability of the Rock's naval base and military airfield." The reason is that were the base to be treated like a U.S. base in Spain, as the Spanish government favors, questions asked would have to be answered, thus impairing the absolute freedom of maneuver now enjoyed by the British and American militaries in a community that has grown up in the shadow of a fortress and sees the military as a way of life. . . . The stakes, then, are not trivial. While the great British naval base, capable of handling repairs to warships as big as air craft carriers, is no longer, and while defense spending has dwindled [since the 1970s] from representing 70 percent of the local economy to a mere 7 percent, around 150 British warships have called at Gibraltar since April 1998. There is a staging post for the Royal Air Force, which is currently undertaking an £8 million refurbishment of the airfield. About one hundred training exercises take place annually, including submarine exercises in the deep waters around the Rock. The use of nuclear berthing facilities is a key activity, as well. The Rock also continues to be the "ears and eyes" of the British—and by extension of the Americans—in an area of the world where potential trouble spots abound. The United States has communications interests here, and the Rock is used by U.S. Marines for training. (Strong Anglo-American influence in the Strait is perhaps why Al-Qaeda chose it as a terrorist target, before timely arrests this past summer [2002] in Morocco apparently foiled their plans.) American interests are quietly looked after by a solitary U.S. liaison officer, whose operational center lies deep inside a tunnel not far from where General Eisenhower commanded Operation Torch. The status of the Rock still matters, not just to the people of Gibraltar, but to the United States, as well.

Is there light at the end of the diplomatic tunnel for this centuries-old Anglo-Spanish confrontation? Proposals by a former chief minister, Sir Robert Peliza, to fully integrate Gibraltar with Britain were rejected by the British Government in the 1970s. The concept of Gibraltar becoming a "Royal City State" within the European Union was promoted in 1992 by the Gibraltar Liberal Party, but without success. Now, a thorough revision of the Constitution has been undertaken by an all-party committee of the mini-parliament here to remove the remaining vestiges of colonialism and gain greater self-government within the British umbrella. But Gibraltarians do not want to boot the British off the Rock and, indeed, any proposed constitutional change will be put to London.

Meanwhile, as Britain and Spain persevere with their talks over joint sovereignty for Gibraltar, Mr. Caruana has opined that the Andorra model may be the sort of solution Gibraltarians could support. He says this not because he wants to be a prince, but because the Principality of Andorra, sandwiched between France and Spain high up in the Pyrenees (those other rocks), "represents full self-determination for the people of Andorra, with sovereignty vested in its people." He added: "Andorra is in no sense a part of Spain nor of Spanish sovereignty. It is an autonomous territory." So what is the problem? "Unfortunately, the modern Andorra model is unacceptable to Spain," Mr. Caruana told me in his Convent Place office. Madrid does not accept self-determination or real autonomy for Gibraltar.

Nonetheless, the Gibraltar government has decided to go it alone and organize an internationally-supervised referendum in late October [2002]. It is understood as a pre-emptive strike against the looming Anglo-Spanish deal "to make Gibraltar's view on joint or any Spanish sovereignty absolutely clear," as Mr. Caruana puts it. Madrid has condemned the Rock's proposed referendum, *and so has London*. So Gibraltar and its people face yet another siege—only this time the British government is not standing like a rock on their behalf. It rather seems reduced to gravel.

Spanish Society Today: Continuity and Change

By Stephen Hugh-Jones

Journalist Stephen Hugh-Jones surveys the changes Spanish society has undergone during the past twenty-five years. Economically, Spain has seen tremendous growth in recent years, particularly after joining the European Union. There have been significant advances in education, television has become a cultural mainstay in Spain, and the roles of men and women have undergone important changes as well. Women in contemporary Spanish society enjoy greater freedom and opportunity. They are more visible in the public sphere, participating in the business world, politics, and higher education. For men, there has been an increase in the sharing of domestic responsibilities.

What sort of society has emerged from the multiple influences of the past 25 years? A far richer one, of course, with more schooling and skills, better jobs, millions of cars, TV sets, mobile phones, holidays abroad: in sum, much like any in Western Europe—that is, greatly altered, in a very short time. But deeper down? Yes, greatly altered too.

Especially for women. Today, some 60% of university students are women, if only 30% of lecturers and 10% of top-level professors. In business, Ms Botin, the banker's daughter, now an e-business venture capitalist in her own right, is far from alone: on official figures, 30% of Spanish businesses are headed by women. Not the big firms, it is true; and unemployment among women is double that among men. Still, what a change from Franco's day, when a wife needed her husband's say-so to go out to work or

Stephen Hugh-Jones, "A Radically New Society," *The Economist*, vol. 357, November 25, 2000, p. 9. Copyright © 2000 by The Economist Newspaper Group. Reproduced by permission.

open a bank account. In politics likewise, Mrs Martinez, of the Andalusian parliament, is far from alone; and [Spain's prime minister] Mr [José María] Aznar has raised women in his cabinet at least as high as [British prime minister] Tony Blair has.

As for family life, the new PSOE [Spanish Socialist Party] leader still won loud applause recently urging Spain's men to share in household tasks. Like men elsewhere, they still beat their partners, and sometimes murder them. Women's complaints of domestic violence indeed have been rising fast. But is that because there is more of it, or because women are readier to speak out? One regional premier set off a lively debate in October [2000] calling for men guilty of violence toward their partners to be publicly "named and shamed".

The statistics of a happier side of life speak volumes. In 1975, the birth rate was much the same as in 1945; today it is half as much. Thank the contraceptive pill, banned in Franco's day, but now widely used. The morning-after pill is not yet on sale; when it is, Andalusia's health service will supply it to any woman over 13. Parliament this autumn debated plans to recognize de-facto married couples, including same-sex ones. The PP [Popular Party] said no; but it, and even the church, would accept a civil contract which, notably, would confer pension rights. Like it or not, all this represents a huge change.

Tolerance is wide. The old savagery of political division has gone. Except at its loony fringe, Basque nationalism rests less on abuse of "them" than the Scottish sort, and against Basques as such, arouses none: when Seville or Madrid march against some ETA [terrorist group] killing, the slogan is *Vascos si, ETA no*. When a homosexual army colonel—a lawyer, it's true, not a tank commander—recently came out, it was a two-day wonder, even in the army (which, in turn, faces little of the dislike inherited from Franco's days).

The immigrants who flock ashore in the south, however, or drift round Barcelona's historic centre, are testing this new tolerance. Opposition parties dislike a tough law planned by Mr Aznar that would draw a sharp line between legal and illegal newcomers. But, as he says, no society has limitless capacity for integration. Some incidents, not only in the south, suggest Spain's is under strain. [In 1999] 430 tonnes of cannabis were seized, 80% of it in Andalusia, and 18 tonnes of cocaine. No one pretends all this was just in transit to countries farther north:

Spain has a big drug problem, with 90,000 arrests last year [1999], but there is evidence for those who want to believe that outsiders and crime go together.

Education, the Media, and Their Uses

The future, as everywhere, lies with two things above all: education, nearly all in regional hands; and the communication that spreads, adds to or destroys it. In both fields, the news is good and bad.

In the schools, Spain has a tiff of its own, over the way Spanish history gets swamped by the regional sort. But it also faces questions raised in many other countries. Are there too many options, not enough core curriculum? And, in the later years of school, what exactly should count as core?

Spain extended compulsory schooling from age 14 to 16 by a law of 1990. The extra two years were introduced gradually. Now one effect is plain: that some kids don't want them. The education minister, Pilar del Castillo, wants to steer these into practical things or vocational training, rather than toward the pre-university baccalaureate. Better for them, she feels, better for Spain, certainly. In 1991 it had 890,000 students in post-school vocational training, today—and not merely because school lasts longer—only 520,000. Even so, in Galicia this autumn [2000], say trade unions there, half of those who wanted vocational training could not get into the course of their choice.

Meanwhile, university numbers have soared; at Madrid's Complutense to 86,000. This, at least, must be good news? Not wholly. Many study only for lack of a job; some are no good at it. Andalusia today has ten universities; too many, hints even an enthusiast for the region's development. Traditional pride in "my son at the university"—often studying that other great Latin tradition, law—cannot easily be redirected into, say, biotechnology or hotel management. The result is an economy crying out for skills, notably in informatics, yet with more graduates than jobs for them.

So be more practical, says Mrs del Castillo. The left suspects discrimination, calling for more bursaries, more social and regional levelling up, and less of what it calls favouring the semi-public sector. And the youngsters themselves? Young Spaniards are wild about the Internet, and learn English from the age of four—indeed the Basque Country, already teaching in two languages, is experimenting with teaching senior classes in English as well.

Yet where does all this education lead? Watch Spanish television and, as anywhere else, you can despair: football apart, this year's rage was "*Gran Hermano*" (*Big Brother*). The press, in contrast, offers lots of weeklies "of the heart" but no dailies of the gutter, just sober regionals, and national papers which read as if all Spaniards were postgraduates in world, Spanish and regional politics. A sharp bout of newsprint-rationing would do the big dailies no harm. Except on Sunday, few people buy them: *El País* leads with 440,000 weekday sales. The reason, it is said, is that Spaniards read papers in the bar, and then mostly for local news. Spain's oldest daily, the *Faro de Vigo*, worries about the port, the mayor and traffic in the *gran via*. On weekdays it sells 33,000 copies in a city of 300,000.

Yet among young adults, only one in seven claims to read any printed medium at all. The real moulder of society—though not of politics—is television: nine public-sector providers (two central, seven regional), two main private channels, plus Canal Plus, a subscription outfit with a digital associate. TVE-1, the state's main channel, gets about 25% of viewers, private Antena 3 and Tele-5 around 20% apiece. Viewers say the public-sector stations are politically biased. In opposition, the PP denounced RTVE, the provider of both state channels. In office, the party put pals in charge of it three times; number three is now a minister, the government spokesman. In turn, Andalusia's socialist Mr Chaves has just sent his spokesman to run the region's channel.

Change may be on the way, however. RTVE is about to join other state businesses under the wing of SEPI. That normally means a shake-up, write-offs, then privatisation. Not for us, say RTVE; and given its debts of $3.6 billion (and rising), that may prove true. Madrid province wants to privatise its channel, Catalonia ought to, if anyone will take on its $500m debt. But anyway there is choice. The Prisa group, publisher of the faintly leftish *El País*, is active in TV and radio. So, in a smaller way, is Recoletos, a subsidiary of Britain's Pearson group that publishes the firmly right-wing *El Mundo*. The monarchist *ABC* is looking for a digital channel. Telefonica has TV and radio interests, and, like every other publisher, is into the Internet. A more justified complaint, though only puritans make it, would be of television's inescapable outpouring of junk. What satellites and the web will do to that is for prophets to say.

An Enduring Force

Yet much endures. Witness the most enduring (and moulding) force of Spain's past 1,000 years: the church. Go to Saturday evening mass in Nervion, a middling suburb of Seville, and you may wonder. The big 19th-century church of the Immaculate Conception is far from crowded. Half the worshippers are women over 50. Is this really, as one bishop says, still "a profoundly Christian country"?

Profoundly, no; but was it ever, even at the peak of ecclesiastical power? Widely, yes. A congregation of around 100 is no packed house, but it is still five times what you would find at such a service in London. In Andalusia, 90% of people call themselves believers, 20% churchgoers. The church has a university centre in Seville, and a seminary with over 75 trainee priests, three times as many as in the 1980s.

Nor is this special to the south. Basques are zealous Catholics; when Pope John Paul II this autumn [2000] canonised a Basque saint, that region's chief minister went to Rome to kiss the papal ring. Barcelona's Gaudi church of the Holy Family may be a wonder of architecture, not religion, but it is pilgrims, not just tourists, who pack Santiago de Compostela, and many of them come from other parts of Spain. Even now, about 40% of Spanish children go to church schools. This is very different from ex-Catholic France or even Italy.

That is odd. For Spain too was torn by the old liberal-clerical divide, and both more recently and far more violently than they. As the priest of Nervion remarks, Franco was profoundly religious "in the old style", and his rebels saw the civil war as, in part, a crusade against godless communism, with some cause. Andalusia's peasants, and urban workers in many places, were deeply anticlerical; early in the war, thousands of clerics were murdered.

Most of the hierarchy readily kissed the future *caudillo*'s ring, and the church was later entwined with the regime, until Franco's last decade. Except maybe in the Basque Country, where it resisted Franco's centralising zeal, the church might have felt a fierce backlash after his fall. That did not happen. The democrats, conservatives and Socialists alike, agreed to maintain Franco's concordat with Rome (which gives the state a say in naming bishops, while the church gets a modest subsidy—and needs it: laden with priceless buildings and works of art, it is short of cash). And what the state accepts, society does, because the church has changed. Though it speaks out on social issues such as abortion, it steers clear of party politics. Our priest and bishop alike talk with enthusiasm of the Vatican Council. Ask about the Muslim immigrants, and their response is that of any sensible cleric in France or Britain.

Today, in Spain as elsewhere, the church's problem is indifference, or, at best, a faith that the believers do not choose to show. But even now, in an indigent parish, the priest is still called upon to be the local problem-solver. In Andalusia's villages, says the priest of the Immaculate Conception, you will see more of the village at mass than you would have done 60 years ago. (He is old enough to remember.) And a nationwide survey found 28% of young people calling themselves practising Catholics.

New Monarchy, Not So Many New Men

In sum, Spain offers humanity's usual mixture of change and continuity, but in unusual proportions.

Change? Take the monarchy: another ancient institution like the church, in far deeper discredit 70 years ago, yet now more widely respected than perhaps at any time since 1800. Why? Because it too is new. . . .

And continuity? Well, for all the changes, perhaps it is time Spain's women mounted a revolution of their own. According to the survey mentioned above, only 10% of young women aspired first and foremost to home and children. But 44% of young men aged 15–29 said they never did any housework, and 18% did not even make their own bed.

CHRONOLOGY

B.C.

40,000s
First humans appear on Iberian Peninsula.

1600s
Iberian immigration into Spain.

1000s
Phoenicians begin to establish colonies along the east and south coasts of Spain.

900
Celtic people move into Spain.

600
Greeks land in Spain and set up trading posts.

400s
Carthage, an African city, conquers most of Spain.

200s
Hannibal, a Carthaginian general, attacks Italy from Spain.

218–201
The Romans drive out the Carthaginian forces and conquer Spain.

A.D.

Late 300s
Christianity becomes the official religion of the Spain province; the Roman Empire splits in two. Spain becomes a part of the Western Roman Empire.

409
Germanic invasions begin.

476
The Western Roman Empire collapses.

480s
The Visigoths invade Spain and conquer the entire peninsula.

711
Arabs and Berbers (Moors) from northern Africa invade Spain.

718
The Moors conquer the Visigoths and establish Muslim al-Andalus. Pelayo stops the Moors at Covadonga.

755–1031
The Umayyad dynasty rules Muslim Spain.

801
Charlemagne and the Franks establish the county of Barcelona in western Spain.

840s
Navarre achieves independence.

850s
Christians reoccupy the region of Castile.

879
Independent Catalonia is established.

910
León becomes a kingdom.

929–1031
The caliphate of Córdoba exists, the height of Muslim power in al-Andalus.

970–1035
Most of Christian Spain is united by Sancho III the Great.

1008–1086
Muslim power begins to wane, and al-Andalus splits into *taifa* (faction-state) kingdoms.

1035
Castile and Aragon become kingdoms.

1043–1099
El Cid fights for the Christian reconquest of Spain.

1086–1143
Almoravids arrive from Morocco and establish power in al-Andalus, reuniting and strengthening Muslim rule.

1128
Portugal gains its independence.

1143
The Almoravid empire breaks up and the *taifa* kingdoms reemerge.

1156
Almohads from Morocco subjugate the *taifa* kingdoms.

1188
The first assembly of a *cortes* (parliament) in León.

1212
The kings of Castile, Aragon, and Portugal defeat Almohad at Las Navas de Tolosa.

1230
Castile and León are united under Ferdinand III.

1236–1252
Ferdinand III conquers Córdoba, Murcia, Jaen, and Seville.

1252–1492
The Muslim territory is reduced to the kingdom of Granada. The Christian kingdoms of Aragon, Navarre, and Castile control the rest of what is now Spain.

1282
The house of Aragon gains control over Sicily.

1323
Aragon conquers Sardinia.

1450–1556
The Spanish cultural renaissance takes place.

1469
Prince Ferdinand of Aragon marries Princess Isabella of Castile.

1474
Isabella becomes queen of Castile.

1479
Ferdinand becomes king of Aragon.

1478–1480
Ferdinand and Isabella establish the Spanish Inquisition, aimed at stamping out heresy among Spanish Christians. Converts from Judaism and Islam are particularly targeted.

1480
Isabella and Ferdinand begin to drive the Muslims from Granada.

1492
The Muslims of Granada are defeated; Spanish Jews who would not convert to Christianity are expelled from the country; Ferdinand and Isabella send Christopher Columbus on a voyage, which will take him to America. This signals the beginning of the Spanish Empire in the Americas.

1494
In the Treaty of Tordesillas, Portugal and Spain agree on a line that would divide the New World between the two countries.

1512
Ferdinand seizes the kingdom of Navarre, uniting all of Spain under his rule.

1513
Vasco Núñez de Balboa crosses Central America and becomes the first European to see the eastern shore of the Pacific Ocean.

1516
Charles I becomes king, bringing the lands of Belgium, the Netherlands, and Luxembourg into the Spanish Empire.

1519
Charles becomes the Holy Roman Emperor and is hereafter known as Charles V.

1521
Hernán Cortés conquers the Aztec nation in Mexico.

1533

Francisco Pizarro conquers the Incan Empire in South America.

1550

Spain controls Mexico, Central America, most of the West Indies, part of the southwestern United States, and much of western South America.

1556

Philip II becomes king.

1560s

The Netherlands rebels against Spanish rule.

1580

Philip invades and conquers Portugal.

1585–1604

Spain wages war with England.

1588

Philip launches the Spanish Armada against the English fleet, but English ships defeat the armada.

Late 1500s

Spain gains control of the Philippine Islands.

1609

The Muslims are expelled from Spain.

1618–1648

Spain finances the Thirty Years' War.

1635–1659

Spain goes to war with France.

1640–1655

The Catalans revolt.

1641

Portugal gains independence from Spain.

1700

Philip of Anjou, a French duke, becomes the heir to the Spanish throne and ascends as Philip V. He is the first Spanish ruler from the French Bourbon family.

1701
The War of Spanish Succession begins.

1714
The War of Spanish Succession ends. Philip remains king, but Spain loses all of its European territory. Aragon, Valencia, and Catalonia lose autonomy.

1763
Spain loses Florida to the United Kingdom.

1778
Spain joins France in fighting against England during the American Revolution.

1779
Spanish troops invade Florida.

1783
The American Revolutionary War ends with the Treaty of Paris. The treaty returns Florida to Spanish control and recognizes Spanish control of the island of Minorca.

1793–1795
Spain wages war against revolutionary France.

1798
British troops capture Minorca.

1802
Spain recaptures Minorca.

1808
French forces led by Napoleón invade Spain and gain control of the government. Napoleón makes his brother, Joseph Bonaparte, king of Spain; the Spanish begin to drive the French forces out during the Peninsular War.

1812
The Liberal Constitution is drafted by the Cortes of Cádiz.

1813
The French are driven out of the peninsula with the help of the English duke of Wellington.

1814

Ferdinand VII is returned to the throne. He rejects the constitution of 1812.

1816

Spain loses control of Argentina.

1820

Cádiz is ordered by Ferdinand to leave on an expedition to reconquer the American colonies. He refuses, and mutiny spreads quickly throughout the country.

1821

Spain cedes Florida to the United States.

1823

With the help of French troops, Ferdinand puts down the uprising.

1825

Spain loses all of its overseas possessions except Cuba, Puerto Rico, the Philippines, Guam, and some outposts in Africa.

1833

Isabella II becomes queen, but her regent, Maria Christina, rules with liberal support.

1833–1839

The First Carlist War occurs.

1841

General Espartero replaces Maria Christina as regent.

1843

A rebellion breaks out against Espartero; General Narvaez gains power.

1848–1852

The Second Carlist War occurs.

1854

The Narvaez regime is overthrown.

1855

A new constitution is promulgated; Narvaez returns to power.

1858–1868
General O'Donnell takes over the government.

1868
A group of army officers leads a revolt that deposes Isabella.

1870–1876
The Third Carlist War occurs.

1873
A republican government is established.

1874
The army overthrows the new government.

1875
Isabella's son, Alfonso XII, is brought back to rule the country.

1890s
Cuba and the Philippines rebel against Spanish rule.

1898
The United States declares war on Spain in favor of Cuba after the sinking of the USS *Maine*; the Spanish are defeated by the United States; Cuba is given its independence; Guam, the Philippines, and Puerto Rico fall under the control of the United States.

1912
Parts of Morocco come under Spanish rule.

1914–1918
Spain remains neutral during World War I.

1921
The Moroccans revolt, killing ten thousand Spanish troops.

1923
General Miguel Primo de Rivera leads a successful military revolt against the Spanish government and becomes the prime minister, but he holds power as a dictator. He restores order in Morocco and Spain.

1930

The army turns against Primo after he fails to reestablish a constitutional government in Spain. He is forced to resign; in December a general strike is called in support of the revolution.

1931

The Spaniards vote for a republican form of government in April; a parliamentary election is held in June; Parliament approves a democratic constitution in December, and Niceto Alcala Zamora becomes the first president of the republic.

1932

The Cortes, or parliament, gives into the demands from nationalists in Catalonia and grants them limited self-government.

1933

The government calls for a parliamentary election. The Conservative Party emerges as the most powerful political force in Spain.

1934

The Socialists and the nationalists of Catalonia lead an uprising against the government. The government puts down the revolt.

1936

The Cortes is dissolved in February; in July the Spanish army stationed in Morocco declares a revolution against the Spanish government; in September General Francisco Franco becomes the commander in chief of the rebels. The revolt develops into a civil war.

1937

Nationalists gain the upper hand in the civil war.

1938

The Soviet Union ends its large-scale aid to the Republicans.

1939

Franco enters Madrid in March. In April he announces that the civil war has ended, and he becomes the dictator of Spain, ruling until 1975.

1939–1945
Spain remains officially neutral during World War II. However, Franco draws close to whichever side is winning.

1945
The Soviet Union calls for a campaign of international opposition to overthrow Franco. Many Western nations support the campaign.

1945–1946
All major countries break off relations with Spain.

1947
Franco declares Spain a constitutional monarchy.

1948–1953
The Cold War makes Spain an ally of the United States and a member of the North Atlantic Treaty Organization.

1953
The United States begins to build air force and navy bases in Spain.

1954–1972
The Spanish economy grows dramatically.

1955
Spain joins the United Nations.

1966
The government relaxes its censorship of the press.

1968
Protests against the government erupt at the universities in Barcelona and Madrid.

1969
Franco declares that Prince Juan Carlos will become the next king of Spain.

1973
Admiral Carrero Blanco is assassinated by radical Basque separatists.

1975
Franco's government executes five terrorists; Franco dies in November; Juan Carlos becomes king.

1976
Adolfo Suarez Gonzalez is made the prime minister by Juan Carlos and begins to transition the country to democracy; the ban on political parties ends.

1977
Parliamentary elections are held.

1978
Spanish voters approve a new democratic constitution. Catalonia and the Basque country receive autonomy.

1980
Basque and Catalonia elect regional parliaments.

1982
The Socialist Party (PSOE) wins elections and Felipe Gonzalez becomes prime minister.

1986
Spain joins the European Community (EC).

1992
U.S. air bases in Spain are closed; Olympic games are held in Barcelona and World-Expo-92 in Seville.

1993
Spain and other EC countries form the European Union; the Socialists lose their majority in elections, but Felipe Gonzalez remains prime minister.

1996
Elections bring the center-right Popular Party to power and leader José María Aznar becomes prime minister.

1997–2002
The Spanish economy grows dramatically, particularly in tourism and the service sector. A decline begins in 2001.

1998
The Basque separatist movement declares a cease-fire.

2000
The Basque separatists resume their terrorist attacks.

2001
Aznar institutes a series of labor reforms in an attempt to stem economic decline; Britain and Spain begin negotiations about the fate of Gibraltar.

2002
The government bans Batasuna, the political wing of the Basque separatist movement.

For Further Research

Books

Rafael Altamira, *A History of Spain: From the Beginnings to the Present Day.* Princeton, NJ: Van Nostrand, 1966.

E. Ramon Arango, *Spain: Democracy Regained.* Boulder, CO: Westview, 1995.

William Atkinson, *A History of Spain and Portugal.* Baltimore: Penguin Books, 1967.

John D. Bergamini, *The Spanish Bourbons: The History of a Tenacious Dynasty.* New York: Putnam, 1974.

Raymond Carr, *Spain, 1808–1975.* Oxford, UK: Clarendon, 1982.

John Edwards, *The Spain of the Catholic Monarchs, 1474–1520.* Oxford, UK: Malden, 2000.

Ronald Fraser, *Blood of Spain: An Oral History of the Spanish Civil War.* New York: Pantheon Books, 1979.

David Gilmour, *The Transformation of Spain: From Franco to the Constitutional Monarchy.* New York: Quartet Books, 1985.

Duff Hart-Davis, *Armada.* New York: Bantam, 1988.

George Hills, *Spain.* New York: Praeger, 1970.

Gabrielle Ashford Hodges, *Franco: A Concise Biography.* London: Weidenfeld & Nicolson, 2000.

Richard L. Kagan and Geoffrey Parker, eds., *Spain, Europe, and the Atlantic World: Essays in the Honour of John H. Elliott.* Cambridge, UK: Cambridge University Press, 1995.

Alan Lloyd, *The Spanish Centuries.* Garden City, NY: Doubleday, 1968.

Salvador de Maderiaga, *Spain: A Modern History.* New York: Praeger, 1958.

Julián Marías, *Understanding Spain.* Trans. Frances M. Lopez-Morillas. Ann Arbor: University of Michigan Press, 1990.

Melveena McKendrik, *The Horizon Concise History of Spain.* New York: American Heritage, 1972.

Roger Merriman, *The Rise of the Spanish Empire in the Old World and the New.* New York: Cooper Square, 1962.

Stanley Payne, *The Spanish Revolution.* New York: Norton, 1970.

Peter Pierson, *A History of Spain.* Westport, CT: Greenwood, 1999.

David R. Ringrose, *Spain, Europe, and the "Spanish Miracle," 1700–1900.* Cambridge, UK: Cambridge University Press, 1996.

Teofilo Ruiz, *Spanish Society: 1400–1600.* New York: Longman, 2001.

Pierre Vilar, *Spain: A Short History.* Oxford, UK: Pergamon, 1967.

Periodicals

Akbar S. Ahmed, "Spain's Islamic Legacy," *History Today*, October 1991.

Fouad Ajami, "The Other 1492: Jews and Muslims in Columbus's Spain," *New Republic*, April 6, 1992.

Jack Beaudoin, "The Mystery of the *Maine* (History of the Spanish-American War, 1898)," *New York Times Upfront*, November 1, 1999.

Holland Cotter, "Coexistence in Medieval Spain, at Least Until 1492 (Convivencia: Jews, Muslims, and Christians in Medieval Spain)," *New York Times*, November 13, 1992.

Economist, "The Conquest (of Mexico by Spain, 1519–1600)," December 25, 1999.

Elisabeth Ferrell, "Spain's Legacy Lives," *Europe*, October 1993.

Paul Heywood, "Why the Republic Lost (the Spanish Civil War)," *History Today*, March 1989.

J. Derek Latham, "The Rise of the Umayyad Dynasty in Spain," *UNESCO Courier*, December 1991.

Eddie May, "Origins of the Spanish Civil War," *Modern History Review*, April 1999.

Richard K. Munro, "A Legend Among Christians and Muslims, Don Rodrigo Diaz de Vivar Became Spain's First National Hero—El Cid," *Military History*, June 1999.

Elizabeth Munson, "Walking on the Periphery: Gender and the Discourse of Modernization (the Rights of Women in Early Twentieth Century Spain)," *Journal of Social History*, Fall 2002.

Sara Schatz, "Democracy's Breakdown and the Rise of Fascism: The Case of the Spanish Second Republic, 1931–6," *Social History*, May 2001.

John Sullivan, "Forty Years of ETA (Basque Homeland and Liberty)," *History Today*, April 1999.

Francesco Vallverdu, "A Thousand Years of Catalan History," *UNESCO Courier*, May 1989.

Websites

American Academy of Research Historians of Medieval Spain, www.uca.edu/aarhms. An affiliated society of the American Historian Association, this site provides a forum in which scholars can discuss their current research on medieval Spain and provides links to important research resources.

Constituting Modern Spain, www.isu.edu/~owenjack/conmodsp/conmodsp.html. This website coincides with a course offered by Professor J.B. Owens at Idaho State University and includes materials on the comparative study of Spaniards' attempts to create a constitutional regime that would provide a stable political framework in the face of serious religious, national, and class divisions, 1808 to the present.

History of Spain, www.emulateme.com/history/spaihist.htm. This site contains information covering all periods of Spanish history from the Library of Congress Country Studies series.

Internet History Sourcebooks Project, www.fordham.edu/halsall. The project includes an index of selected and excerpted texts for teaching purposes and full texts of historical sources arranged according to type and time perioed.

Library of Iberian Resources Online (LIBRO), www.uca.edu/ aarhms. LIBRO is a joint project of the American Academy of Research Historians of Medieval Spain and the University of Central Arkansas. Its task is to make available to users the best scholarship about the peoples and nations of the Iberian peninsula. Consequently, the book list is principally drawn from recent, but out-of-print, university press monographs. In addition, the collection includes a number of basic texts and sources in translation.

The Spanish Armada of 1588, http://tbls.hypermart.net/ history/1588armada. This site explores the story of Spain's King Philip II's attempt to invade England, which resulted in what is regarded as the longest naval battle in history. It also contains a searchable online database containing records of more than three hundred ships involved in the armada campaign.

The Spanish Empire, www.isu.edu/~owenjack/spemp/spemp. html. A companion to a course offered by Professor J.B. Owens at Idaho State University, this website includes materials on the geographic, cultural, economic, administrative, and military dimensions of the encounters and conflicts among the peoples of the Spanish Empire from its medieval beginnings to its final collapse in the Napoleonic era.

INDEX